ORPHEUS
THE METAMORPHOSES OF A MYTH

ORPHEUS

THE METAMORPHOSES OF A MYTH

EDITED BY JOHN WARDEN

UNIVERSITY OF TORONTO PRESS

TORONTO • BUFFALO • LONDON

© University of Toronto Press 1982
Toronto Buffalo London

First published in paperback 1985
Printed in Canada

ISBN 0-8020-6593-7 (paper)
ISBN 0-8020-5518-4 (cloth)

Canadian Cataloguing in Publication Data

Main entry under title:
Orpheus : the metamorphoses of a myth

Includes index.
ISBN 0-8020-5518-4 (cloth)
ISBN 0-8020-6593-7 (paper)

1. Orpheus – Legends – History and criticism –
Addresses, essays, lectures. I. Warden, John, 1936–

BL820.07076   398.2'2   C81-095140-1

This book has been published with the help of a grant from the Canadian
Federation for the Humanities, using funds provided by the Social Sciences
and Humanities Research Council of Canada, and a grant from the
Publication Fund of University of Toronto Press.

Contents

JOHN WARDEN

Introduction

THE AIM OF THIS BOOK is to look at the myth of Orpheus in movement from antiquity to the end of the Renaissance, to bring together from different disciplines and media a conspectus of the myth's career, and to show how the myth grew and changed to meet changing demands. The book started from an undergraduate course which was held at Scarborough College in the University of Toronto some years ago, and which drew together scholars from many areas. Indeed, all of the contributors except Professor W.S. Anderson (of the University of California at Berkeley) still teach at the University of Toronto. We felt as a result of that experience that it would be useful to put together a collection of essays, each contributor writing on the aspect of the myth that interested him. Thus the intention is not to provide a continuous or an exhaustive account. Nor is there any attempt to impress uniformity of approach; treatments range from historical synthesis through critical evaluation to detailed interpretation.

The Orpheus myth is defined for the purposes of this book as consisting of those stories in which Orpheus appears by name as a central figure. This is not quite as obvious as it seems. For there is a collection of stories from all over the world that could be described as of the 'Orpheus type.' That is to say they handle the same themes or contain the same motifs, or have a resemblance in structure to the myth of Orpheus. The musician who can tame the wildness of nature, the shaman who visits the land of the dead, the quest for the lost beloved, the last-minute breach of taboo, the severed and prophesying head – these motifs can be found in the mythologies of many different cultures. This recurrence raises some very interesting questions – how far can it be accounted for by diffusion? do these motifs correspond to archetypes in the human consciousness? does myth as a structure of communication inevitably give rise to stories of the same shape? or are the problems that man confronts and seeks to ease through myth sufficiently common to explain a similarity of response?

The limitations we have imposed on ourselves require that these questions remain for the most part not only unanswered but unasked. This loss however can be turned to advantage. The ultimate questions about myth distract from its continuing life. We become greedy for answers, impatient to grab onto a formula and carry it off to our lair. We should remember that if myth is a language it has a literature as well as a grammar. Those who study the content for itself and not for its structure have tended to back away in shame from the sharp-edged tools of the new scientists. But the anthropologists should not have it all their own way. Myth has an immediate importance to us, not just as a static phenomenon to be studied. It is the currency in which our culture is transmitted. To understand this we must be conscious of myth in movement.

The original myth of Orpheus is not available to us. By the time that Orpheus emerges as a figure with a recognizable physiognomy and biography his myth has already been through the hands of generations of artists literary and plastic. For myth is the raw material of artists: the straight narration of given myth is obsolete by the time of literacy – if not before. Homer was adapting pre-existent myth to his artistic purposes, no less than Aeschylus or Calderón or Cocteau. There is, however, what might be called a standard version of the myth – a version, that is, that most people at most times would have recognized as the myth of Orpheus, and this is what follows.

Orpheus was born in the generation before the Trojan War, the coeval of Heracles and Peleus. His father was the god Apollo, or, more commonly, a Thracian river-god, Oeagros. His mother was a Muse, usually Calliope. He travelled with Jason and the Argonauts to recover the Golden Fleece from Colchis. He was a singer and player of the lyre who could charm and soften the violence of nature. Trees and animals came to his song. Birds flew above his head and fishes swam behind his boat. He was a prophet and religious teacher who knew the secrets of the world of the dead; a shaman and magician who had crossed over into that world and used his spells to bring the dead back to the world of the living. In particular the story tells how he descended to the underworld in quest of his wife, Eurydice, who had died of a snakebite, how the beauty of his music persuaded the king and queen of the dead to release his beloved. In the best-known version of this story he has a solemn injunction laid on him that he must not look back at his beloved until he has reached the world of the living; but the power of love is too strong for him, he turns, and Eurydice is lost. Following this second loss of his wife he retreats into the wilds of Thrace, abjures womankind and laments. Eventually he meets his death at the hands of the Bacchants, who scorn him for his neglect of Dionysus or hate him for his neglect of women. His head and lyre, still playing and singing, float down the river Hebrus. They are carried across the Aegean to the island of Lesbos. There the lyre is dedicated to Apollo; the head is buried, but continues to prophesy until forbidden to do so by Apollo.

Orpheus was a great prophet and religious teacher, founder, at least according to legend, of a religious sect called Orphism. In the historical development of the myth, Orphism tends to take a different route from the stories associated with Orpheus the man. The one becomes a quarry for eastern Neoplatonism, the other for western moralists and romancers, though at certain key moments they are reunited. Orphism, floating free of its putative originator, suffers from centuries of loose usage, until it becomes, as it tends to be today, a vague catch-all term for certain kinds of mystical attitude.

For this reason among others it is extremely hard to pin it down in retrospect. A controversy, described in the opening chapter, rages between sceptics and believers. One side maintains that there was a firmly established sect with a fixed body of doctrine and mythology in existence by the sixth century BC. The other holds equally strongly that there is no evidence that any such thing existed until many hundreds of years later, and that 'Orphic' at this early period is nothing more than a convenient term for describing certain types of ritual or belief. I seek to avoid the controversy by offering a brief description of the nature and content of Orphism as it was passed down from the ancient world.

In the first place it was generally accepted that there was a canon of sacred writings associated with Orphism. These are for the most part ascribed to Orpheus himself. The most important of these for present purposes is the so-called *Rhapsodic Theogony*.[1] From this source we can piece together the Orphic mythology – and a strange one it is, a sophisticated amalgam of primitive ingredients. In the beginning was water and slime; and out of the water and slime was born Chronos (Time), brooding over the universe, a serpent with the head of a bull and a lion at the side and the face of a god between. 'Of this Chronos, the ageless one ... was born Aither [the bright shining air] and a great yawning gulf' and in the 'divine aither great Chronos fashioned a silvery egg.' The egg splits open, and from it hatches Phanes, the first creator deity who is also called Erikepaios, Eros (Love), Dionysus, Zeus, or Protogonos (first-born). Phanes is the shining one, the revealer; he has 'four eyes looking this way and that ... golden wings moving this way and that ... and he utters the voice of a bull and of a glaring lion.' He is 'the key of mind' who 'cherishes in his heart swift and sightless Love.' He is bisexual, beyond difference, a 'very whole animal.' As 'female and father' he brings forth Night; darkness and light unite to produce Heaven and Earth (Uranos and Ge). At this point normal 'Hesiodic' mythology takes over with the tale of the mutilation of Uranus, the birth of the Titans, and the struggles of Zeus with his father Kronos. Zeus establishes himself as ruler and in a rather remarkable manner re-creates the world. This is the so-called κατάποσις Φάνητος, the 'swallowing of Phanes.' 'Engulfing the might of Erikepaios, he held the body of all things in the hollow of his own belly; and he mingled with his own limbs the power and strength of the god. Therefore together with him all things in Zeus were created anew.' By thus reabsorbing the world into himself and re-creating it, Zeus makes it his own. In the words of the Hymn to Zeus: 'Zeus became first, Zeus ... last, Zeus is head, middle and from Zeus all things have their being. Zeus became male, Zeus was an immortal maiden ... Zeus is king and Zeus himself first father of all.'

Zeus begets Dionysus, whose birth brings to a close the process of Theogony. The Titans, of the generation older than Zeus, jealous of his power and of his son, beguile the young Dionysus with toys and mirror, and while he is thus distracted they tear him apart. His heart is saved by the goddess Athena, and from it Dionysus is brought back to life. The Titans who have eaten the flesh of Dionysus are burnt to cinders by the thunderbolt of Zeus. From their ashes man is born.

Man then is of twofold nature, the Titanic and the Dionysiac, the earthly and the divine. The aim of the Orphic life is by purification, asceticism, and ritual to purge away the Titanic part of us and to prepare ourselves to become fully divine. The body is the source of evil and contamination. It is a tomb from which the soul of the Orphic initiate will finally be released to find the true life. The body is also seen as a prison house, and life is a period of punishment and trial. Man must purify himself through a succession of re-births and thousand-year cycles in order to be freed at last from the wheel of birth. At each death he is tried before the three judges of the underworld. Those who are initiated in the Orphic mysteries are sent to the fields of Bliss; the uninitiated are to lie up to their necks in 'a mass a mud and ever-flowing filth.' When the soul is finally purified it is 'brought to the life of blessedness' – the divine in man rejoins the divine.

> I have paid the penalty for deeds unrighteous ...
> I have flown out of the sorrowful weary circle.
> I have passed with swift feet to the diadem desired.
> I have sunk beneath the bosom of the Mistress, the Queen of the Underworld.

And now I come as a suppliant to holy Persephoneia,
that of her grace she send me to the seats of the Hallowed.
Happy and blessed one, thou shalt be god instead of mortal.
A kid I have fallen into milk.

The first essay attempts, through an examination of the early Greek evidence, to 'fix' Orpheus before metamorphosis can take place. The chapters that follow describe the progress of the myth through three main periods, Augustan Rome, the Middle ages, and the Renaissance. Historical periods have a dubious reality which tends to dissipate as you approach their borders. But there are certain characteristics that distinguish the mental habits and attitudes of these large blocks of time when viewed from a distance. It might be useful to try to determine with what presuppositions about its nature and function the three ages approach myth in general and the myth of Orpheus in particular.

For the Augustan Age myth is first and foremost a literary tool. Faith in the creed to which the myths belonged was weak; and the poets of the period were the inheritors of the highly sophisticated and self-conscious treatment of myth developed in the Hellenistic period. Myth was to all intents and purposes the matter of literature. So it is used to do all the different jobs that literature is required to do – to explore the human soul, to express the tragedy and comedy of life, to map out man's relationship with powers beyond him, and above all to create a world of the imagination. It is a common language, a common world of reference into which the poet can invite the reader by a single word. One might add that the poets of the Augustan Age were poets' poets, highly conscious of their place in a long tradition, eager to do something new with well-worn themes, competitive, sensitive to parody, and alert to any chances of literary play. These qualities will become apparent in the study of Virgil and Ovid in the second essay.

Christianity brings a new directness and a new *naïveté*. Christian doctrine is the only point of reference, and myth will either diverge from it (and thus be the work of the Devil) or conform to it (and thus be God's prefiguration of the truth). Reactions of the early apologists tend towards the former; but with increasing confidence they learn to accommodate within their faith the pleasures of myth. (The third essay shows us Clement's ambivalence.) Allegory becomes rampant, myth is wrenched and cannibalized to fit into the Christian message. But this Philistinism has the virtue that myth is preserved; and with the passage of time there is an integrative tendency, the parts of the myth being brought together again to give a continuous and coherent interpretation. But the allegorical meaning is paramount; there is no respect for the lines of the story. It is in the romantic tales of courtly love that the figures of myth regain their vitality. And in the process they are fully medievalized. Orpheus as troubadour or noble lover is no longer strained by the need to stand in for the word of God or Beautiful Voice. He is himself again. And the further the author can move from the trammels of classical tradition, the greater the vigour. *Sir Orfeo* from the fringes of the European cultural world, shot through with Celtic influence, is Orpheus reborn.

The Renaissance is characterized by a renewal of interest in the classical world. The preoccupation with the recovery of ancient works of art and the careful emendation of texts – this antiquarianism and precision lead to rediscovery of the original figures of myth; their concrete forms and the details of their stories become of interest for themselves.

There is however another side to the Renaissance attitude to myth. In many respects the intellectual world of the early Renaissance was closer to late antiquity than it was to the classical period. One reason for this is that a number of very influential works taken to be classical were in fact forgeries of the second and third centuries AD – the Hermetic Writings, the Sibylline Oracles, much of the Orphic Corpus. These brought with them a heady brew of syncretist mysticism. In this tradition myth was an enigma to be unravelled, a veil protecting truth from profane eyes, to be drawn aside by the philosopher or poet.

These two attitudes are really contradictory. But in both Orpheus plays a central role. As tamer of beasts he is the champion of humanism, symbol of the power of the word to soften the wild hearts of man and bring civilization. As prophet and mystagogue he is the spokesman for an exotic mysticism which offers space to both Christian and Neoplatonist. For a few years the two sides hold together. Singer and theologian are united.

But the positivist approach of the humanist scholar tends towards disintegration. It is no longer assumed that the myth can tell the whole story. Calderón's *autos*, where the myth is an allegory for the sacred history of the world, are the last hurrah. For now the story is treated piecemeal and serves many purposes – rather as it did in the Augustan Age. This is well illustrated in the chapters on art and music. Where the myth does tell a story to the age it is a disquieting one. Milton the puritan rejects it as a vehicle for the Christian message. Bacon the scientist reads it as a symbol of the failure of civilization – Orpheus must die because culture must die. The confidence of the early humanists has all run out.

That is the end of our story. But it is by no means the end of Orpheus. His career since the Renaissance would fill at least another volume. Perhaps most dominant is the romantic and post-romantic Orpheus, visible already in the paintings of Giorgione and Titian: the self-absorbed artist, the quester after the unattainable. Art is the last refuge of the shaman. The artist by his magic descends into himself to seek a world of absolutes.

Orpheus in this mood can grow uncomfortably like Narcissus. But let us take leave of him with the vision of Rainer Maria Rilke, perhaps the most successful in our own century at restating and reintegrating the myth. Orpheus' scattered remnants after his dismemberment by the Maenads become the mouthpiece for the dumb objects of nature:

> Sound of you lingered in lions and rocks you were first to
> enthral, in the trees and the birds. You are singing there still.

No longer the champion of a humanism that shapes all things to man's pattern but 'a mouth through which nature may speak,' Orpheus is the go-between, narrowing the gap between person and thing, between living and dead. Such is the power of song.

> Raise no commemorating stone. The roses
> shall blossom every summer for his sake.
> For this is Orpheus. His metamorphosis
> in this one and in that. We should not take
>
> thought about other names. Once and for all,
> it's Orpheus when there's song.[2]

NOTES

1 See Otto Kern *Orphicorum fragmenta* (Berlin 1922); the translations are taken from W.K.C. Guthrie *Orpheus and Greek Religion* (London 1935) 137–42.
2 *Sonnets to Orpheus* tr J.B. Leishman (London 1936) Part One 26.10–11 and 5.1–6. I owe my discovery of Rilke's sonnets to Professor Horst Wittmann.

ORPHEUS
THE METAMORPHOSES OF A MYTH

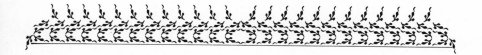

EMMET ROBBINS

Famous Orpheus

ORPHEUS. Few names from Greek myth are so evocative. Few figures have so appealed to later ages. For us the name has immediate and automatic associations. We think first of the lover who harrowed hell to win back his beloved, second of the minstrel whose sweet music enchanted all nature. We may, if we have made particular study of antiquity, be able to add a third role to the first two. Not only lover and musician but priest: the name of Orpheus is regularly linked in antiquity with mystery religion and special illumination, with initiation into knowledge of the secret workings of the universe. These three facets of this astonishing character account for the universality of his appeal, for in them myth, folklore, and legend come together.[1] Myth, folklore, and legend are not mutually exclusive categories and definitions of each might be disputed. But it would probably be reasonable to claim that Orpheus the revealer of the mysteries is the most truly mythical figure: myth, if it is to be separated from folklore and legend, may most easily be recognized as distinct by its more speculative nature and by the seriousness of its preoccupations.[2] Orpheus the lover is the folklore figure: the motif of the lover who braves the powers of darkness to find his loved one is common to many parts of the world, as is the taboo against looking back or speaking to her which the lover must observe if he is to be successful in his quest.[3] Orpheus the musician is the figure of legend, for legend comes closer to history than do myth and folklore, and the story of the gentle singer whose gift makes savage nature tame is certainly none other, on one level, than the story of the advance of civilization and the arts. The Roman poet Horace knew this:

> When men lived wild, a spokesman of the gods,
> The sacred Orpheus, scared them from their foul

And murderous ways; and so the legend says:
Ravening lions and tigers Orpheus tamed.[4]

The triple personality which European art and literature inherited from antiquity is a complicated amalgam which took centuries to emerge. Most of Greek tradition, we shall see, knew or cared little about Orpheus the lover. Of Orpheus the religious teacher there was certainly much talk among the Greeks, but it has proved notoriously difficult to establish anything definite regarding the beliefs and traditions that accompanied his name. Orpheus the musician is the best attested of all – early art and poetry know this figure well. The final product was the patient work of centuries, perhaps of more than a millennium. And the centuries that followed the end of classical civilization were left in possession of a composite personality they could in turn dismember, faithful to the Greek tradition of Orpheus' end, selecting whatever aspect best suited the purposes of different ages and different artists. In the succeeding chapters of this book we shall see what various periods of European history made of Orpheus. In the Middle Ages he became a type of Christ, overcoming death, a psalmist or a troubadour, courtly lover and singer of pretty lyrics.[5] From the Renaissance on, Orpheus is the very incarnation of the power of music, an art in which scientific and mathematical precision creates a language intelligible on a plan that transcends reason: since the voice of Orpheus is the voice of Music, he presides over the transformations and interaction of poetry and science in the period 1600–1800.[6] In the very same period he becomes the patron of the newly emergent art of opera, from the time of Monteverdi to that of Gluck, again in his role as Music Incarnate.[7] To the Romantics and to our own century he has been the eternal seeker beyond the threshold: different Eurydices summon, new hells yawn.[8]

Priest, lover, musician – a figure of myth, folk-tale, and legend. Does a real person stand behind this great name or is Orpheus simply the product of the imagination of a nation that has bequeathed to us other names equally evocative but almost certainly fictitious? To some the matter is of no consequence, for the real value of many great names – Oedipus, Odysseus, Hamlet, Don Quixote, Robinson Crusoe, to list but a few – is undiminished even if there is no historical personality that can be disinterred for our scrutiny. Orpheus, however, is somewhat different, for he is not only a figure whose exploits have furnished substance to poets and artists. The Greeks persisted in regarding him as a great poet and one of the spiritual founders of their nation. Aristophanes, writing in the late fifth century BC, accords Orpheus a place with Homer and Hesiod.[9] Socrates, a few years later, could, as he faced death, put Orpheus on a par with Homer and Hesiod as someone he looked forward to meeting in the realm beyond the grave provided life did not end with bodily death.[10] And Orpheus, in both cases, is mentioned before Homer and Hesiod. It appears highly likely that he was regarded as more ancient and more venerable than the two poets whose works are our first surviving monuments of Greek literature. No Greek of any period, certainly, ever questioned the existence of Homer or Hesiod. As poets and teachers they enjoyed an honour that no hero we might describe as purely mythical could ever claim.

And so one is inevitably tempted to look for a historical reality behind the great name, inclined to suspect that there was, once, a real Orpheus whose memory lived on, first in the hearts of his countrymen. When and where, if at all, can he be located?

Our first literary mention of the name of Orpheus occurs in the mid-sixth-century poet Ibycus. A brief mention in a lyric fragment is all we have: 'famous Orpheus.' The name is, thus, celebrated one hundred and fifty years before Aristophanes and Socrates mention him, though we are given no indication why. More intriguing yet is the first representation of Orpheus in art. It antedates the first poetic reference by perhaps a quarter of a century and is thus the first certain appearance of Orpheus that we know. It allows us to make some fascinating, if cautious, surmises.

About the end of the first quarter of the sixth century BC, the people of Sicyon, a town in the northwestern Peloponnese, dedicated, under their tyrant Cleisthenes, a 'treasury' or small temple at Apollo's famous shrine at Delphi. On one of the metopes or relief sculptures from the frieze, surviving in badly damaged state and visible today in the museum at Delphi, are the mutilated outlines of a ship, shown in profile and flanked by two mounted horsemen. Two lute players are standing on the ship, one of them with his name, Orpheus, clearly visible beside him. The ship has been plausibly identified as the Argo, the two horsemen as the twins Castor and Pollux. The tradition is well-established, certainly, that Orpheus formed part of the crew of the illustrious expedition that set out to bring back the Golden Fleece. Pindar, in 462 BC, gives us the first detailed account of the voyage of the Argo and he lists Orpheus, as well as Castor and Pollux, among the heroes who sailed from Greece on the great venture.[11] All later accounts give special prominence to Orpheus too. Notable among later versions is a fourth-century BC epic by Apollonius of Rhodes, a work which we still possess in its entirety. So long as classical civilization lasted Orpheus was linked with the Argo. An account of the voyage of the Argo, difficult to date but most probably from the early centuries of the Christian era, is put into the mouth of the singer Orpheus. This poem is regularly called the *Orphic Argonautica*.

The association of Orpheus with the Argo is secure from the very beginning. Another lyric fragment, by the poet Simonides (556–468 BC), is our first definite literary reference to Orpheus after that by Ibycus and it is most easily understood if taken as presupposing his presence on board the Argo:

> Over his head flew innumerable birds and to
> his beautiful song fish leapt straight out of
> the blue sea.[12]

Orpheus' link with the fabulous Argonautic expedition is both early and certain. It is, in fact, the earliest incident in his biography for which we have evidence and it would seem reasonable to look more closely at this myth and to attempt to understand its import.

No other Greek myth is so venerable in its antiquity. The voyage of the Argo was already famous when Odysseus met Circe and received navigational advice from her on his way home from Troy:

> One of two courses you may take,
> and you yourself must weigh them. I shall not
> plan the whole action for you now, but only
> tell you of both.
>   Ahead are beetling rocks
> and dark blue glancing Amphitritê, surging,
> roars around them. Prowling Rocks, or Drifters,
> the gods in bliss have named them – named them well.
> Not even birds can pass them by, not even
> the timorous doves that bear ambrosia
> to Father Zeus: caught by downdrafts, they die
> on rockwall smooth as ice.
>   Each time, the Father
> wafts a new courier to make up his crew.
> Still less can ships get searoom of these Drifters,
> whose boiling surf, under high fiery winds,
> carries tossing wreckage of ships and men.
> Only one ocean-going craft, the far-famed
> Argo, made it, sailing from Aiêta;
> but she, too, would have crashed on the big rocks
> if Hêra had not pulled her through, for love
> of Iêson [Jason], her captain.[13]

It has long been understood that Odysseus' men are Argonauts in disguise, that many of the episodes in the wanderings of Odysseus were taken by the poet we call Homer from an earlier epic, no longer surviving, about the Quest for the Golden Fleece and transferred to Odysseus.[14] That the borrowing occurred is no longer doubted, though there must necessarily be some uncertainty regarding the exact nature of the original poem. It is probable that the poem known to the poet of the *Odyssey* supplies him with a good deal of geographical information about the Propontis, the Black Sea, and the land of Helios the Sun (the father of Circe and the grandfather of Medea) – in a word, about the eastern extremities of the world known to the Greeks. This information may well have been, in the pre-Odyssean *Argonautica*, the record of information brought back to the shores of Ionia by explorers and colonizers and thus current in the land where the *Odyssey* seems to have taken, at a date somewhere around 700 BC, the form in which we know it. But even if there were details of mariners' travels to the Black Sea area embedded in the *Argonautica* in question, and thus in the later *Odyssey*, there is no necessity to believe that the story of the voyage to Colchis and of the Argonauts' return with the grand-daughter of the Sun was primarily the story of an actual voyage of exploration to the Caucasus. There are too many archetypal elements in the story to permit us to reduce it to a simple record of historical fact. We have, in the myth of the Argonautic expedition, too much that seems to jump the confines of possible history and land us in the realm of pure imagination: the evil king (Pelias) who deprives a young hero of his throne and sends him on an impossible mission; the never-never land at the end of the world, complete with beautiful princess, golden treasure, fire-breathing dragon; the perilous voyage, especially the passage through the Clashing Rocks that threaten to pulverize the traveller and his crew.

Something in all this suggests experience psychological more than historical. It has been argued that the myth of the Quest for the Golden Fleece is the oldest and most significant of all Greek myths, that it is essentially the account of the voyage out and return of the shaman, that figure familiar to so many cultures, who mediates between this world and the beyond and whose most extraordinary characteristic is his ability to bring souls back from the realm of the dead.[15] Jason is such a figure, his mission to rescue and repatriate a lost soul. Pindar's King Pelias sends Jason forth with the following words:

> You have the power to lay the wrath of those in earth.
> Phrixos is calling, that someone redeem his ghost,
> And, going to the hall of Aietas, fetch
> The thick-piled Fleece
> Of the Ram, by whom he was saved of old
> From the sea.[16]

'Redeem his ghost' (the Greek for 'ghost' here is *psychê*). And so Jason is a psychopomp, the voyage of the Argo a voyage through the narrow passage to the furthermost bourne in search of a wraith.

The presence of Orpheus on the Argo becomes, thus, of particular interest. For he, par excellence, was remembered as an intermediary between this world and the next; he more than any other was famous for his descent to the underworld and his mission to redeem a ghost. The Greeks remembered Orpheus as the first of their great poets and spiritual teachers. They remembered him as an Argonaut and placed him on a boat the commander of whose crew curiously resembles him as psychopomp. Argonautic poetry stands behind Homeric poetry just as the Argonautic myth is well known to the author of the *Odyssey*. It would not, it seems, be rash to believe that there was once an Orpheus, a shaman and poet, himself a traveller to the other side and expounder of its secrets to those to whom he returned. His teaching may have been contained in poetry – the attribution to him of musical gifts is ubiquitous – and one of his works may, in all likelihood, have been a poem about the Argo, the skipper of whose crew is so like himself. His 'signature' survives, even if the original poem does not, in his continuing association with the Argonautic myth in the art and literature available to us.

To return to the metope of the Sicyonian treasury at Delphi. The Argo is there flanked by the twins Castor and Pollux, two of the most haunting figures of Greek myth. Theirs is a union which holds life and death, this world and the next, in eternal, fixed conjunction. The mortal twin Castor was redeemed from death by his brother who sacrificed, in part, his immortality that he might live. The twins, as a result, either live together, one day on Olympus alternating with one day in Hades, or they take turns to die, one replacing the other with regularity in the underworld. The association of these figures with the voyage of the Argo is surely no more gratuitous than the inclusion of Orpheus in its crew. They are the patrons of mariners to whom they appear 'bearing light in the grievous night.'[17] These figures link the nether world with the upper air, the dark land of the dead with the bright land of the living. Life and death are not so much opposites as the complementary halves of a single whole, the twins holding in their embrace knowledge of both sides of the tomb. They represent, symbolically, the two terms of the shaman's voyage, this world and the beyond. Orpheus, like Jason, is privy to their knowledge and, like them, straddles the grave.

The Greeks of the classical period have been much admired by some for their 'direct and unequivocal acceptance of man's mortality.'[18] There is not much in the Greek myths, we are told, that probes the boundaries between mortal and immortal as does the Mesopotamian *Epic of Gilgamesh*. Shamanic figures, who exist to explore and to initiate into a world beyond the grave, are exceptional, the established Olympian religion being hostile to any attempt on man's part to overcome death. One suspects, in the admiration, a reading of contemporary religious feelings into the distant past: in an age when belief in an afterlife has, for the most part, considerably weakened, we are reassured to find that the Greeks demanded in their myths what we demand today – acceptance of the finality of death.[19] But if this 'freedom from illusion' is 'most often admired,'[20] it has been criticized too.[21] The Olympian religion, the product of an invading patriarchal society, superseded and suppressed an earlier Aegean religion, dominated by the figure of a Mother Goddess who generously shared her deathlessness with her devotees. The sky gods of the Indo-Europeans were jealous of their prerogatives, most important of which was their immortality, and demanded that man should recognize his limits. His limits were fixed in this life and he was forbidden to seek knowledge beyond it. Value judgments apart, it is accurate enough to explain the relative absence of immortal longings in the Greek myth we find in classical literature as the product of a historical process in which Olympian dynastic gods replaced powerful female deities as Indo-Europeans assumed a parallel dominance, in the second millennium BC, over native Aegean stock.

This consideration may help us in establishing an approximate period for Orpheus. Every attempt to resurrect this shadowy figure must be, to a considerable degree, speculative. But if we believe, as Greeks of the classical period were wont to do, that an actual Orpheus preceded the poets Homer and Hesiod and if we are inclined to see in him a shaman who could penetrate the world beyond the grave, we shall also be tempted to place him in the Bronze Age, in the second millennium BC, and to see in him a shaman-priest connected with the cult of the Mother Goddess.

A particularly tantalizing fresco from the Throne Room of the late Bronze Age Palace of Nestor at Pylos in the southwestern Peloponnese shows a seated bard, attired in a long garment, playing a five-stringed instrument and appearing to charm a large, winged creature. The excavator of this site, C.W. Blegen, himself suggested that this might be Orpheus.[22] The invading Indo-Europeans, or Mycenaeans as they are generally called, took many mythical and religious motifs from the people they subdued. One of the most prominent of recurring themes in Greek myth is the story of the recovery of an abducted princess: examples are Persephone, Helen, Eurydice. The leading twentieth-century scholar of Greek religion has, in fact, suggested that the myth of a Maiden snatched from the embrace of Death is one that the Mycenaeans took over from the older religion.[23] They found in the area they occupied a religion not haunted by thoughts of the finality of death: its central divinity was the Mother Goddess who ever grants continuing life, just as the earth, with which she is always associated, is both tomb and womb, restoring the life it takes. The Indo-Europeans, a warrior people, secularized at least one of the myths that tell of the recovery of a stolen princess and transferred it from the divine to the heroic level. Helen is not, for those of us familiar with the *Iliad*, a divinity. But divine she undoubtedly was in her origins, and there survive in Greek myth stories of her abduction by Theseus – that same Theseus who carried off the Cretan princess Ariadne and who, in some versions, attempted to carry off Persephone. In the story of Theseus' attempted abduction of Persephone it was the new religion, which insisted on maintaining the distinction between this world and the next, which would not allow Persephone to come to the shores of light but forced Theseus to remain among the dead. Orpheus may well be another figure, taken for the Throne Room at Pylos from the repertory of the pre-Greek natives. Orpheus is, after all, a successful *revenant* from the beyond. The earliest versions of the Eurydice story known to us tell of his recovery of her, as we shall see.

The case for a Mycenaean origin for Orpheus has been extensively argued in the most recent contribution to Orphic studies, R. Böhme's *Orpheus: Der Sänger und seine Zeit* ('Orpheus: The Singer and His Age'). Response to the book has been guarded, the prevailing opinion on the topic being sceptical, but Böhme's ideas have received favourable notice from W.K.C. Guthrie, who refuses to accept the minimalist position and whose own book, *Orpheus and Greek Religion*, remains the most widely read work on the subject in the English language.[24] Guthrie, in his book on Orpheus (1935) and in a chapter of his later work *The Greeks and Their Gods* (1950), is also disposed to believe that there was a historical Orpheus even though he would not place him so far back in time as would the more recent writer on the subject. The most impressive part of Böhme's treatment, Guthrie feels, is his minute analysis of remarkably similar, often virtually identical, passages in Homer and Hesiod and other early poets which argue a common archetype rather than mutual borrowing. One example among many might be cited.

In Hesiod's *Theogony* we read of:

> the place where Night and Day
> Approach and greet each other as they cross
> The great bronze threshold.[25]

In the eighth book of the *Iliad* there are 'gates of iron and a brazen doorstone'[26] before the entrance to Tartarus while in the *Odyssey* the Laestrygonians of Book Nine, living at the extreme end of the known world, are placed where 'the courses of Night and Day lie close together.'[27] Another parallel is provided by the poem of the pre-Socratic poet-philosopher Parmenides. He describes his voyage from the House of Night into the presence of a goddess who reveals to him the truth. The way lies through 'the gates of the paths of Night and Day.'[28] All four passages speak of a threshold. If they have a common source could it be in the songs of Orpheus, the figure on the threshold between this world and the next?

The past century has seen an enormous amount of controversy over the possibility of believing in a historical Orpheus. Guthrie and Böhme, convinced by circumstantial evidence, have held for an actual historical figure who gave rise to the stories associated with his name. An important work written in the period between the books of Guthrie and Böhme, I.M. Linforth's *The Arts of Orpheus* (1941), sifts all the available evidence and arrives at absolutely minimal conclusions: no justification for believing in a historical Orpheus; so little uniformity in the information to be gleaned from studying the texts, mostly of late antiquity, that claim Orphic inspiration, that it is impossible to construct a coherent doctrine recognizable as the product of a single religious teacher. There is a bewildering miscellany of religious writings, conveniently collected for those who have the Greek to read it, in O. Kern's *Orphicorum fragmenta* (1922). Guthrie and Linforth deal with the same evidence but reach different conclusions, the latter arriving at the position that we have no right to believe in any religious institution founded by a historical figure, the former unable to avoid the conclusion that a sect did exist in historical times and that the impulse behind it was an actual religious teacher.

Linforth finds the term 'Orphic' completely vague and virtually meaningless. It has no utility as a label and is better avoided. We know that the mythical figure was a fabulous musician and an Argonaut, that stories were told of his descent to the underworld, that a host of philosophic and religious doctrines were promulgated with his name attached to them. None of this warrants the assumption that the mythical figure was more than a convenient referent for mystical, ritual, eschatological, and philosophic doctrine and we simply cannot know how early he was popular in the Greek imagination. The argument does not lend itself to summary, for Linforth's book is essentially a detailed examination of individual items of evidence, avoiding all but negative conclusions. The reader who tackles it will find it stringent and difficult, tough-minded and chary of broad generalizations. Its effect has been considerable, as one example will suffice to demonstrate.

E.R. Dodds, in his epoch-making book *The Greeks and the Irrational*, admits that Linforth was largely responsible for disabusing him of almost everything he once thought he knew about Orphism. Dodds is quite willing to believe that there once was an Orpheus. He thinks too that this Orpheus was a shaman, but he is quite unwilling to attach to him the fantastic theogonical speculation that went on for a thousand years in the ancient world and he finds himself quite lacking the tools necessary to separate the wheat from the chaff in the vast amount of 'Orphic' material.[29] The trouble with most of the evidence is its lateness. Some, of course, is comparatively early, but Linforth has detected, even in the earliest material, nothing more than a desire to foist upon an august name the most disparate doctrine. Orpheus was associated with the mysteries from an early date, hence anything liturgical, ritualistic, or speculative was loosely called Orphic. But there is nowhere in antiquity a clearly discernible Orphic sect, generally acknowledged and admitted and identifiable by a characteristic body of doctrine.

Guthrie, in contrast, does not see a nebulous mass of popular tradition and loose speculation that disintegrates upon close examination but is impressed by a core of belief evinced in many writers, some of whom ascribe the teaching to Orpheus, others of whom do not. Most prominent are a belief in transmigration and in an afterlife in which good is rewarded and evil punished, and a belief in the necessity of catharsis or purification to free our immortal soul from the fleshly tomb in which it is incarcerated. Abstention from eating flesh and reliance on the efficacy of scrupulously performed ritual were likely to go along with these beliefs. Multifariousness or lack of doctrinal coherence and absence of canonical scripture is, for him, the hallmark of practically all of Greek religion outside Orphism, and Orphism was the direct antithesis of the common attitudes. It was structured, dogmatic, authoritative, based on holy writings that were inspired by the teaching of a great religious reformer, if not his own composition, and ever peripheral or esoteric, the property of a sect whose ideas never filtered very far down into the general consciousness of a nation whose religious life was not characterized by holy books, a priestly caste, personal piety, and moral injunctions, in other words, the very things which those of us reared in a Judaeo-Christian tradition expect of religion and which Orphism alone in the classical period of Greek culture provided.

Guthrie is convinced that a historical figure spawned the myths, legends, and teachings associated with his name. But rather than place him at a point remote in time from the writers of classical Greece, in the Bronze Age hundreds of years before our first explicit mention of him, he places him, or at least the most important incident in his biography, at a point geographically remote from the life of the civilized Hellenes. Orpheus is, for Guthrie, a Greek missionary preaching his Apolline religion of catharsis and asceticism among the wild barbarians of Thrace, the orgiastic devotees of the un-Greek Dionysus. He came to grief at the hands of the women votaries of the god of ecstasy. An Alexandrian author of a treatise on the constellations, one Eratosthenes, tells us the story of Orpheus' end and in so doing mentions a lost play of Aeschylus, the *Bassarids*, probably written early in the fifth century BC and taking its name from the chorus of women in tragedy. He writes as follows:

He [Orpheus] paid no honour to Dionysus but considered Helios to be the greatest of the gods and addressed him as Apollo. Hastening through the night he reached the summit of Mount Pangaeus and waited there to see the rising sun. Dionysus in his anger set the Bassarids against him, as the poet Aeschylus says, and they tore him to pieces and scattered his limbs broadcast. The Muses gathered his remains and buried them in what is called Leibethra [a mountain district of Thrace]. Having no one to whom to give his lyre they asked Zeus to set it among the stars as a memorial to him and to themselves.[30]

Fifth-century vase paintings show both Orpheus playing his lyre among the Thracians and Orpheus being attacked by hostile women.[31] The reason for the hostility of the women is difficult to understand, but it is a well-attested part of his story; Plato alludes to it, a century after Aeschylus, in the famous Vision of Er with which the *Republic* ends. Er, witnessing the souls of the departed preparing to return to this world after a long period of purification, sees among them the soul of Orpheus choosing the life of a swan for his next incarnation because of his refusal to be born of the sex that had been responsible for his death (x 620 a). Guthrie assumes that there was something profoundly misogynistic[32] about the religion that Orpheus preached. He offended not only Dionysus, the mighty antagonist of Apollo, but along with him the entire female sex which the god admitted enthusiastically to his following but which the ascetic preacher outraged by his anti-feminism as he ensorcelled their husbands through his music and his summons to a celibate community.

How to reconcile the view that Orpheus was a Bronze-Age shaman (Böhme) and the view that he was a missionary among the Thracians (Guthrie)? The Mycenaean figure appears to have a reality more psychological than historical, as we have seen. And no doubt the story pattern and the ritual experience are older than the name we attach to them. At some point – it is difficult to say when – the stories became attached to a name, as did poetry and a body of religious doctrine. It is interesting to note a possibly similar pattern in the case of Heracles. First, a shamanic figure and Master of Animals whose origins may go back even beyond the Bronze to the Stone Age;[33] then, perhaps, a real man who became the focal point of the tradition and who contributed the name by which the character, partly historical and partly mythical, was to be known.[34] Scholars are unlikely to come to complete agreement regarding who the historical Orpheus was and when he lived. But Homer is a vague figure too, though the Greeks never doubted that there had been such a man, even if modern scholars have. So it is in the case of Orpheus.

Whatever truth there may be in Guthrie's interpretation, it is interesting to note that the Romans, who inherited a much impoverished Orpheus, concentrating as they did almost exclusively on the love story of Orpheus and Eurydice, made much of the hostility of the female sex towards poor Orpheus. Virgil, in the *Fourth Georgic*, the first and still the most beautiful account of the unsuccessful attempt of Orpheus to bring Eurydice back from the nether world, describes the antagonism of the women of Thrace. For Virgil the hatred of the women is simply the result of the singer's undying attachment to the woman he has lost, his death at the hands of the Thracian women a motif directly subservient to a romantic story:

> No thought of love
> Or wedding rites could bend his inflexible will.
> He wandered lonely through the icy North,
> Past the snow-encrusted Don, through mountain fields
> Of unadulterated frost, conveyed the grief
> At Hell's ironic offerings, and rapt
> Eurydice. By such unwavering faith
> The Thracian women felt themselves outraged,
> And at their sacred exercise, nocturnal
> Bacchanals, they tore the youth apart,
> And scattered his limbs around the spacious fields.
> But even then his voice, within the head
> Torn from its marble neck, and spinning down
> The tide of his paternal River Hebrus,
> The cold-tongued voice itself, as life fled away,
> Called out 'Oh, my forlorn Eurydice!
> Eurydice!' and the shoreline answered back
> Along the river's breadth, 'Eurydice!'[35]

Ovid, at the beginning of the eleventh book of the *Metamorphoses*, tells in lurid detail the story of the dismemberment of Orpheus by the spurned women – the motif here too grows out of the romantic story – and adds the detail that Orpheus' head was washed up on the island of Lesbos. The story of Orpheus' extreme devotion to his wife was what the Romans best liked, and they combined it with the mysterious story, as least as old as Aeschylus, of his being rent asunder by Thracian women. The detail of the severed head floating down the river Hebrus and being washed ashore on Lesbos is in all likelihood an old one too. The head of Orpheus was buried in a temple at Antissa on Lesbos, where it continued to give oracles, and his lyre was preserved in a temple of Apollo. These illustrious relics were widely held to have inspired the flowering of poetry on the remarkable island that produced Terpander, Sappho, and Alcaeus, the first lyric monodists of the Greek world (late seventh and early sixth centuries BC). A fragment of Alcaeus, frustratingly incomplete, mentions the river Hebrus:

Most beautiful of rivers, Hebrus, are you, as you pour forth beside Aenus into the purple sea surging through the land of Thrace ... And many maidens visit you, with delicate hands [? to bathe] their beautiful thighs; they are beguiled ... wondrous water like unguent ... [36]

The invocation of the river would in all probability suggest the story of Orpheus, and the poem may well have gone on to tell it. A singing head endowed with oracular powers is something which points towards shamanism again. In all parts of the world, in addition to having the ability to travel to the Beyond and recover lost souls and a not infrequent power to summon birds and beasts to listen to their music, the shaman lives on after death as a magical head which gives oracles that are but a continuation of the incantations he practised while alive. [37]

The love story of Orpheus and Eurydice, so important to the Romans and to us, seems quite clearly the tail-end of a centuries-old tradition that knew Orpheus, shaman and Argonaut, as traveller to the world beyond and master of its mysteries. Romantic love was of little interest to the early Greeks. It was essentially a creation of the Alexandrian Age and forms part of its legacy to Rome. The first truly romantic narrative in European literature is, in fact, the love story of Jason and Medea in the *Argonautica* of Apollonius of Rhodes. Nowhere before do we find the intimate analytical handling of a love theme which makes the third book of this poem so much more interesting than the story of the voyage within which the love story is contained. The Romans inherited the Alexandrian interest and turned it to account, no one more splendidly than Virgil, who could use Apollonius' handling of Jason and Medea as model for his own story of Dido and Aeneas and who has given us the classical account of Orpheus' tragic love for Eurydice. The unhappy ending has been, since Virgil, an essential ingredient of the great love story: passion and death are indissolubly linked. But if the Virgilian story has the unhappy ending which we have come to regard as the regular one when we think of Orpheus and Eurydice, it is likely Virgil's own invention or something he took from a lost Alexandrian source. Ideas of taboo, so prominent in folk-tales, are rare in Greek myth and are not likely early ingredients of stories in which they are found at a late date.[38] The Greeks, in a period before interest in romantic love demanded the unhappy ending, seem to have known Orpheus – and this is what we would expect – as one who was successful in bringing his wife back from the underworld.[39] The name Eurydice, which means 'Wide-Ruler,' may well be late. It is used for the first time in literature in the *Lament for Bion*, probably of the first century BC. Earlier she had been called Agriope, 'Savage Watcher,' by the poet Hermesianax in the third century. The names are rough equivalents, both being obviously names of the Queen of the Night, Persephone. The Bronze Age archetype discussed earlier would suggest that the lost princess was released and recovered, that the earth gives back life, that the shaman is not defeated in the House of Death. Both in the *Lament for Bion* and in Hermesianax Orpheus is successful in bringing back Eurydice/Agriope. And so it is not surprising to learn that the first passing reference to Orpheus' descent for his own bride is a reference to a successful recovery. In Euripides' play, the *Alcestis* (438 BC), the poet puts into the mouth of Admetus, the husband of the doomed Alcestis, the following words:

> Had I the lips of Orpheus and his melody
> to charm the maiden daughter of Demeter and
> her lord, and by my singing win you back from death,
> I would have gone beneath the earth, and not the hound
> of Pluto could have stayed me, not the ferryman
> of ghosts, Charon at his oar. I would have brought you back
> to life.[40]

There can be no doubt that Euripides is referring to a story, already well known, in which Orpheus was successful in bringing back his wife. If the commonly known story had been one in which he had failed, reference to it on the part of Admetus would have been totally inappropriate at this moment.

Almost contemporary with the reference in Euripides' *Alcestis* is a late fifth-century Attic relief extant in three copies, the finest of which is in the National Museum in Naples. The three figures in the relief are identified by inscriptions above their heads as Hermes, Eurydice, and Orpheus, though it is likely that the inscriptions were not on the original. In any case the figures are clearly identifiable. Orpheus is holding his lyre in his left hand. Hermes looks on as Orpheus, with his right hand, touches Eurydice's left, apparently lifting the veil from her face. Interpretation of this famous piece of sculpture is uncertain. Is Orpheus here portrayed in the act of breaking the taboo which causes him to lose Eurydice a second time? Is he simply taking his first farewell at her death? Or are we shown the moment of his triumph in the underworld? The most natural interpretation would seem to be the last: the lyre suggests that Orpheus has just finished singing, the veil brushed aside that he has learned the secrets of the afterlife and is united to Eurydice, whom he is to escort back.[41] A remarkably similar scene, clearly a scene of union rather than of separation, is visible on one of the reliefs from the frieze of a temple at Selinus in Sicily. This metope, today in the National Museum in Palermo, shows the Holy Marriage of Zeus and Hera. Zeus, like Orpheus, touches the veil and the left wrist of his bride with his right hand. The pieces in Naples and Palermo both date from approximately the middle of the fifth century BC.

Plato speaks in the *Symposium* of the failure of Orpheus, but not in the manner familiar to us from Virgil. In this dialogue the speaker, Phaedrus, contrasts Alcestis, who was brave enough to die for Admetus, with Orpheus, who was sent back from Hades 'without accomplishing his mission' (*atelê* 179d). The underworld gods show him a phantom rather than give him his wife since they found him a poor-spirited fellow, as lyre players are wont to be. The story in the *Symposium* is probably Plato's own invention: it would be hazardous to regard it simply as something taken over intact from the current stock of myth. Plato may be influenced here by the well-known story, mentioned by the poet Stesichorus (c 630–c 555 BC) and repeated by Plato himself in the *Republic* (IX 586 c), that the war at Troy was fought over a phantom, Helen never having been at Ilium. The Orpheus story in the *Symposium* relies for its effect on the shock value of the word *atelê* ('unsuccessful') at the beginning of the passage in which it is told. It presupposes, surely, an accepted version in which Orpheus was successful, stands the known story on its head, and surprises us by informing us that what Orpheus found was a phantom, not his real wife. In other words, the tale of the phantom explains the word 'unsuccessful.'

Of especial interest in this version is the notice that the gods found Orpheus reprehensible as being insufficiently heroic. Something in this seems to pick up a preoccupation older than Plato. A commentator, or scholiast, on the *Argonautica* of Apollonius of Rhodes[42] has a fascinating discussion of authors who mentioned Orpheus' connection with the Argo long before Apollonius. It appears to have been of major concern to explain just how

Orpheus, generally so unlike most Greek heroes, could have sailed with the Argonauts. One fifth-century writer, Pherecydes, had, according to the commentator, been quite unwilling to believe that Orpheus was in the company of the stalwart crew that sailed with Jason and had, accordingly, made the striking statement that Orpheus had never really been on the Argo. There is, without any doubt, something about Orpheus that sets him apart from all the other great figures of Greek myth. Greek myth is pre-eminently heroic myth, myth that enshrines martial values: courage, killing, blood-lust. Not surprising in the legacy of a male-dominated warrior society that produced, in the *Iliad*, the world's supreme battle epic and whose agonistic, competitive impulse never faltered for a moment. The finest products of classical Greek poetry, a thousand years after the Indo-European invasion of the peninsula, are plays, produced at competitive festivals, and victory odes for triumphant athletes. The contest dominated Greek life in all its aspects, from the Gymnasium and the law-courts to dialectic. A modern theologian points out that there is even an intimate connection between the characteristic competitive impulse of the Greeks and their concept of love, always seen as a striving or an *agôn*.[43] Orpheus clearly belongs to another world, as has been suggested above. All the other great figures of Greek myth, whatever else they may be, are great killers: Achilles, Heracles, Jason, Perseus, Oedipus, Odysseus, Agamemnon – the list could be extended indefinitely and would show not a single figure of note who is not blood-stained. Orpheus is unique and he seems to have puzzled the Greeks. He did not particularly interest the poets of the classical period and he seems not to have escaped the charge of cowardice when compared with his fellows. Prometheus is not a killer, certainly, but he is undeniably aggressive and his hands reek of the blood of sacrifice: the two most important items in the myth concerning him are his contest of wits with Zeus and his establishment of the laws of sacrifice. A recent book by W. Burkert, *Homo Necans*[44] ('Man the Slaughterer'), is an intriguing study of the Greek obsession with animal sacrifice and its relation to aggressive biological drives found in animals and in primitive hunters. And certainly there is no honest way of minimizing the role of blood-letting either in Greek heroic myth or in Greek religious practice. Every hero fleshes his sword. Altars were steeped in the blood of animals of all sorts. Priests were butchers, temples slaughterhouses. The Greeks were fortunate in having these outlets for their murderous instincts. On the ritual level animals could be slaughtered instead of human beings; in myth the same impulse was discharged in fantasy, in stories of war and of dragon-slaying. Both these channels were innocent and socially beneficial.

But Orpheus cuts a strange figure among the heroes. He seems tame if not weak in comparison, as the Greeks themselves noticed. He restores to life instead of killing; he is surrounded by the fiercest of animals which, far from slaying, he leads from savagery to docility and meekness by his music. Claude Lévi-Strauss and his followers in the structuralist school of anthropology have asserted that mental and social processes are fundamentally binary, coded in mythical examples which, when deciphered, reveal simple polarities. The psychic life of a people sends up directly contradictory impulses that will crystallize in antithetical figures. If there is any truth in this, it may be reasonable to see in Orpheus the necessary and precious counterpiece to his numerous more ferocious brethren. One of Lévi-Strauss's disciples has written a fascinating essay on this very theme, comparing Orpheus, the unnaturally gentle – his subjugation of wild animals through the power of music is contrary to expectation and all normal experience – with Orion, the excessively savage, whose thirst for blood knows no bounds.[45] On this interpretation the musician is, as he appears to be judged in the *Symposium*, a cowardly creature, though as inevitable a product of the mythical imagination of antiquity as is his equally extreme opposite number. The mean would lie somewhere between the extremes, the mythopoeic imagination creating the embodiments of opposite and discordant qualities and inviting that reconciliation or repose which is created by the presence of balance and stress.

It is, of course, not necessary to view the matter this way. If Orpheus is viewed as a culpable extreme by a speaker in a Platonic dialogue or by a modern structuralist, he may be, and most often is, received without any pejorative value-judgment clinging to him. When George Steiner describes Lévi-Strauss himself as 'Orpheus with his myths'[46] he is being highly complimentary: Lévi-Strauss is Orpheus in his traditional and time-honoured role, both musician (the various parts of Lévi-Strauss's work correspond to musical forms and the author continually turns to music to provide the best analogy for myth as he understands it) and prophet who reveals, in difficult and enigmatic language, a vision which ranges beyond that of the generality of men. The *Mythologiques* of Lévi-Strauss are, for Steiner, Orphic in the best possible sense of the word, advancing the cause of harmony where there is silence (death) or discord (savagery). One is tempted to add another Orphic point to all this. The closing paragraph of the third volume of the *Mythologiques* shows its author's urgent concern to turn European civilization back from the hell ('enfer') in which it has become imprisoned by self-centredness.[47] Who better than Orpheus to perform such a task?

The Orpheus that the ancients knew was priest, lover, musician. Most times one or two of the three, rarely all in combination. There is one avatar of Orpheus in European art who is quintessentially all three, the perfect amalgam that is nowhere else so fully present, even on the stage of antiquity. Since his name is not Orpheus and since he will, thus, not appear in the succeeding pages of this book, he must not be passed over here. There can be little doubt that his creators had the ancient myths in mind when they designed him. He is the perfect Orpheus, lacking only the traditional name.

Mozart's opera *The Magic Flute* was written in 1791, in the last months of the composer's life. The author of the libretto, Emmanuel Schikaneder, worked closely under the composer's supervision, the result being an opera in which Mozart was able to exercise the greatest degree of control over the text he set to music. One of the composer's closest friends at this time was the master of the Masonic Lodge to which he belonged. This remarkable person, Ignaz von Born, was learned in countless fields and had a knowledge of ancient myth and ritual that was unmatched in the Austria of his time. He influenced Mozart as Mozart influenced his librettist, and the result is the most profoundly felt of all the composer's great works.

In the First Act, Tamino, the hero of the opera, charms, by the power of his music, the beasts of the wild wood; in the Second Act he quells, by the same magic, the hostile forces, here fire and water, that threaten to engulf him. Further, he gains his beloved princess Pamina through his steadfastness in refusing to break the taboo imposed on him if he is to win her. Through a succession of trials he moves from the Realm of Night – Pamina is the daughter of the Queen of the Night – to membership in the brotherhood of the Temple of Light. His progress is transparently a successful emergence from the underworld, successful because he observes the prohibition enjoined on him. Pamina pleads with him but he is adamant. Only thirty years earlier (1762) Viennese audiences had seen a Virgilian Orpheus, the Orfeo of Gluck's opera *Orfeo ed Euridice*, lose his princess because he was unable to persist in observing the taboo. The audience that saw Pamina pleading with Tamino to speak to her will certainly have remembered Euridice pleading with Orfeo in Gluck's opera. Most important of all, Tamino, in Mozart's work, moves through his self-mastery and asceticism into possession of the mystic secrets of an esoteric sect (much influenced by Masonry, a society in many ways comparable to the Orphic sect for the existence of which in ancient Greece scholars like Guthrie have, as we have seen, argued). Goethe wrote a dramatic sequel to Mozart's opera. In it he elevated Tamino to the role of High Priest and mediator of salvation for humanity. Nothing could correspond more closely than this to the role assigned to Orpheus by those who have seen in him an authentic religious teacher of the Greeks, revealing truth and instituting ritual. In Tamino all the attributes of Orpheus have been blended in fairly equal proportions.

Orpheus entire or Orpheus dismembered. The figure is fascinating however we take him. We have seen what he was to the Greeks. Let us now see in some detail what he has been since.

NOTES

1 Cf M.O. Lee 'Orpheus and Eurydice: Myth, Legend, Folklore' *Classica et Mediaevalia* 26 (1965) 402–12.
2 There is a good discussion of these matters in G.S. Kirk *The Nature of Greek Myths* (Harmondsworth 1974) 30–8.
3 See, eg, Stith Thompson *Motif-Index of Folk-Literature* (Bloomington 1933) F 81.1 and C 331.
4 *The Art of Poetry* 391–3 (tr John G. Hawthorne), in L.R. Lind ed *Latin Poetry in Verse Translation* (Boston 1957) 140
5 See J.B. Friedman *Orpheus in the Middle Ages* (Harvard 1970).
6 See E. Sewell *The Orphic Voice: Poetry and Natural History* (New Haven 1960) especially Part II.
7 See J. Kerman *Opera as Drama* (New York 1956) 25–50.
8 See W.A. Strauss *Descent and Return: The Orphic Theme in Modern Literature* (Harvard 1971).
9 Aristophanes *Frogs* 1032ff
10 Plato *Apology* 41a
11 Pindar *Pythian* 4. 171–7
12 Simonides fr 62 in D.L. Page *Poetae Melici Graeci* (Oxford 1962) tr C.M. Bowra *Greek Lyric Poetry* (2nd edn; Oxford 1961) 364
13 *Odyssey* 12. 57–72 tr R. Fitzgerald (New York 1961)
14 See K. Meuli *Odyssee und Argonautika* (Basel 1921); D. Page *Folktales in Homer's Odyssey* (Cambridge, Mass 1973) chapters 2 and 4.
15 J. Lindsay *The Clashing Rocks; A Study of Early Greek Religion and Culture and the Origins of Drama* (London 1965)
16 Pindar *Pythian* 4.158–61 tr C.M. Bowra *The Odes of Pindar* (Harmondsworth 1969). The passage is discussed by W. Burkert in his article on Greek shamanism 'ΓΟΗΣ. Zum griechischen Schamanismus' *Rheinisches Museum* 105 (1962) 36–55.
17 Alcaeus fr 34.11 in E.-M. Voigt *Sappho et Alcaeus* (Amsterdam 1971)
18 G.S. Kirk *Myth: Its Meaning and Functions in Ancient and Other Cultures* (Berkeley and Los Angeles 1970) 231–2
19 One example among many possibilities might be cited: N.O. Brown's influential book *Life against Death: The Psychoanalytical Meaning of History* (New York 1959).
20 Kirk *Myth: Its Meaning and Functions* 231–2

21 J. Campbell *The Masks of God: Occidental Mythology* (New York 1964) Part One 'The Age of the Goddess'

22 'The Palace of Nestor Excavations of 1955' *American Journal of Archaeology* 60 (1956) 95

23 M. Nilsson *The Mycenaean Origin of Greek Mythology* (rpt New York 1963) 74–6, 171–4

24 R. Böhme *Orpheus: Der Sänger und seine Zeit.* An earlier book, *Orpheus: Das Alter der Kitharoden* (Berlin 1953), is reviewed by Guthrie in *Gnomon* 26 (1954) 303–7.

25 Hesiod *Theogony* 748–750 tr D. Wender (Harmondsworth 1973)

26 *Iliad* 8.15 tr R. Lattimore (Chicago 1951)

27 *Odyssey* 9.86

28 Parmenides fr B 1.11 in H. Diels and W. Kranz *Die Fragmente der Vorsokratiker* (11th edn; Zurich and Berlin 1964)

29 E.R. Dodds *The Greeks and the Irrational* (Berkeley and Los Angeles 1951) 147ff

30 Kern *Orphicorum fragmenta* Test 113 (my translation)

31 See Guthrie *Orpheus and Greek Religion* (rpt New York 1966) figures 4 and 5, plates 4 and 6.

32 Ibid 49

33 See W. Burkert *Structure and History in Greek Mythology and Ritual* (Berkeley, Los Angeles and London 1979) chapter 4.

34 H.J. Rose *A Handbook of Greek Mythology* (6th edn; London 1958) 205

35 Virgil *Georgics* 4.516–27 tr S.P. Bovie (Chicago 1956)

36 Alcaeus fr 45 (tr D.L. Page); see D.L. Page *Sappho and Alcaeus: An Introduction to the Study of Ancient Lesbian Poetry* (Oxford 1955) 285–8.

37 M. Eliade *Shamanism: Archaic Techniques of Ecstasy* tr W.R. Trask (New York 1964) 391; E.R. Dodds *The Greeks and the Irrational* 147.

38 See Martin P. Nilsson *A History of Greek Religion* (2nd edn; rpt New York 1964) 52–7.

39 The tradition of the unsuccessful return of Orpheus is discussed by P. Dronke 'The Return of Eurydice' *Classica et Mediaevalia* 23 (1962) 198–215. Dronke is primarily interested in the use of the myth in medieval poetry where Orpheus is a type of Christ. He argues that the dominant tradition remained strong and was never eclipsed by the Virgilian version.

40 Euripides *Alcestis* 357–362 tr R. Lattimore (Chicago 1955)

41 Rilke's account of the second loss of Eurydice by Orpheus in the poem 'Orpheus. Eurydike. Hermes' is probably inspired by the sculpture discussed here: see Strauss *Descent and Return* 172. Rilke clearly interprets the sculpture in accordance with the tradition of the unsuccessful attempt to restore Eurydice

to life. But the bas-relief is not explicit: much of its fascination comes precisely from the fact that it must be interpreted in accordance with a view of the myth formed by literary versions. Rilke accepts the Virgilian version.

42 C. Wendel *Scholia in Apollonium Rhodium Vetera* (2nd edn; Berlin 1958) 8–9

43 M. Scheler *Ressentiment* tr W.W. Holdheim (New York 1972) 84–6

44 W. Burkert *Homo Necans: Interpretationen altgriechischer Opferriten und Mythen* (Berlin and New York 1972). A rather different position is taken by J. Huizinga in his famous book *Homo Ludens: A Study of the Play-Element in Culture* tr R.F.C. Hull (Boston 1955). Huizinga thinks that the Greeks were no more competitive or aggressive than other peoples and criticizes scholars who have maintained that they were (71ff): for him war, contests, sacrifice are but manifestations of a play-impulse that is ubiquitous in world culture. But when Huizinga posits the superiority of Greek civilization to others (eg p 174) he does so on the grounds that the play-element in Greek culture was more lively and imaginative than it was elsewhere. It appears to be chiefly a question of the value-judgment attached to the agonistic habit; Burkert's 'necans' is less complimentary than Huizinga's 'ludens,' but both authors find special evidence among the Greeks for what they are seeking.

45 M. Détienne 'Orphée au miel' *Quaderni Urbinati di Cultura Classica* 12 (1971) 7–23. Perhaps the tradition of Orpheus' death at the hands of women is no more than a further proof of his untypical, unheroic nature. Normal heroes (eg Achilles, Heracles, Bellerophon, Theseus) are superior even to Amazons: only a weakling could fall to female assailants. In the *Odyssey* it is Aegisthus who kills Agamemnon. In Aeschylus, where Clytemnaestra commits the murder, there is a reversal of normal roles, Clytemnaestra being masculine, Agamemnon effeminate. And the Pentheus of Euripides' *Bacchae*, before his murder by the women, has himself been virtually turned into a woman by Dionysus.

Of interest in this respect, perhaps, is the possible existence of a tradition that sees Jason as weak and unheroic; see M. Hadas 'The Tradition of a Feeble Jason' *Classical Philology* 31 (1936) 166–8. This may provide another link between Jason and Orpheus. It is noteworthy, certainly, that these two Argonauts became the two Greek 'heroes' most famous for their loves. Something in their very nature seems to have lent itself especially well to romantic exploitation by Apollonius and Virgil.

46 G. Steiner *Language and Silence: Essays on Language, Literature, and the Inhuman* (New York 1967) 239–50

47 C. Lévi-Strauss *Mythologiques III: L'origine des manières de table* (Paris 1968) 422

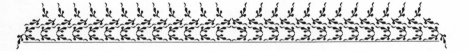

W.S. ANDERSON

The Orpheus of Virgil and Ovid: *flebile nescio quid*

SHORTLY AFTER OCTAVIAN won the battle of Actium and Civil War gave place to Golden Age, the poet Virgil, whose earlier collection of pastoral poems had given such promise, published his *Georgics,* a didactic work of four books that indeed justified the high expectations of his friends. No small part of his achievement, though covering barely seventy-five lines in *Georgics* 4, was his narrative of Orpheus. Many readers, if they recall nothing else in detail from the poem, remember with strong emotions the affecting story of Orpheus' tragic loss of Eurydice and the inconsolable mourning that marked his pathetic life thereafter and that coloured his death. Virgil's account, concentrating as it does on violent and ultimately thwarted passions, is an emotional tour de force.

Not long after the turn of the century, Ovid embarked on his *Metamorphoses*, and no doubt before his exile in AD 8 he had completed his own story of Orpheus, roughly thirty-five years after Virgil's. It is a story of great charm and wit, typical of some of the best material in Ovid's delightful poem, but, like so many of Ovid's passages, it cannot be fully savoured without the knowledge of Virgil that Ovid of course could assume in his earliest Roman audiences. Quite consciously viewing the mythic materials in a different way from Virgil, placing his story in a long poem quite different from Virgil's didactic work, and setting his story in a context at variance with Virgil's, Ovid has given the same myth a new interpretation. He has concentrated on the grief of Orpheus, like Virgil, but, unlike Virgil, he cannot or will not immerse himself subjectively in that tearfulness, at least not for long. The final song of the dead Orpheus, which haunts Virgil and Virgil's reader as the epitome of tragedy, is carelessly tossed off by Ovid as 'something or other pathetic' ('flebile nescio quid' in *Metamorphoses* 11.52). The change in the narrator's attitude toward Orpheus, striking in itself, necessarily entails a new perception of the mythical figure, a new literary appropriation of the myth.

With these two richly different views of Orpheus, the products of the two greatest poetic talents of Rome, I shall be concerning myself in this essay. These views mark the beginning of a tradition of reinterpretation of Orpheus and Eurydice, which has shown extraordinary vitality well into our own century.

I ORPHEUS IN *GEORGICS* 4

Virgil's story of Orpheus is an obvious intrusion into the basic format of the *Georgics*. The narrative style of the tale is not in keeping with the didactic approach; its mythical contents are patently at odds with the realistic subject of *Georgics* 4, that is the day-to-day problems of a farmer tending bees; and the high emotionality of the account differs appreciably from the sensible, often good-humoured irony with which Virgil views the 'monumental problems' of the diminutive bees in their anthropomorphic society. Virgil justifies his story as follows: he proposes to explain how to cope with the crisis when an entire swarm of bees dies. Therefore, he describes an Egyptian practice which supposedly generates bees from the putrefying hide of a dead calf (4.281ff). Having done this, he introduces the originator of this practice, mythical Aristaeus, and embarks on a long mythological elaboration of how it all began (315ff). Aristaeus, when all his bees died, complained bitterly by the riverside, and his mother, the nymph Cyrene, brought him down to her home beneath the surface, fed and comforted him, then sent him off to Egypt to learn the reason for the death of his bees (333ff). In obedience to her commands, he captured the wise sea-god Proteus and compelled him to speak the truth (415ff). Proteus told him that he was suffering the consequences of inadvertently causing the death of Eurydice; he had tried to rape her, it appears, and, while running away from him, she accidentally had gone too close to a poisonous snake on the river bank (453ff). When Proteus had impressed upon Aristaeus his guilt, Cyrene gave him instructions in the way to placate Orpheus, Eurydice, and the angry Nymphs who were her friends (530ff). Four bulls and four cows were slaughtered on the altars of the Nymphs; their corpses were left to rot; and after eight days a swarm of bees rose from the bodies, ready to serve Aristaeus. Thus, the immediate reason for the story of Orpheus is to explain to Aristaeus the loss of his bees: he has accidentally caused Eurydice's death, and as punishment, his bees have been killed.

I shall come back later to the deeper poetic reasons for introducing Orpheus in this context. For the present, however, let us ignore the context and concentrate on the story itself. It may be briefly summarized, because Virgil has established the outlines for all successive versions of Orpheus' loss of Eurydice; and these details will sound very familiar to most readers.[1]

Bitten by a poisonous snake, Eurydice died, amid general lamentation from friends and her devoted husband Orpheus. After mourning her day and night, Orpheus resorted in desperation to Hades, appealing in passionate song to the powers of the Underworld. They were deeply moved and granted him Eurydice, on condition that she follow him out of Hades and that he not turn to look at her until they reach the open air and daylight. Unable to contain himself, Orpheus turned near the surface, and Eurydice was snatched from him, back to Death. This time, none of the powers of Hades would grant him a hearing. When he continued his mourning and refused to make the best of the remainder of his life by remarrying, his violent rejection of Thracian women resulted in his death by dismemberment at their hands. Most of the pieces of his corpse were scattered about the fields, but his head fell in the Hebrus River and floated out to sea, still singing its pathetic lament for lost Eurydice.

Although Virgil's is the first surviving account of Orpheus and Eurydice which specifically focuses on his failure to recover her entirely, there are good reasons, in my opinion, to believe that the Latin poet was working in a familiar Greco-Roman myth.[2] In the first place, Virgil does not develop his account with the fullness that one would require in an unfamiliar tale, not even in the sequence of the fatal turning-around of Orpheus, precisely where, according to some scholars, *new* material enters. In the second place, the total economy of *Georgics* 4.281ff makes it evident that Orpheus' experiences play a distinctly subordinate role to those of Aristaeus, so much so that the familiar Orpheus seems called upon to elucidate unfamiliar details in Aristaeus. Indeed, it is highly likely that the *new* features invented by Virgil inhere in the Aristaeus-story, that he is the first to link Orpheus and Aristaeus. Perhaps the link suggested itself because the given, familiar motifs of Orpheus' tragic experience offered rich material for colouring and interpreting the unfamiliar and novel story assigned to Aristaeus. Exactly when the story of Orpheus' failure originated remains a point of contention among scholars. I myself am inclined to agree with those who go back before the Hellenistic period as early as fifth-century Greek literature (presumably tragedy) and art for the source.

Virgil does not tell of Orpheus' experiences as though the details of the story were unfamiliar to his readers. Rather, he relies on the familiar, and introduces his own special emphases. From the beginning, the narrative focuses on Orpheus. Although, at the time of Proteus' narration, the husband is quite as dead as his wife, nevertheless he, not Eurydice, is said to have caused Aristaeus' punishment. Orpheus is said to be still raging ('saevit' 456) over his loss; the feelings of Eurydice are not mentioned. Since Virgil is probably the first to link Orpheus and Aristaeus, the narrator must explain Aristaeus' guilt and Orpheus' anger at him. These are shown briefly by means of a common story-motif appropriate to the rural world: Aristaeus (obviously with erotic intent) pursued the nymph Eurydice, who, while trying to escape him, failed to see a poisonous snake, which bit and killed her. Virgil renders this episode in three relatively bland lines (457–9), and minimizes the role of Eurydice by not naming her and by avoiding qualifying details other than calling her 'girl doomed to die' ('moritura puella' 458), an 'elegiac' phrase which serves more to replace a full, pathetic description of her death than to make us weep. Indeed, the snake gets more emphasis in the three short lines than either Aristaeus or Eurydice. Once the narrator has removed Eurydice, without any notice of the death-scene itself, he can establish his desired emphasis on lamentation. Four lines suffice to report the way her friends the Dryads weep for her and how the pastoral scenery echoes this grief (460–3). That general grief serves to preface the more powerful and, for the narrator, more significant misery of Orpheus:

> ipse cava solans aegrum testudine amorem
> te, dulcis coniunx, te solo in litore secum,
> te veniente die, te decedente canebat. (464–6)

(Orpheus himself, attempting to console the agony of his love on the hollow shell of his lyre, sang of you, darling wife, of you on the lonely shore by himself, of you as the sun rose, of you as it set.)

It is clear from the context that the participle 'solans' does not denote the success of his consolation, but the effort that unfortunately proves vain. The love of Orpheus, which determines all his subsequent acts, is sick ('aegrum' 464), and it prescribes the kind of song he sings; song does not charm away his grief. Virgil uses his subjective style in 465–6 to express through repeated apostrophe ('te' at the beginning of both lines and at the central caesurae) his sympathy with the situation. However, although ostensibly he addresses Eurydice, it seems to me that the apostrophe serves rather to characterize the way Orpheus continuously but vainly sings, pathetically addressing his dead Eurydice, 'dulcis coniunx' to him while alive. Still inconsolable, Orpheus goes down to Hades. Virgil does not directly explain why, presumably relying on his audience's familiarity with the story. Only in his indirect description of the powers below as 'hearts that do not know how to be softened by the prayers of men' (470), does he suggest that Orpheus pleads for Eurydice's release.

Virgil does not cite the words of Orpheus' musical prayer. He prefers to indicate its dramatic effect by describing the way various residents of Hades were moved ('cantu commotae' 471). From the diverse classes of dead, whose reactions he further qualifies by simile (471–80), the poet goes on to note select figures of mythical Hades (Cerberus, the Eumenides, and Ixion) who were struck dumb and motionless by the charm of Orpheus. Then without pausing over the decision of Hades and Proserpina to release Eurydice or the conditions they set – another indication of familiar details – the narrator jumps directly to the journey back to life. We are suddenly shown the pair as they are about to emerge into the daylight (485). As Virgil tells it, though, Eurydice is the subject of the three lines that deal with the journey; it is she who had almost escaped her misfortunes, almost reached the upper air. Apart from focusing on Eurydice, the poet does not colour the description by a single qualifying adjective or adverb or by a verb, metaphorical or not, that might capture our feelings. In sharp contrast are the four lines that follow, accounting for Orpheus' fatal action in turning around; these are the most densely packed lines in the entire story:

> cum subita incautum dementia cepit amantem,
> ignoscenda quidem, scirent si ignoscere manes:
> restitit, Eurydicenque suam iam luce sub ipsa
> immemor heu! victusque animi respexit.   (488–91)

(... when sudden madness possessed the heedless lover, surely pardonable if the powers below knew how to pardon: he stopped, and by the first light from above, forgetting, alas, the conditions, his reason overcome, he looked back toward his own dear Eurydice.)

Orpheus' backward glance, for all the poet's qualifications, cancels out the journey of Eurydice. Virgil's seven-line sentence (485–91) is a brilliant example of the utility of the so-called *cum-inversum* structure. The three lines about Eurydice, which seem to be carrying the main events of the passage, lull the audience into security. However, the *cum* clause of 488, far from subordinating what follows to what precedes, in fact focuses on the principal actions: first 'restitit,' then 'respexit.' Two verbs, and the rest is qualification. Orpheus is a victim of madness and love together, pardonable by human standards but unpardonable here where gods were judging, of irrationality and failure to remember the penalty. The light, which alone gives a setting, comes, as my translation makes emphatic, not from the subterranean world but faintly penetrates from above to the travellers. In the Latin, Virgil has violently separated object from verb in 490–1; the separation connotes the total impossibility of Orpheus' rash desire. He looked back at Eurydice, his beloved ('suam'), and at that very moment, by consequence of the act itself, she ceased to be his. Indeed, he hardly saw her and failed utterly to touch or embrace her.

Orpheus' rash deed of irrational passion receives a generalized comment from the narrator and a triple roll of thunder wells up from Hades below. Then comes the more poignant comment of Eurydice. For Virgil, who has

wisely avoided trying to duplicate Orpheus' charmed song among the dead
and only indirectly suggested some elements of his lament above ground in
464ff now produces the only direct speech of the entire story, the last pathetic
words of Orpheus' wife.

> illa 'quis et me' inquit 'miseram et te perdidit, Orpheu,
> quis tantus furor? en iterum crudelia retro
> fata vocant, conditque natantia lumina somnus.
> iamque vale: feror ingenti circumdata nocte
> invalidasque tibi tendens, heu non tua, palmas.'   (494–8)

'What is this, what great madness,' she said, 'has destroyed both poor me and you,
Orpheus? Now again the cruel fates summon me back, and sleep (of death) drowns my
swimming eyes. Goodbye: I am carried off, surrounded by massive darkness, holding
out powerless hands to you, alas not yours to have.')

Virgil allows her to protest at the 'furor' which has caused such damage,
but she does so in such a way as to attenuate Orpheus' guilt. Although we
know, and he does also, that it is *his* madness which she names, Eurydice
sounds as though she could be blaming a cosmic force that has victimized
them both. Apart from that initial outcry, her speech is more a means of narrative than of fixing her misery. New symbols replace the hopeful ones that had
begun during the journey upward: instead of light, night and sleep now
surround, bury, and drown their victim; instead of upper air, the cruel fates
below possess her; instead of acting as the subject of free, vigorous verbs of
motion, Eurydice now becomes the helpless object of the verbs of 494–6, the
unhappy passive subject of 'feror' in 497, and the only active verbal form is the
final participle 'tendens,' which epitomizes her pathetic condition. As she
vainly holds out her hands to him, she answers his passionate actions of 491
and also of 501 ('prensantem nequiquam umbras'). The hyperbaton separating 'invalidas' from its noun 'palmas' and the inserted pathetic 'heu non tua'
accomplish similar results with, and echo, the hyperbaton of 490–1. Orpheus
tried to make Eurydice 'his' rashly and prematurely; therefore, she has ceased
to be 'his' forever.

   After this unique speech, Virgil maintains Eurydice as subject for another
four lines (499–502), in order to describe her disappearance from Orpheus.
He has looked back at her and caused her disaster, so Virgil appropriately
stresses her loss in visual terms: she vanishes from his sight, and correspondingly she cannot see him, as he desperately tries to hold on to her and speak
to her. She had almost reached the upper air, where she would have become
warm flesh and blood again; now she slips away from his sight and grasp, like
smoke dispersed into thin air. By making Eurydice subject, Virgil elegantly
conveys the reversal of affairs. Orpheus' action has victimized her; now, as

death once again takes her, her involuntary act of departure punishes and ruins him. With that, our attention shifts to him and his pathetic situation, his feelings of love and loss compounded by an inevitable sense of guilt. He has hardly caught a glimpse of her, and he is frustrated in his attempt to touch her or to speak to her the many things he obviously has to say. Virgil remembered this poignant context and reused it when describing the final encounter of Aeneas and his 'dead' wife Creusa in the nightmarish horror of burning Troy: like Orpheus, Aeneas is made the object affected by her departure, vainly expressing his emotions and trying to communicate with her ('lacrimantem et multa volentem / dicere deseruit' Aeneid 2.790–1).

Virgil neatly compresses events now by co-ordinating Eurydice's departure ('neque illum ... vidit') with the refusal of Charon to transport Orpheus across the Styx for another appeal ('nec passus transire' 502–3). It is easy for us to imagine how Orpheus rushed back to the Styx and tried to reach Hades again, but Virgil's attention fixes on Orpheus the helpless, suffering lover, unable to act, only to be affected. That helplessness is further stressed by a series of deliberative questions:

> quid faceret? quo se rapta bis coniuge ferret?
> quo fletu manis, quae numina voce moveret? (504–5)

(What should he do? Where should he go now that his wife had been snatched away a second time? With what tears could he touch the Shades, what gods could he move with his song?)

The answer comes in unmistakable fashion in a final lapidary line about Eurydice, indeed lost forever:

> illa quidem Stygia nabat iam frigida cumba. (506)

(She was already cold, swimming now in the Stygian skiff.)

He cannot cross in Charon's boat to recover his beloved, warmly responding Eurydice, because she is a cold spirit departing from him in that very boat.

It has taken Virgil scarcely fifty lines to cover this portion of the narrative. In the remaining third of the story, we watch Orpheus lamenting once again, this time in the sure conviction that he has lost Eurydice forever. He heads back to Thrace, finds a lonely, chill, bleak spot under a hollowed-out cliff by the Strymon River, and month after month he sings of his pathetic loss. (Virgil says nothing of his guilt, but inevitably, from the way the narrative elaborated the motives behind his looking back, we are entitled to assume that his anger at Aristaeus has been mixed with anger at himself.) The song still exerts a powerful charm, though it serves no purpose whatsoever: Orpheus tames wild tigers and stirs oak trees (510). In a five-line simile, the narrator catches some of the chief elements by which this protracted grief may be assessed:

> qualis populea maerens philomela sub umbra
> amissos queritur fetus, quos durus arator
> observans nido implumis detraxit; at illa
> flet noctem, ramoque sedens miserabile carmen
> integrat, et maestis late loca questibus implet. (511–15)

(Like a grieving nightingale in a shady poplar tree, which complains of her lost young, which a tough plowman has spied and snatched, still fledglings, from her nest. She weeps all night long; perched on a branch, she keeps repeating her unhappy song and fills the forest far and wide with her mournful complaints.)

Here one finds unquestionable sympathy for the nightingale and for Orpheus. The bird is the innocent victim of the unfeeling farmer, robbed of her young, and her complaint is patently justified. It is conventional to think of the nightingale's song as beautiful and sad, especially since it is associated with the gloom of night-time. To that extent, she matches and colours the pathetic plight of the human singer. Orpheus, however, is not merely a victim. He is a man with the capacity to make rational choices, to deal creatively with his grief, and not to go on indulging himself eternally in vain lamentation. He could have a future. The bird indirectly points to such a future, because nightingales mate again, construct new nests, and tend new nestlings in instinctive response to nature's ever-continuing vital process. Moreover, Orpheus is not a guiltless victim. Although Aristaeus may be somewhat comparable to the 'durus arator,' Orpheus himself mainly bears the responsibility, as we have seen, for the conclusive loss of Eurydice. He has failed to come to grips with his own 'furor.' The bird also indirectly points to that complex background of guilty passion, for, by calling it 'philomela,' Virgil inevitably reminds his audience of the well-known myth in which mother and sister killed the son of Tereus, to punish his outrageous crimes of lust, and were then transformed into birds, the mother into a forever mourning nightingale.[3] Thus, Orpheus' grief is certainly pathetic, but somehow an inadequate response to the human situation, as the simile suggests.

From the simile, Virgil returns to renewed description of the inconsolable singer. Rejecting any thought of marriage, any love (516), Orpheus continues to haunt the lonely, icy Thracian landscape, and continues to sing his monotonous complaints on the loss of Eurydice. A woman scorned is dangerous enough. But when Orpheus spurns all the Thracian women, they turn on him and tear him limb from limb. A grotesque tradition had it that only his head escaped the wrath of the women: it fell into the river Hebrus and somehow floated out to sea, and, in some versions, across to the island of Lesbos. With marvellous finesse, Virgil manages to use this tradition to catch and epitomize the tragedy of Orpheus, in the last five lines of his narrative:

> tum quoque marmorea caput a cervice revulsum
> gurgite cum medio portans Oeagrius Hebrus
> volveret, Eurydicen vox ipsa et frigida lingua,
> a miseram Eurydicen! anima fugiente vocabat:
> Eurydicen toto referebant flumine ripae.   (523–7)

(Then, too, his head was torn from his marble-white neck, and as the Thracian Hebrus carried it along, rolling it in the midst of its wild waters, 'Eurydice' the voice and cold tongue called out, 'poor Eurydice,' with its failing breath; and the banks along the river echoed back: 'Eurydice.')

The main theme of this story is the pathetic, but essentially futile and ultimately suicidal, grief for a loss that cannot be altered. Virgil exhibits that complicated narrative technique which is later so powerful an element of the *Aeneid*: he conveys his strong sympathy for the deep feelings of a human being, but he does not shirk the necessity to judge 'furor' as human inadequacy. Men possess both rich feelings and reason with which to control and channel those feelings; mere indulgence in sentiment is wrong.

This story of Orpheus, which Virgil puts in the mouth of the prophetic Proteus to explain to Aristaeus why pestilence has wiped out his bees, has deeper functions. The fact that the theme conveys both sympathy and negative judgment for Orpheus and that the details of the story make more of Orpheus' guilty act of insane passion than of Aristaeus' attempt to rape Eurydice suggests that Proteus has been made to say things which serve the poet's larger purposes. Those purposes are to elaborate the meaning of Aristaeus' myth, namely, the resurrection of the beekeeping activities by renewal of the swarm. It does not take much effort to realize that the story of Orpheus has been told in such a way as to replace the guilty Aristaeus rather swiftly with the passionate and hence guilty Orpheus; and that is because Virgil aims to develop significant parallels and contrasts between the two men.[4] Both Aristaeus and Orpheus experience serious losses; Aristaeus is as deeply disturbed in his way by the death of his bees as Orpheus is by Eurydice's death. Like Orpheus, Aristaeus takes his stand by a river and pours out his complaints (319–20). Aristaeus like Orpheus has no desire to live and invokes a curse on surrounding nature that is comparable to Orpheus' dedication to cold, lifeless landscape. Aristaeus descends beneath the surface of the water, in order to recover his bees, much as Orpheus descends to Hades in pursuit of his wife.

It is at this point, in the circumstances surrounding these descents, that the

ways of Orpheus and Aristaeus part, and the poet now starts to stress the
differences between the two. Whereas Orpheus plunges into a dark and alien
realm, but manages to affect it by his passionate appeal, Aristaeus is welcomed
into a friendly domain presided over by his mother, the nymph Cyrene, is
wined and dined, then is given advice and encouragement by which he
eventually achieves his goal. Orpheus by his passion compels those stern rules
of Hades to soften, though they were conditioned never to grow soft at the
appeal of human beings; but because of that same passion, he loses Eurydice,
being unable to follow the inflexible law set by Proserpina. Aristaeus,
however, no longer acts on the basis of passion or grief after he leaves his
mother's realm, and therefore he proceeds along a direct, though difficult,
course to secure new bees. First, he must exert himself to use heroic violence
and master the sea-god Proteus, in order to force from him an explanation of
his loss. Virgil patently models this particular Proteus-sequence on the
famous episode of *Odyssey* 4, in which Menelaus captured Proteus and forced
key information from him.[5] The implication is that Aristaeus is taking on the
character of an active epic hero.[6]

When he has learned that his guilt toward Eurydice has earned him his
punishment, that the gods have in effect avenged Eurydice by killing the bees,
Aristaeus can face that guilt and act to reverse it. In this, he differs strikingly
from Orpheus, who never, as Virgil tells it, analyses or understands his grief
and so, by simply indulging his misery day after day, month after month,
fixed in that cold and solitary Thracian setting, becomes an emblem of inertia
and death. He is 'miserabilis' as we first hear of him (454); his powerful lament
is comparable to the 'miserabile carmen' (514) of the nightingale; he hears
Eurydice call herself 'miseram' (494) as a result of his 'furor'; with dying
breath his separated head moans out 'a miseram Eurydicen' (526), and these
last words are echoed back by the river banks. In sharp contrast to this
protracted unhappiness, pathetic but inert, the mood of guilty Aristaeus
changes swiftly from wretchedness to brisk and hopeful resolution. Cyrene
dismisses both his anguish and his guilt. Her very first words after Proteus
ends his story and vanishes, his task done, work upon those feelings: 'Son,
don't let your unhappiness get you down,' to put it a bit freely ('nate, licet
tristis animo deponere curas' 531).[7] There are precise acts he can initiate which
will earn him forgiveness from the angry gods, free him from guilt, and then
win him new bees.

To further the contrast with Orpheus, the ritual acts enjoined on Aristaeus
by his mother involve sacrifice of bulls, cows, a sheep, and a calf, whose
deaths, appeasing the hostility of the dead, become the means to life. Leaving
the corpses by the altars where he has slaughtered them, Aristaeus returns
nine days later to pacify the shades of Orpheus by a sheep, of Eurydice by a

calf, and discovers buzzing in the 'wombs' ('utero' 556) of the eight cattle-corpses a swarm of bees that rise in a cloud and hang from the branch of a tree, ready for him to possess. Out of death new life has been 'born,' thanks to the benevolent advice of Cyrene and the vigorous, unemotional, purposeful actions of Aristaeus. Orpheus almost resurrected Eurydice, but his irrational passions caused her final death, and then those same passions froze him in inactivity and ultimately brought about his death.

Thus the tragedy of Orpheus serves to establish the 'heroic' stature of Aristaeus and to provide a foil which sets off the values he embodies. For the myth of Aristaeus, designed by Virgil to conclude the thematic development of the *Georgics*, epitomizes some of his key insights into the complex moral significance of the farmer.[8] The ultimate purpose of the beekeeper and all the other specialists in the farming world is to make Nature productive, to enhance life-giving and life-continuing forces and control as much as possible destructive forces. The means by which he operates to gain his end are not gentle; he cannot afford to indulge his own sentimentality (like Orpheus) or to permit destructive passions in his beasts or luxurious growth in the wrong plants. The beekeeper, for instance, calmly observes a 'duel' between two would-be 'kings' of the swarm, then calmly kills the loser (4.90). To prevent the swarm from dispersing, he should pull the wings from the 'kings' (4.106–7). He doesn't have to deal with erotic passions such as those which plague horses and bulls, for bees possess a nature superior to that of beasts in that (according to Virgil's time) they are free of sexual needs: 'neque concubitu indulgent, nec corpora segnes / in Venerem solvunt' (4.198–9). As he works for the total productivity of the swarm, the beekeeper deals unsentimentally with individual bees and, in the perspective of general renewal, feels no surprise or regret at the deaths of single insects. When one works with Nature, death is a regular phenomenon, but one can be dispassionate about individual deaths if one knows that the swarm, the herd, or the species lives on. At best, a single bee will survive hardly seven years, but, under intelligent management, the swarm can be considered deathless: 'genus immortale' (208).

Virgil views the farmer as the symbol of the compromised individual in a world of responsibility. He must act responsibly and intelligently and morally to ensure the productivity of his fields, trees, animals, and bees; he must also act ruthlessly and unsentimentally, subordinating the individual to the larger group. If one concentrates exclusively on the farmer's ruthlessness, one can represent him as a guilty enemy of Nature, a rough unfeeling plowman like the one in the simile (512) who robbed the nightingale's nest. However, when we place this ruthlessness, this destructiveness of individuals, this 'guilt' in the total context of creative purposefulness, the pathetic individuals must be regretfully rejected, even the passionately loving Orpheus, that singer of the most moving songs myth has ever imagined. The '*durus arator*,' the guilty but energetically purposive Aristaeus, should be our model. Orpheus, Virgil's first elaborate dramatic character, is the prototype of those magnificently flawed individuals Dido and Turnus of the *Aeneid*.

II OVID'S ORPHEUS IN THE *METAMORPHOSES*

Born in 43 BC and raised in his native Sulmo, Ovid came to Rome as a young man to further his education and, by his father's wishes, to prepare for a career based upon mastery of rhetoric.[9] It was just in this period that Virgil published his *Georgics*, and this poem will have exerted strong influence upon the young Ovid. But poetic activity in Rome was not confined to Virgil: in this same vital decade of the 20s, Horace completed work on his *Satires* and *Epodes* and then devoted his efforts exclusively to the *Odes*, which he published in 23; Tibullus and Propertius were shaping the genre of Roman elegy. Ovid's genius was such that, having assimilated without apparent effort the rhetorical techniques his father had commanded, he deliberately chose to give himself to poetry, whose various styles and conventions he also quickly assimilated. The two poets who most impressed him throughout his long career were those complex and persuasive students of passion and moral obligation Propertius and Virgil. At the age of forty, a mature poet, indeed the only talented poet still alive of those who had worked during the 20s, Ovid began composition of the *Metamorphoses*. When Augustus suddenly exiled him, in AD 8 at the age of fifty, to the shores of the Black Sea, he had all but completed the fifteen books of that hexameter masterpiece of myth. Although in earlier works like the *Heroides* and the mock-didactic *Ars Amatoria* Ovid's stylistic and thematic obligations to, and ambiguous attitude toward, Virgil manifest themselves, it is in the *Metamorphoses* that we encounter the fullest use of Virgil, indeed one of the most ingenious adaptations of one masterful poet by another.[10] Ovid uses both the *Georgics* and the *Aeneid*, but, for our purposes, study of the way he adapts Virgil's Orpheus is especially significant, because, as we have seen, the unhappy singer not only epitomizes major themes of its poem but also anticipates Dido and Turnus of the *Aeneid*. What will emerge is that Ovid transforms the Virgilian tragic failure into a character entirely appropriate to his different poem: a melodramatic, egoistic poet of overblown rhetoric and shallow self-indulgent sentimentality. Ovid's Orpheus serves as a particularly ironic comment on poets and their personalities, on the poetic environment of Augustan times.

It will be useful, I think, to show how Ovid has taken the story told by Virgil and organized it to suit his own purposes. The two parallel columns summarize the key elements of each poet's lines on Orpheus.

Virgil *Georgics* 4	Ovid *Metamorphoses* 10–11
	Orpheus marries Eurydice under ominous conditions. (1–7)
Aristaeus tries to rape E. (457) In flight, E. fails to see a snake. Her death not reported. (458–9) General mourning of E.'s friends and surrounding nature. (460–3)	E. wanders in meadows with friends. (8–9) A snake bites E. in the heel, and she dies. (10)
Focus on Orpheus' grief. (464–6) O. even enters the jaws of Taenarus and braves the fearful darkness of Hades in an effort to soften the heart of the powers of Death. (467–70) [He sings, but Virgil leaves that fact implicit and gives no details of what he included in the song.]	O. sufficiently mourns E. above earth. (11) O. decides to try his luck with the Shades, and so boldly descends through the gate of Taenarus past the 'simulacra functa sepulchro' [phrase from *Georgics* 4.472–5] to Persephone. (12–16)
The effects of O.'s marvellous song: a) The bodiless dead crowd around him ('simulacraque ... defunctaque corpora vita') like birds taking refuge from darkness or a winter storm. (471–80)	O. strokes the strings of his lyre and sings at length, a supremely clever *suasoria* to persuade Death to give back E. (17–39) The effects of O.'s marvellous song: a) The bloodless spirits weep. (41)
b) Legendary monsters, Cerberus and Eumenides, are charmed; archetypal tortures (Ixion alone cited) briefly stop. (481–4)	b) All five of the archetypal tortures (Tantalus, Ixion, Tityos, Danaides, Sisyphus) are halted; the Eumenides weep for the first time. (41–6) Persephone and her husband cannot resist O.'s plea. (46–7) They summon E., who limps in. (48–9) O. gets E. back, on condition ('legem') that he not look back until he has emerged from Hades. Otherwise, the gift will be cancelled: 'aut irrita dona futura.' (50–2)
[Virgil leaves the business with the gods implicit; he refers to the conditions of E.'s return, 'legem' 487, only in a retrospective parenthesis.]	O. and E. start up the dark path and almost reach the edge of the earth above. (53–5) In fear and love, O. looks back. (56–7)
O. and E. have almost reached the upper air, and E. is on the verge of escaping Death. (485–7) In a storm of complicated emotions, O. looks back. (488–91) All O.'s efforts are nullified; thunder of doom sounds. (491–3)	

E. voices her criticism of 'furor,' her feelings of desperation, then adds 'vale' as she dies again. (494–8)
She disappears, like smoke into thin air, away from O., who tries to hold her and speak to her. (499–502)

Ovid specifically denies that E. complains about her husband. (60–1) She merely whispers the single word 'vale.' (62)
As soon as O. looks back, E. slips away from his grasp. (57–9) He can barely hear her last word as she goes back to Hades. (62–3)
The effect of this second death ('gemina nece') on O. is conveyed by reference to two obscure characters of myth. (64–71)

O. tries to get Charon ('portitor Orci') to ferry him across for a new appeal. But he has to recognize that E. is indeed lost. (502–6)

O. appeals to Charon, but the 'portitor' bars his passage. (72–3)

He goes back to Thrace, sits down at the foot of a bare cliff by the lonely Strymon, and for seven months weeps out his misery to the cold stars. (507–9)
O. charms tigers and trees. (510)

O. remains seven days on the bank of the Styx, without food, weeping. (73–5)
He climbs up into the mountains of Thrace, to complain of the gods of Death, for three years. (76–9)

Simile of nightingale. (511–15)
No love, no thought of marriage can distract O. (516)

[This motif, much expanded, added later, 86–144.]

O. avoids women's love, either from despair or because he has promised E. (79–81)

He continues to haunt the frozen, bare Thracian fields, lamenting the loss of E. and the vain gifts of Dis ['irrita dona,' model for *Metamorphoses* 10.52]. (517–20)
The Thracian women resent rejection. (520)

Thracian women are resentful. (81–2)

O. advocates pederastic love. (83–5)
[The remainder of Book 10, some 650 lines, represents O. singing his advocacy of boy-love and, conversely, his misogynistic conclusions about women's love.]

Women tear O. apart. (521–2)	Even more resentful, Thracian women attack O. and tear him apart. (11.1–50)
His head floats down the Hebrus to the sea, still lamenting E. (523–6)	Carried down to the sea by the Hebrus the head and lyre combine to moan out 'flebile nescio quid,' a veritable marvel. (50–3)
River banks echo the name of E. (527)	River banks echo the 'flebile.' (53)
	The head floats across the Aegean to Lesbos, where Apollo prevents a snake from attacking it. (54–60)
	O.'s shade rejoins that of E., and at last the couple can walk in security. (61–6)

From this summary presentation of the two narratives, it should be evident that Ovid expects his audience to know Virgil's poem and to relish the changes that he the later poet has made, not only in detail and organization but also in tone and theme. Using these parallel columns, we may quickly discern where details and organization vary, then look more closely to determine the effect on theme and tone.

To begin with, Ovid abandons the Aristaeus-frame for his story. Since that was, as we saw, probably the invention of Virgil devised to make Orpheus a significant foil to the beekeeper, we may be sure that, in abandoning it, Ovid has found a new thematic context for Orpheus. His justification for introducing the tale is a naïve contrast with the previous one, that of Iphis and Ianthe, which ended with two lovers marrying, destined to live, as they say, happily ever after. From happiness to misery: terrible omens surround the marriage of Orpheus and Eurydice. Therefore, Eurydice's snakebite comes as she is quietly walking through the meadows, not running in panic from a lecherous pursuer. By eliminating the guilt of the would-be rapist, it seems to me, Ovid has streamlined his narrative and potentially given it a more tragic form. Without another character for us to blame, Orpheus could be depicted in heart-rending manner.

In fact, having 'improved' Virgil, Ovid ostentatiously ignores his opportunity and the pathos of the bereaved husband. We note first that he does not use the device chosen by Virgil, namely, an ample description of general grief among Eurydice's friends (who were with her when she suffered the bite and died) and in the surrounding landscape, to prepare for Orpheus' even profounder grief. Instead, he briefly and indifferently refers to those initial lamentations of Orpheus alone, merely to emphasize the decision to visit the Underworld. This follows directly on his objective report of Eurydice's death in the single matter-of-fact 'she died' ('occidit' 10). Ovid continues: 'When

the Rhodopeian bard had sufficiently bewailed her to the upper air ... '
('Quam satis ad superas postquam Rhodopeius auras / deflevit vates'). That
adverb 'satis' is damning, no matter how one views it, whether as the thought
of the narrator or as the feeling of Orpheus. For us who have read Virgil, it
seems incredible that Eurydice could ever be mourned sufficiently.

The most obvious distinction between Virgil and Ovid resides in Virgil's
restraint and Ovid's total exuberance at the point in the story where Orpheus
sings in Hades. It would be simple-minded to sneer at Ovid for failing to
realize that he could never equal what was by definition in the myth unique,
namely, a song that overcame the flinty hardness of Death. Ovid knew it as
well as Virgil did. And so the song he assigns Orpheus is anything but unique:
it makes no emotional appeal whatsoever, but works with cheap, flashy, and
specious rhetoric to persuade Hades to go against his own nature. As a
consequence, Orpheus strikes us as a third-rate poet-orator who, assigned the
task of creating an inimitable song and trying to regain Eurydice, can only
mouth commonplaces or try to devise clever but lifeless points ('colores') and
so win applause. He starts off in canonic fashion by swearing that he speaks
the truth (19–20). Then, he carefully denies that his purpose there is either to
be a tourist or, like Hercules, to capture Cerberus: he has come to recover his
wife. 'I wanted to be able to endure her death,' he asserts (25), thereby
stressing again the chasm that lies between him and Virgil's inconsolable
singer, who never even thought of enduring his misery. 'I tried, but Love
conquered' (25–6). It is the first time in this strangely told story that the
concept of love has been mentioned, and Ovid presents it as a chill abstract
noun, a calculated point in persuasive discourse that has nothing in the
previous narrative or in Orpheus' character to support it.

Orpheus affects to wonder whether love is known in the Underworld,
until he conveniently remembers – Ovid wittily refers to an earlier episode in
Metamorphoses (5.346 ff) – that *Amor* had united Persephone with her
husband. However, to compare the romantic passion supposedly linking him
and Eurydice with the mere lust and rape by which Pluto secured his wife, to
force the comparison on us by explicitly alluding to the familiar version of
rape, 'veteris rapinae' (28), suggests the shallowness of Orpheus' love and the
awkwardness of his rhetoric. Ovid will not let him speak affectionately and
convincingly of his wife. Invoking the fearful, cavernous silence of the
Underworld (29–30), ridiculously inept, Orpheus finally asks for Eurydice
back. Why should the request be granted? We could easily imagine dozens of
compelling reasons that are based on human needs, on the tragedy of life cut
short and marriage just begun. And yet Ovid makes Orpheus turn tragedy
and genuine grief into tawdry rhetoric:

omnia debentur vobis paulumque morati
serius aut citius sedem properamus ad unam.
tendimus huc omnes, haec est domus ultima, vosque
humani generis longissima regna tenetis.
haec quoque, cum iustos matura peregerit annos,
iuris erit vestri: pro munere poscimus usum.   (32–7)

(All things are owed to you; after lingering a little, sooner or later we all rush to the same place. We all head in this direction, this is our last home, and you two possess the longest mastery over the human race. This woman, too, when she has completed her proper span of years, in the maturity of age, will come under your control. I merely ask to borrow her; I'll count it as a gift.)

Almost every phrase in these six lines was a commonplace for Roman ears, the trite baggage of expectable words about death. For three lines, Orpheus rings the changes on the topos: We all must die. The next three lines focus on the metaphor of Death's dominion over us. But what turns this into inimitable rhetoric for Orpheus is the way he inverts its normal usage, exploiting his unusual dramatic opportunity. At the human level, those commonplaces function in protreptic (very often, for example, in Horatian *Odes*) to urge us to make the most of our lives while we can, or, in consolations, to encourage us to accept death, the common lot of all men. Orpheus 'cleverly' turns this all around: he addresses it not to mortals, but to the very deities who are never threatened by Death, the lords of Death themselves. They are thus obsequiously reminded of their power and asked to 'loan' Eurydice for a few years. This song has plumbed the depths of bathos; it is utterly frigid. In the Roman audience, it should have elicited smiles; Persephone should have burst into laughter. From the smaller earlier changes of emphasis, we may have suspected it; now we know that Ovid has taken away the tragic mood that Virgil sought. He has not allowed this Orpheus to express any sincere feelings for Eurydice.

In the way the two poets reported the effects of the song, there are two phases. Virgil spent ten lines describing the way Orpheus moved the lifeless spirits, as if he almost vitalized them by his warm human passion; hence, the symbolic value of the bird-simile (473–4). As Virgil realized, the responses of these masses of dead human beings would far more effectively convince us of the magic of Orpheus' singing than would the fabulous reacting of mythical monsters and incredibly tortured figures. Ovid quite consciously chooses to emphasize the fabulous: after three words to dispose of the normal dead ('exsangues flebant animae' 41), he elaborates five lines of striking changes among the damned. Whereas Virgil contented himself with saying that the wheel on which Ixion was spread stopped rolling (484), Ovid not only 'outdoes' Virgil – Ixion's wheel is stunned ('stupuit' 42) – but also reviews the other archetypal damned. He ends up with a hilarious alliterating apostrophe to Sisyphus: 'You sat down on your stone, Sisyphus' ('inque tuo sedisti, Sisyphe, saxo' 44).

We studied the way Virgil brought all his poetic powers to bear upon the moment when Orpheus looked back at Eurydice and lost her forever: the complex sentence he constructed, the dense series of moral terms, the blend of sympathy and blame, the emphasis on Eurydice as victim both through the unique speech he assigned her and through the device of 'seeing' the whole experience through her dimming eyes.[11] Virgil devotes eighteen superbly crafted lines to this critical sequence (485–502); Ovid handles it neatly and objectively in eleven (53–63). By limiting Orpheus' motives to fear, eagerness, and love ('metuens,' 'avidus,' 'amans' 56–7), Ovid rules out the powerful Virgilian theme of 'furor' and all the guilt which compounds the husband's later laments. He obviously knows what he is doing, for he goes on to reduce the fine Virgilian speech of Eurydice to the bare 'vale' and to state expressly (as if correcting Virgil) that Eurydice had no reason to complain of a husband actuated solely by love (60–1). Thus, a grand human tragedy becomes simplified into insipidity. However, when Ovid so ostentatiously denies Orpheus' guilt and so clearly refers back to Virgil's narrative, he invites us, I think, to look at things another way, to view Orpheus as a shallow, self-satisfied, self-indulgent 'lover' who could never perceive his own guilt, who would have to imagine Eurydice being grateful to him for his (doltish) passion even in her final moments!

Ovid has prevented Eurydice from playing any meaningful role in his narrative. He has eliminated her superb Virgilian speech; he has not allowed Orpheus to apostrophize her, to speak to her directly, or to describe her movingly in his laments. His only memorable detail about her was the bathetic innovation, that at Persephone's command she limped up (49). If Ovid's tale does this to Eurydice, we should not be surprised that it taints Orpheus' grief after her final disappearance. We can see this best in the comparative effects of the similes inserted at this juncture by the two poets. Virgil creates a convincing narrative framework concerning Orpheus' lonely song under the icy stars of Thrace, within which he sets the richly suggestive simile of the nightingale.[12] Our sympathies and our critical faculties are brought into play, and the wider thematic relevance of the story is called to our attention by the key detail of the 'durus arator.' Ovid's tactics tend to remove us from Orpheus, to make him an object of distant, learned mythology. He starts from a clever phrase: the 'double death' of Eurydice ('gemina nece' 64); and here, as elsewhere, cleverness produces a frigidity which destroys appropriate feeling in the audience. Then, instead of describing warm active feelings of grief, he capitalizes on the opportunity to record a secondary metamorphosis, as he often does elsewhere, and has Orpheus so stunned ('stupuit' 64) by misery and shock as to seem petrified. We may perhaps be thankful that this unusually loquacious Orpheus has been rendered wordless here and relish the note of black humour. According to our narrator, then, Orpheus may be likened to a pair of men who indeed changed into stones: one man who saw Hercules carry up the monstrous Cerberus out of Hades and became stony in terror, a second who saw his wife metamorphosed into stone as punishment and prayed successfully, in innocence and love, that he might share her metamorphosis.

As we look more closely at these comparisons, recondite allusions to otherwise unknown myths, we suspect that Ovid has something else in mind than to provide a double insight into the way that Orpheus was petrified at the loss of his wife. Terror *could* be natural emotion, but here it is manifestly inept, because it calls attention to the selfish nature of the husband rather than to his regrets for her. (If we chose to be irreverent or insisted on Ovid's irreverence, we might suggest that the analogue for Eurydice in this simile is the three-headed Cerberus!). The second comparison seems more complex and insidious. Ostensibly it deals with Orpheus' love, but it also stresses the 'crimen' of the wife. Since, though the story itself is unknown, its basic elements parallel those of other tales, we can reconstruct the outlines as follows: Lethaea was beautiful, too beautiful, and in her foolish pride ('confisa figurae' 69) she provoked the anger of some female deity, most typically of Juno or Venus, who turned her into an ugly stone. Now absolutely none of that fits Eurydice. She may have been beautiful, but that detail is irrelevant to, and not mentioned by, either Virgil or Ovid. She certainly never did wrong or provoked a goddess's jealous fury. Lethaea's husband willingly took on her fate. Orpheus does no such thing. Indeed, as we shall see, Ovid changes the ending and makes the bard die not for his love of his wife but from his hatred of women. Thus, while Virgil unflinchingly requires us to perceive Orpheus as guilty (though pathetic), Ovid deflects the motif of guilt here most naughtily on to Eurydice.[13]

Both Virgil and Ovid follow Orpheus back to the banks of the Styx, where he appeals in vain to Charon to ferry him over again. Virgil subjectively conveys the man's torment by a series of so-called rhetorical questions that help to capture our sympathy. The stark line (506) about Eurydice, cold in death, aboard the very skiff that Orpheus longs to take, produces a strong contrast and implies Orpheus' realization of the finality of his loss. No time is specified. Ovid, however, all too realistically observes Orpheus for seven days after Charon's refusal. As befits a man in mourning, he must be 'squalidus,' his beard growing more and more unkempt. Then, since he is spending seven days in a region that cannot provide him food, the poet must call attention to that fact and immediately extract a rhetorical point from it: grief and tears were his 'food' ('cura dolorque animi lacrimaeque alimenta fuere' 75). Again, the cleverness forces us to savour the wit of the narrator at the expense of the mourner's grief. It seems like a pattern of calculated frigidity to alienate us from Orpheus.

Another insidious 'improvement' on Virgil appears soon after. Virgil said that Orpheus spurned 'Venus' (which has to be sex with women) and marriage (516); then, after another three lines about the continuing lament, he quickly comes to the resentful Thracian women ('spretae matres' 520) and their fatal attack on the bard. Ovid records the same rejection of sex with women, very pronouncedly and redundantly specifying 'femineam Venerem' (80), and he reports the women's resentment: 'multae doluere repulsae' (82). But he also speculates, and invites us to do so too, as to the reason for Orpheus' decision. Our options are: either he had promised Eurydice or he was discouraged, disgusted, or somehow 'turned off' by his abortive first marriage. This speculation and the highly indefinite rationale for the alternative I have cited second ('seu quod male cesserat illi' 80) raise the spectre of an egoistic husband who literally blames his wife for dying, even though he has been the cause, and then decides that marriage isn't worth the trouble. And now Ovid finishes off Orpheus by revealing the reason for the unusual and seemingly needless stress on *female* sex in 80: Orpheus reacts against women and marriage by deciding to gratify his sexual needs hereafter with boys. Ovid makes him the originator ('auctor' 83) of male homosexuality, a stereotyped shrill advocate who soon will couple his argument for pederasty with a violent misogyny. Not only does that alter our impression of Orpheus' grief, but it also decisively colours our view of the Thracian women's resentment and wild attack on the bard later. He has not only spurned them, as in Virgil, from loyalty to Eurydice; he has actively attacked them and viciously twisted the idea of female sexuality, having forgotten Eurydice. He deserves their hostility.

The long gap in Ovid's narrative between this final perverse development of Orpheus' selfish grief and his death further weakens any latent sympathy. As those who analyse the structure of the *Metamorphoses* comment, Orpheus' personal experiences dwindle and appear to function as a mere frame of little import for a series of very effective stories in 10.106ff.[14] However, the stories, which are mainly told by Orpheus and which are *all* relevant to his new pederastic and misogynistic attitudes, cumulatively function to make us ignore his feelings about Eurydice (as over and dead) and force us to concentrate on the new interests, which cause his murder.[15]

Earlier, Ovid had skipped over the Virgilian detail of how nature responded to the husband's lament. Now, as his Orpheus begins to advocate love of boys, a host of trees come running (90ff). In themselves, the trees emphasize the new setting for Orpheus' song, no longer icy mountains but a shady, level patch of grass on a green hill, a cheery pastoral environment. Then, to make it clear that both singer and theme have changed, we hear that young Attis, now a pine tree, and Cyparissus 'puer,' now a cypress, have joined the throng of trees which respond to Orpheus' song. It seems obvious that this song features pretty young boys, not Eurydice.

It has frequently been noted by scholars that, unlike his contemporaries, Ovid shows no personal interest in pederasty. Therefore, when he builds Orpheus up in this fashion, we might well expect him to undercut the homosexuality. In fact, as the stories of boy-love unfold, Ovid's inescapable conclusion forces itself on us, if not on silly Orpheus, that boy-love ranks far below heterosexual love in terms of affection, mutual concern, and chances for extensive happiness. Cyparissus dies out of ridiculous grief for a dead deer rather than living for the satisfaction of Apollo. Apollo tries again with the boy Hyacinthus, but accidentally kills him while they are competing in the discus-throw, and again he is balked of his love (162ff). At the end of Book 10, Orpheus further contradicts his theme by singing of Adonis, who much prefers hunting to dallying with Venus, and consequently gets himself ripped open by a boar's tusk and dies in lamenting Venus' arms. Only one boy manages to survive to gratify his lover, and that is Ganymede, whom Jupiter snatches up to Olympus to be his cupbearer and who becomes the cause of discord with Juno ('invita Iunone' 161). Thus, Orpheus' advocacy of pederasty has proved self-contradictory: three out of four instances end with the death of the silly unresponding boy and the concomitant lamentation and frustration of the divine lover. Thus, this kind of love results in frustration similar to that from which Orpheus supposedly reacted in revulsion.

In support of his pederasty, Orpheus proposed to sing the misogynistic theme of how 'girls were driven wild by illicit passions and earned punishment by their lust' (153–4). Three stories, which are non-pederastic, might be considered in connection with this theme: those of Pygmalion (243ff), Myrrha (298ff), and Atalanta (560ff).[16] The first of these starts from supreme misogyny and ends with perfect romantic love: Pygmalion reacts immaturely against all women after seeing a few prostitutes, tries to find satisfaction not with boys but with a statue of a beautiful woman, and ends by preferring the mortal and fallible woman to the statue. Here there is no illicit passion, and the ideal love of man and woman leads to happy marriage. The second story does indeed portray Myrrha acting on illicit passion and committing incest with her father, for which she is punished. However, the account also undermines Orpheus' misogyny, because Myrrha exhibits a rich moral awareness and struggles against her passion; and, once her turpitude has been exposed, she willingly faces her penalty, and instead receives mercy, if not a kind of honour: she becomes a tree of precious myrrh. As for Atalanta, she clearly constitutes no argument for misogyny. She tries to avoid marriage because of a threatening prophecy, and she causes the deaths of numerous suitors until Hippomenes softens her heart. Against her own interests, with a maidenly modesty that earns our approval, she lets herself by defeated in the race and awarded as prize to the male, whose passions have been emphasized. Orpheus the singer fails to single out anything illicit in her behaviour, and indeed it is Hippomenes who by his lust brings punishment on them both. Thus, the stories of this supposedly incomparable bard fail to prove his points: boy-love ends in lamentation, not happiness; girl-love refuses to be reduced to a simple formula of libido and punishment, and in two cases out of three the girl is innocent and worthy of the romantic feelings of her husband. Ovid's Orpheus is weirdly incompetent.

When finally the bard stops singing, the moment comes for the Thracian women to exact their revenge. Ovid elaborates a marvellous scene in which Orpheus at first charms all the missiles the women hurl at him. Then, as the uproar drowns out the music, the women close in, first disposing of the audience of animals, snakes, and birds before tearing the singer apart. At this death, Ovid introduces the detail which he had refused to Eurydice, namely, the general mourning of nature (11.44ff). He follows this by his last significant parallel with Virgil:

> membra iacent diversa locis; caput, Hebre, lyramque
> excipis, et (mirum!), medio dum labitur amne,
> flebile nescio quid queritur lyra, flebile lingua
> murmurat examinis, respondent flebile ripae.   (50–53)

(His limbs lie here and there about the fields; but his head and lyre are welcomed by you, river Hebrus, and – a veritable marvel – while they float down the river, the lyre laments something or other tearful, the lifeless tongue mutters a tearful message, and that tearful something is echoed back by the river banks.)

Ovid warns his audience of his tone by the apostrophe to the river and then by his ingenuous parenthetical 'mirum.' It is evident that this Orpheus cannot, as Virgil's could, sing with dying breath of poor Eurydice. For this one has long ago forgotten Eurydice and made the silliest of adjustments to grief by turning against women to boys. Ovid rejects him, and invites us to also, as he indifferently describes the last song of his 'hero,' once so flashily rhetorical and never before at a loss for clever words, as 'flebile nescio quid.'

In the total mass of the *Metamorphoses*, Ovid's eighty-two lines about Orpheus' loss of Eurydice at the beginning of Book 10 and the long-postponed sequel about the singer's death at the opening of Book 11 do not possess major significance. They certainly do not operate in rich thematic antitheses with the chief themes of the epic, as Virgil made his Orpheus-story function. Nevertheless, Ovid did develop, I would maintain, more than a facile parody of Virgil. Whereas Virgil had made his central object the portrayal of irrational love as 'furor,' faulty though pathetic, Ovid inspects Orpheus' love and finds it wanting.[17] He ignores the love of husband and wife at the time of marriage and scants Orpheus' grief when she first dies: Orpheus laments 'enough' to the upper air! Love first appears as an uncoloured abstract noun in the rhetorical argument for the release of Eurydice, in a context that makes Orpheus a cheap orator-poet, not a convincing lover. Love returns a second time as a participle ('amans' 57) to qualify the act of looking back. By this point, however, our impression of the shallowness of Orpheus' feelings should be well formed, and we cannot respond with the sympathy that Virgil generates in us. By his organization alone Ovid has revealed his emphasis: twenty-three lines for the rhetorical song in Hades versus eleven lines for the entire episode of losing Eurydice the second time. Thus, when he affects expressly to 'correct' Virgil and to insist that Eurydice had no cause of complaint (except that she was 'loved' 61), the irony is hard to mistake. Somebody is protesting too much. Guilt, which here is ostentatiously denied for Orpheus, is next implicitly shifted to Eurydice by the simile about Lethaea (68ff). Finally, Orpheus rejects Venus altogether and advocates that men should transfer their *amor* to boys. This seems a carefully planned thematic development. Orpheus' love lacks *furor* because it lacks genuine commitment; it is a self-indulgent masculine love that cannot perceive or feel the woman as a person, that blames Eurydice for dying, and that gives up women because they aren't worth the inconvenience. Ovid, exploring the tension between male and female, has opened up a rich vein for future adaptations of the myth.

But Orpheus is for Ovid more than a flawed lover: he is also a flawed poet. Virgil lays little emphasis on the poetic side of his Orpheus; it is subordinated entirely to the theme of unwise passion and uncreative grief. Hades and the animals and trees do not respond so much to his art as to the vital human warmth of his love. Ovid's Orpheus is a performer, egotistic, calculating, self-dramatizing. Having decided that he has sung enough to the unresponding upper air, he descends to Hades and tries his dubious art on a new audience. His patent devices turn passionate love into clever frigidity, but, ironically, his audience is so undiscriminating – like so many contemporary Roman audiences of performing poets and *rhetores* – that he bewitches it. We should not be fooled. For lack of an audience after Eurydice's disappearance, he cannot emote: he is struck dumb, petrified ('stupuit' 64).[18] When, after three years of singing to the icy mountains, he comes down to grassy hills and a pastoral setting and tries out his new self-serving pederastic themes, he captures a prejudiced audience, a thicket of trees that include some metamorphosed boys who were once loved by gods. He continues this song and elaborates it with its antithesis, a misogynistic perversion of women's feelings of love, and now he miscalculates his audience. Even though the song gets out of hand and promotes a conclusion quite other than he intends, nevertheless the Thracian women take Orpheus according to his proclaimed misogyny and destroy their enemy.

Elsewhere in the poem, Ovid studies artists at work, and he is obviously delighted to expose the inadequacies of those whose reputations in myth seemed most secure. The Muses in Book 5 take on the challenge of the Pierides to a poetic competition. Thanks to a prejudiced panel of judges, the interminable, ill-planned, unfocused song of Calliope triumphs, but we are not convinced. Athena competes in Book 6 with Arachne in weaving, and even she, for all her prejudice, can find no fault in Arachne's tapestry. She has to resort to her superior force to win. Thus, the exposure of the mythical marvel, Orpheus, is not surprising: he is viewed in the perspective of the all-too-familiar contemporary phenomenon of corrupt rhetoricizing poetry. Ovid, who himself was often tempted to exploit his rhetorical talents and to impress his audience by superficial cleverness, would have been particularly sensitive to this kind of poetic inadequacy. As Ovid knows, the artist cannot remove feelings from existential situations and weave cold-blooded clever arguments around an abstract Love: one loves a person. Pygmalion's failure as an artist and his success as a human lover are Ovid's potent response to the myth of Orpheus. And here again Ovid has opened up a rich vein for future adaptation: the tension between lover and artist. Thanks to Virgil and Ovid, the story of Orpheus and Eurydice became a subject for sophisticated presentation in art.

NOTES

1 I assume, with most scholars, that the story of Orpheus and Eurydice recounted in *Culex* 268–95 is post-Virgilian, indeed derivative from *Georgics* 4.453ff.
2 I follow the argument of K. Ziegler 'Orpheus' in Pauly-Wissowa *Real Encylopädie* 18:1 (Stuttgart 1939) cols 1268ff. For a different viewpoint, see the introductory essay of this collection.
3 Earlier, in *Eclogues* 6.79, Virgil had already described the tragic actions of Philomela before she and her husband Tereus were metamorphosed. In *Georgics*

4.15 he refers to her sister, changed into a swallow, her breast stained with blood.

4 For important discussions in English on the connections between Orpheus and Aristaeus, see B. Otis *Vergil, a Study in Civilised Poetry* (Oxford 1963) 190ff; C.E. Segal 'Orpheus and the fourth *Georgic*: Vergil on nature and civilisation' *American Journal of Philology* 87 (1966) 307–25; and D.S. Wender 'Resurrection in the fourth *Georgic*' *American Journal of Philology* 90 (1969) 424–36. L.P. Wilkinson in his *The Georgics of Vergil, a Critical Survey* (Cambridge 1969) 120 expresses considerable scepticism about multiple relationships between the two figures. See now M.C.J. Putnam *Vergil's Poem of the Earth: Studies in the Georgics* (Princeton 1979) 290ff.

5 Cf *Odyssey* 4.351ff. For analysis, see Otis *Vergil, a Study* 196–7.

6 As Otis also notes, when Aristaeus weeps helplessly by the seashore, then receives help from his mother, he parallels Achilles in *Iliad* 18.22ff. Achilles is in the depths of despair over the death of Patroclus, and he has lost his armour (worn by Patroclus into battle). The sea-nymph Thetis, Achilles' mother, starts him on his recovery of heroic position. A somewhat analogous situation occurs in *Odyssey* 2.26off: Telemachus, after his tearful failure in the Ithacan assembly, believing his father lost, goes disconsolately to the seashore and prays for Athena's help. Her prompt assistance initiates his successful development toward maturity.

7 We are earlier led to believe that Proteus will supply Aristaeus with the precepts necessary to cope with his guilt and recoup his losses (398). In fact, Virgil portrays Cyrene as the one who gives the relevant *praecepta* (cf 548). By this change, he intensifies the picture of benevolent concern for Aristaeus and for his life-giving tasks; and this increases the contrast with Orpheus. See Otis *Vergil, a Study* 209ff.

8 I am assuming that the story of the revised ending of *Georgics* 4 is untrue or, if true, not demonstrable in the present finished state of the text. The final lines, 559–66, are not part of the thematic development; they produce a familiar ancient coda of autobiographical data, by which the poet brings his audience back from the world of the poem to everyday life.

9 Our basic information about Ovid's career comes from his autobiographical poem, *Tristia* 4.10.

10 For Ovid's use of Virgil in general, see the recent work of S. Döpp, *Virgilischer Einfluss im Werk Ovids* (Munich 1968), especially his valuable review of relevant scholarship in his first chapter. G.K. Galinsky *Ovid's Metamorphoses, an Introduction to the Basic Aspects* (Berkeley 1975) 217ff, analyses 'Ovid's *Aeneid*' in *Metamorphoses* 13 and 14. For the relationship between Virgil's and Ovid's Orpheus, see B. Otis *Ovid as an Epic Poet* (Cambridge 1970) 74 and 184–5; my edition of Ovid's *Metamorphoses, Books 6–10* (Norman, Okla 1972) 475ff;

and C.E. Segal 'Ovid's Orpheus and Augustan ideology' *Transactions of the American Philological Association* 103 (1972) 473–94). See now A. Primmer 'Das Lied des Orpheus in Ovids *Metamorphosen*' *Sprachkunst, Beiträge zur Literaturwissenschaft* 10 (1979) 123–37.

11 See above p 29.

12 See above p 32.

13 Ultimately, this reference to joint metamorphoses of Lethaea and husband may also look forward to Ovid's plan in Book 11 to reunite Orpheus with Eurydice after his death.

14 Cf Otis *Ovid as an Epic Poet* 183ff.

15 The story of young Cyparissus, handsome and beloved of Apollo (10.106–42), is told by Ovid himself, but it clearly anticipates Orpheus' announced theme of 152–3: boys beloved by gods ('pueros dilectos superis').

16 The brief story of the Propoetides (238ff), who were punished as prostitutes, is by definition exempt from passion and female libido.

17 Ovid does not view 'furor' as so easily culpable as Virgil tends to. Ovid's characters who are afflicted with passion, usually women, are aware of its dangers, but struggle in vain to overcome it. Ovid could have represented Orpheus in this manner, had he wanted to. Ironically, though, it is Orpheus' portrait of Myrrha that epitomizes Ovid's special sense of 'furor.' Myrrha, despite her incest, emerges a far more sympathetic person than Orpheus.

18 Note that Ovid eliminates Virgil's affective phrase, 'multa volentem dicere,' from his list of Orpheus' reactions. Orpheus, as Ovid presents him, apparently had *nothing* to say to Eurydice at this critical moment any more than at other times. He never speaks to her alive or apostrophizes her dead.

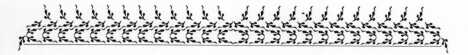

ELEANOR IRWIN

The Songs of Orpheus
and the New Song of Christ

ORPHEUS, THE SINGER whose music moved animate and inanimate creatures, is a figure by which Christ and his power may be understood. Such was the interpretation of Clement of Alexandria, a Christian Apologist and a student of Greek philosophy. Other writers from the New Testament period on had used Old Testament figures as types of Christ: Melchizedek as a type of Christ's high priestly function and Isaac as a type of Christ's sacrifice, to name only two. But Clement took the daring step of typifying Christ through a figure of Greek mythology.[1]

Clement was writing near the end of the second century of the Christian era, when Christians were at times severely persecuted and at times merely despised by the world in which they lived.[2] Many Christian writers of this period defended their community against the attacks and insinuations of their pagan neighbours. This defence usually took the form of showing that Christians were doing no harm to anyone and that, because the sources of their faith were older than in other cultures, their beliefs were superior to those of their opponents. Some of these writers attempted to demonstrate a dependence of Greek ideas on Jewish thought.[3]

Clement wrote his *Protrepticus* or *Exhortation to the Greeks* to explain to his readers in terms which were familiar to them the meaning of his faith and its superiority to their religious beliefs and practices.[4] In this work he shows himself conversant with Greek literature and Jewish Scriptures, with Greek cults and Christian tradition. Quotations and verbal reminiscences are woven into his text with missionary zeal; for however much he may have admired Greek culture, he was quite certain that the Greeks had so far missed the 'greatest of good things' – salvation through Christ the Word (*Protrepticus* 12, 262; 1.86.25–6). Odysseus had his men bind him to the mast of his ship so that he might be restrained from responding to the Sirens who lured sailors to their doom as his ship sailed past their shore. Instead of emulating Odysseus Clement's readers ought to depend on the power of the cross to protect them from evil. 'Bound to the wood [of the cross],' he tells them, 'you will be freed from all corruption' (12, 252; 1.83.25–6). In a later section he compares the experience of becoming a Christian to initiation into a mystery religion – but one which was far superior to the rites of Dionysus (12, 254–6; 1.84). Clement manages to convey a genuine appreciation of Greek literature and culture, yet he refuses to be seduced by it.

Clement begins his *Exhortation* by references to famous singers of antiquity: Amphion who was said to have used music to move stones into position to build the walls of Thebes; Arion of Methymna who attracted a dolphin by his singing and with its help was rescued from wicked sailors; and Orpheus, more ancient and renowned than these, who tamed wild beasts and moved mighty oak trees by the power of his music. We learn of another singer, Eunomus, who was competing at Delphi when one of the strings of his lyre broke. Thereupon a grasshopper which had been chirping in the shade of the leaves jumped up on Eunomus' lyre and twittered there.[5] Eunomus, so the story goes, adapted his music to the grasshopper's song, and thus compensated for the loss of the string. The Greeks thought that the insect was charmed by Eunomus' song, but Clement disputes that. Instead, he would have it that the grasshopper was singing praises to God spontaneously.

Eunomus and the grasshopper make an odd fourth with the others; stones, fish, animals, and trees are surely not to be compared with one small insect. Eunomus himself is a dwarf beside the great musicians. By suggesting a different interpretation of the story of the grasshopper, Clement implies without stating that the supposed influence of music in the other accounts may be susceptible to other interpretations.

Clement's next section deals with the contrast between myth and truth. The Greeks believed myths such as these about the power of song, but they did not recognize the 'shining face of truth' (1, 4; 1.3.24). They held that certain mountains were sacred and they enjoyed watching the stories of past misfortunes made into tragedy. But Helicon, Cithaeron, and the mountains of the Odrysians and Thracians[6] have been replaced by the holy mount Sion and a drama greater than any tragedy has been enacted, with the chief actor, the Word of God, 'crowned in the theatre of the whole world': ὁ γνήσιος ἀγωνιστὴς ἐπὶ τῷ παντὸς κόσμου θεάτρῳ στεφανούμενος. (1, 16; 1.4.15–16) The Word, the title which Clement gives to the second person of the Trinity, is the true *agonistes*, a word which often means 'champion,' although it occasionally means 'actor,' a meaning attested to by the Aristotelian *Problemata*.[7] In this passage the appearance of the Word is contrasted with the dramas of the Greeks; the whole world – not just the tragic stage – is the theatre in which he acts; and the chorus is the company of the holy prophets who have interpreted his coming as the chorus in a tragedy comment on the action of the play (χορὸν [τὸν] ἅγιον τὸν προφητικόν 1, 16; 1.4.9). The crowning mentioned by Clement is a symbol of the reward which, in Christian writings from the New Testament on, comes from God to the faithful.[8] Clement seems to abandon the theatre in this detail and to think rather of the crowning of the victor. By this change he emphasizes the difference between re-enactments of past (untrue) stories in tragedy and the actual, historical unfolding of truth through the activity of the Word. Herein lies the suitability of the term *agonistes*. The Word is more than an actor who represents someone else's action; he is himself both actor and champion.

As the Word is the true champion, not merely an actor, so for Clement he is the (true) singer: 'my Eunomus' in Clement's words (1, 6; 1.4.17). The song of the Word is not an old Greek one, nor is the mode Greek; it is the eternal song, with new harmony, bearing the name of God. It is the new song, the Levitical song, which in the words of Homer is the 'banisher of pain and anger, causing all evils to be forgotten': νηπενθές τ᾽ἄχολόν τε κακῶν ἐπίληθες ἁπάντων.[9] It is typical of Clement that he should introduce a Greek verse just at the moment when he is most insistent on the uniqueness of the Christian message. But his argument is that as Old Testament prophets wrote without complete understanding about Christ, so Greek poets may without comprehending have seen the truth. The words of Homer are truer of the song of the Word than of the poet's original application of them to Helen and the drugs she learned about in Egypt.

The other singers, Orpheus, Amphion, and Arion, deceived mankind by relating stories of violence and sorrow, and led them into idolatry by the enchantment of their music. But 'far different is my singer,' Clement continues. Unlike those musicians honoured by the Greeks, the Word frees those who listen to his music. He tames not wild beasts but human beings who resemble them: birds who represent the 'unstable,' reptiles the 'cheaters,' lions the 'passionate,' pigs the 'pleasure-lovers,' wolves the 'plunderers.'[10] People without sense are wood and stones; just as it was recounted that those famous singers moved trees and stones, so God the Word transforms senseless people. Clement introduces into his presentation quotations from the Gospels to justify his interpretation. Jesus said that God could raise up from stones children to Abraham (Matthew 3:9, Luke 3:8). These stones which could be transformed into Abraham's children are interpreted by Clement as Gentiles who trusted in stones or idols, and who are spoken of as Abraham's children by faith elsewhere (for instance, in Galatians 3:7-9). Pharisees and

Sadducees were called a 'generation of vipers' (Matthew 3:7, Luke 3:8) and false prophets were 'wolves in sheep's clothing' (Matthew 7:15). Clement declares that even these can repent and be transformed.

Non-Christian writers previously had made Orpheus a bringer of civilization, but Clement claims that the taming of beasts is an allegory, not of Orpheus, but of the activity of the Word in dealing with mankind. Clement's treatment of this interpretation suggests that he feels that he is breaking ground. He is explicit about identifying animals and birds with kinds of human beings, he relies on quotations from Scripture to back him up, and his claim that the Word is the only one to tame human beings suggests that he is unaware of attempts to allegorize Orpheus.

The new song does more than tame the savage and revive the insensible; it gives order to the universe. Clement reminds his readers of the tempering of the extremes of heat and cold, the stability of the land, and the limits fixed to the encroachment of the sea. The word here used for world or universe is κόσμος, which basically means 'order' and in a derivative sense 'universe,' because of its order.[11] The harmony in the universe extends from the centre to the edges and from the limits to the centre. One is reminded of the Pythagoreans' concept of harmony in the universe, and in particular of their theory of the music of the spheres, music produced by the revolution of the heavenly bodies.[12]

The Pythagoreans were speaking of literal music, though the ear did not hear it, being accustomed to it from birth. Clement, however, makes it clear that the music he means is not produced on instruments like the lyre and cithara, but that the Word uses the macrocosm and the human microcosm to make music to God. He quotes from an unidentified source, 'You are my cithara, my flute, and my temple,' and interprets this to mean '[you are my] cithara because of the harmony, flute because of the breath/Spirit, and temple because of the Word – God's purpose being that the music should resound, the Spirit inspire, and the temple receive its Lord.'[13] The line quoted by Clement must be addressed by God to a human worshipper. The metaphor of the believer as a temple is found in the New Testament (cf 1 Corinthians 6:19). Prophets were used by God 'as a flautist might blow into a pipe' according to a contemporary of Clement, Athenagoras.[14] A worshipper touched by God was compared by the heretic Montanus to a lyre awakened by the plectrum. What is true of the individual is also true of groups of believers and of the whole of creation.[15]

Having established that the Word does not use a musical instrument like Orpheus or Jubal 'father of those who play the lyre and pipe' (Genesis 4:21), but that he uses his creation as an instrument, Clement focuses briefly on

David 'the sweet psalmist of Israel' (2 Samuel 23:1), who is both like and unlike Orpheus. Like him, David played a stringed instrument, and composed and sang actual songs, but unlike him he did not sing false songs to enslave men to idols. Rather he drove away daemons by the power of his music, as his healing of Saul illustrated (1 Samuel 16:23). It is important to establish that David differed from Orpheus, because the Word incarnate was considered to be 'of the house and lineage of David' (Luke 2:4, 3:23, 3:31) and was to sit on 'the throne of his father David' (Luke 1:32).

As the created order is the instrument of the Word, so the Word is the instrument of God. By this figure Clement means that God revealed himself or 'spoke' through the Word (cf Hebrews 1:2). The Word is the Singer in that he brings order to the world and to people by his music; he is the Song, in that he sings of himself and of God; and he is the Instrument in that he is being used to reveal God. Using the figures of Orpheus and other musicians and the idea of the power of music, Clement has drawn forth a number of pictures by which Christ may be understood. I have made explicit in my discussion what is only implicit in Clement, in order to show how he has explained Christian theology through ideas familiar to his Greek readers.

Clement turns to expound the activity of the Word, both incarnate and pre-incarnate. He does not entirely forget the figure of the singer though he combines it with other figures, such as the doctor (1, 20; 1.8.25) and the teacher (1, 18; 1.7.30). But the imagery of music continues to appear as the Word 'sings to some' ($\overset{\checkmark}{a}\delta\epsilon\iota$ $\delta\grave{\epsilon}$ $\overset{\prime}{a}\lambda\lambda o\iota s$); is 'many-toned' $\pi o\lambda\acute{v}\phi\omega\nu os$; and 'encourages [people] by singing to his instrument' ($\psi\acute{a}\lambda\lambda\omega\nu$ $\pi a\rho a\kappa a\lambda\epsilon\hat{\iota}$ 1, 20; 1.8.25–30). At the end of the first chapter of his *Exhortation,* Clement returns to Greek religious imagery. He urges each of his readers to be purified 'not with laurel leaves and fillets adorned with wool and purple, but bind righteousness [round your head] and wreath yourself with the leaves of self-control.'[17]

Laurel leaves and fillets, if they are meant to have a specific association, may speak of Apollo to whom the laurel was sacred and who presided over purifications.[18] Since Orphics, who claimed Orpheus as their founder, were forbidden to use wool,[19] this cannot be a reference to the singer and is best taken as general imagery.

Throughout this first chapter of the *Exhortation,* wherever the singer appears or Orpheus is mentioned, the power of music to influence is the point of comparison. Later Christian writers compared the story of Orpheus descending into the lower world to rescue his dead wife, Eurydice, to the action of Christ rescuing souls from the power of death. So Eurydice is analogous to the human soul, the snake which caused her death to 'that old serpent,' the devil, and Orpheus to Christ.[20] At times this becomes a general statement of the salvation of the soul, but more frequently it is applied to the rescue of the souls of those who died before Christ's coming and who were released by him when he 'descended into Hell.'[21] In most, but not all, versions of the myth, Orpheus failed to bring his wife back to the upper world; this failure is contrasted with Christ's success, as in a fourth-century hymn by Ephraim of Syria. In it Death scornfully denies the power of music to charm him: 'as for the wise that are able to charm wild beasts, their charms enter not into my ears.' Later in the hymn, 'the voice of our Lord sounded in Hell and he cried aloud and burst the graves one by one.'[22] Death, according to Ephraim, had not given up his prey to one who was able to charm wild beasts, that is Orpheus, but he was defeated by Christ, in the harrowing of Hell. Clement makes no use of this part of the Orpheus story, even in the one place in the *Exhortation* (1, 18; 1.8.3–14) where we might have expected it. There he describes the serpent who 'buries people alive' through worship of idols, who also 'carried off Eve to death.' 'Our rescuer and helper is the Lord' he adds, but he makes no use of the figure of the singer.[23]

For Clement, then, Orpheus is the singer, not the psychopomp he became for later Christian writers. The emphasis which later ages placed upon his great love for Eurydice and his attempted rescue of her from death, though not unknown in the ancient world, is overshadowed by the tradition of the power of Orpheus' music over animals.

Clement is not alone in comparing Christ to Orpheus and his activities to that of the singer's. Eusebius in the fourth century in his speech 'In Praise of Constantine,' the first emperor to identify himself as a Christian, includes in that speech an extended comparison of Christ to Orpheus.[24] He says that Christ used an instrument, man, 'as a musician displays his skill by his lyre.' Thus the human body assumed by the Word at his incarnation is treated as an instrument by which he acted. He refers then to Orpheus 'who tamed all kinds of wild beasts by his song and softened the anger of fierce creatures by striking chords on an instrument with a plectrum.' The Word, however, who is 'all-wise and all-harmonious' strikes up 'odes and epodes' which 'soften the fierce, angry passions of the souls of Greeks and barbarians.' Wild animals are, as in Clement, compared to human beings, but not in the same detail. One feels that it has become a more common and accepted comparison by this time.[24]

Elsewhere in this speech, Eusebius refers to creation as the 'system of perfect harmony which is the workmanship of the one world-creating Word' and compares the harmony of a properly-tuned stringed instrument to the harmony of the world in God's hands. Those who honour what is created and fail to honour the creator are like children who admire the lyre and pay no attention to the musician who produces the music.[26] These are themes which have been used by other writers.[27] They show us the power of music in the minds of these early writers as well as the use of a pagan figure to interpret and symbolize Christ.

Beside these two explicit comparisons of Christ to Orpheus, there are references to Christ as a musician, maintaining harmony in the universe or revealing himself by joining 'various tongues in one song.'[28] There are also references to the untamed nature of human beings without Christ, but these are not explicitly connected to the figure of the singer or Orpheus.[29]

The usual figures for Christ – Teacher, Physician, and Shepherd – can all be traced back to scripture. There are many examples of teaching and healing in the Gospels; and the title 'The Good Shepherd' is familiar from John 10. But none of the Gospel writers describes him as singer or musician. Where then does the Singer come from?

First of all we should consider singing and playing of instruments in the worship of God in the Old Testament. One whole book, the book of Psalms, is a collection of songs addressed to God. There are a few secular songs: David's lament for Saul and Jonathan (2 Samuel 1:17–27) or the popular song comparing the military prowess of Saul and David (1 Samuel 18:7). Most songs, whether in Psalms or elsewhere, praised God, and it is evident, therefore, that God was pleased with music and singing.

Many psalms were attributed to David; to succeeding generations he was the shepherd boy anointed to be shepherd over Jacob, or Israel (Psalms 78:70–1), and skilled in playing the lyre (1 Samuel 16:18). As son of David, Christ inherited his kingship and was also, like him, known as a shepherd. It would not be a great step to attribute David's musical skill allegorically to Christ, especially when one recalls the way David soothed Saul's savage spirit with his music (1 Samuel 16:23).

This blending of the figures of Orpheus, David, and Christ can be seen in early Christian art.[30] The singer is usually clothed in the style of Orpheus: short tunic, Phrygian cap, lyre held to one side. But although sometimes he is accompanied by the kind of animals which in myth he is said to have charmed, at other times his audience is reduced to sheep or increased to include centaurs and satyrs. Many 'Orpheus-Christ' figures are found in the catacombs, and some are set among otherwise biblical scenes. In the Jewish synagogue at Dura-Europos there is a figure with a lyre in a wall-painting which is interpreted variously as Orpheus or David.[31] Goodenough in his *Jewish Symbols in the Greco-Roman Period* has shown that Jews borrowed a vocabulary of pagan symbols during this period and used them on official

Jewish structures, because, as he argues, they represented the same mystic and eschatological hope for Jews, pagans, and Christians, too. He suggests that the lyre player in the synagogue at Dura-Europos symbolizes the power of the spiritual to calm the turbulence of our material nature.[32] He compares the use of the lyre on nine coins of the second Revolt period (AD 132).

Finding the lyre and lyre player outside the Christian community confirms its significance as a symbol rather than as a representation of a particular figure. One might conclude, then, that 'David' in the synagogue painting is not the historical king, but an idealized musician who symbolizes the coming 'peaceful kingdom' when natural enemies will become friends (cf Isaiah 11: 1–9 and 65:25). Similarly when the figure of the Singer appears in Christian art or writing, it symbolizes the harmony of God which is at work now through the activity of Christ the Word but will be better seen in the future.

Music and the lyre in particular represent harmony; the Musician or Singer also represents this harmony. But according to Clement, the Word is not only Singer, he is also the New Song (1, 14–16; 1.6.26–7.28). In the Old Testament many times the Lord and his mighty works are the subject of song and he is the one who inspires the singers. Three times we read: 'The Lord is my strength and song, and he has become my salvation' (Exodus 15:2, Isaiah 12:2, Psalms 118:14). Clement surely had in mind these and other verses when he called the Word the New Song. Six times in Psalms a new song is mentioned: 'sing to him a new song' (33:3); 'he put a new song in my mouth' (40:3); 'O sing to the Lord a new song' (96:1, 98:1); 'I will sing a new song to thee, O God' (144:9); and 'Praise the Lord! Sing to the Lord a new song' (149:1). The phrase recurs in Isaiah (42:10) and in the New Testament in the Revelation (5:9, 14:3). Judith in the Apocrypha (16:2) sings a new song of praise for her deliverance. The new song may be called forth by a recent act of deliverance (as at Psalms 40:3 and 98:1) or by a change in circumstances (Revelation 5:9). These are implicitly contrasted with the 'old song' (not so called), which sang of God's deliverance from Egypt.

When Clement calls the Word the New Song, he means that he recently took human form and brought salvation to all. He reminds his readers specifically that the Word is not new 'in the same sense as a tool or a house' is new (1.14; 1.7.4); the Word is eternal, existing in the beginning.

The redeemed in heaven 'sing the song of Moses, the servant of God, and the song of the Lamb' (Revelation 15:3–4). The song of Moses here must surely be a song of praise for the deliverance from Egypt, the great deliverance of the Old Testament; the song of the Lamb is a song of praise for the deliverance which is its spiritual parallel, salvation wrought by Christ. Similarly Clement speaks of the 'Levitical song' together with the new song

(1,6; 1.4.17ff). The Levites supplied the singers and musicians in the temple worship (1 Chronicles 15:16, 2 Chronicles 5:12). 'Levitical song' as a category includes praise for all God's acts in the Old Testament period; in this connection it is essential to remember that for Clement God acting in the Old Testament was always God the Word. The Levitical song praises the pre-incarnate Word; the new song, the Word incarnate.

Christ the Singer and Song in Clement is a complex figure. First, he is compared to musicians of mythical powers, especially over the world of nature. The debt to Orpheus here is obvious and openly acknowledged; I have suggested that David as a musician who soothed Saul acts as a kind of intermediary in the comparison between Orpheus and Christ. Secondly, the instrument itself in the hands of the musician represents harmony and the subjugation of evil, as we see it in the stories of David and Orpheus. The lyre is also used as a type of the harmony found in creation. Thirdly, the song praises God and his deliverance, and because the Word brought deliverance, he is the Song. He can sing of himself because he is God the Word. The Song is the Word set to music.[33]

There are prophecies of an age of peace when a descendant of David would come as a righteous judge, and when natural enemies in the animal world would become friends and be so tame that a little child could lead them (Isaiah 11:1–9). Reconciliation of the animals also occurs in the promise of new heavens and a new earth (Isaiah 65:25). Mosaics with animals and inscriptions from these passages have been preserved: a lion, a leopard, and a goat with Isaiah 11:6; a lion and an ox with Isaiah 11:7.[34] Since these prophecies looked forward to the coming of the Christ, it was natural that Christ should be placed in the midst of animals he had tamed. Orpheus in the midst of wild animals was accepted as a prototype of Christ in the peaceful kingdom.

Clement's figure of the Singer is more complex than would appear from his choice of Orpheus and the others as his starting-point. Instead of narrowing the discussion to a strict comparison, he widens it to cover more adequately the activity of the Word. Eusebius, whose comparison is reminiscent of his, is not so successful; nowhere else in this period does Orpheus foreshadow so majestically the divine Singer.

NOTES

1 My thanks are due to the Canada Council, who granted me a Leave Fellowship for 1974–5 when the first version of this paper was written, and to Scarborough College for research leave; also to Peter Toon, Oak Hill College, London, England, for a fresh look at psalms and songs in the Old Testament.

For a general discussion of music and the figure of Orpheus in early Christian writings, see Robert A. Skeris ΧΡΩΜΑ ΘΕΟΥ *On the Origins and Theological Interpretation of the Musical Imagery Used by the Ecclesiastical Writers of the First Three Centuries, with Special Reference to the Image of Orpheus* (Altötting 1976).

2 Christians might be brought into the arena as at Vienne and Lyon in AD 177 (Eusebius *Historia Ecclesiastica* 5.1.3–2.8) or might be regarded with suspicion as baby-eaters and committers of incest (cf Tertullian *Apology* 7.1).

3 Eg Moses was supposed to have influenced the Greeks. The *Testament* of Orpheus, quoted only by Christian writers, shows Orpheus repenting of polytheism and embracing monotheism through the influence of Moses. O. Kern *Orphicorum fragmenta* (Berlin 1922) 255–63 distinguishes three versions (his fr 245–47) preserved by Justin, Clement, and Eusebius. Undoubtedly this poem smoothed the way for Christians to compare Christ and Orpheus.

4 *Protrepticus* 12, 254; 1.84.7. First part of the reference is to the section of the work, followed by the page number in Clement of Alexandria, ed and tr G.W. Butterworth (Loeb edn; London and New York 1919); second part of the reference is to volume, page, and line number of the standard edition of *Clemens Alexandrinus* ed O. Stählin (4 vols; Leipzig 1905–36). References to *Protrepticus* will be given in this manner throughout.

5 I have translated τέττιξ as 'grasshopper' and κιθάρα as 'lyre,' although the former might also be translated 'cicada' and the latter 'lute' or 'cithara.'

6 J.B. Friedman *Orpheus in the Middle Ages* (Cambridge Mass 1970) 55 attempts to link all these mountain references to Orpheus: he is the son of Calliope, a Muse with her home on Helicon; he sang hymns and codified the theology of Dionysus on Cithaeron; and he tamed savage beasts and men in the mountains of Thrace and Odrysi. But a careful examination of Clement shows that he is not thinking solely of Orpheus.

7 *Problemata* 918b28; Liddell-Scott-Jones (*LSJ*) *A Greek-English Lexicon* (Oxford 1940) sv ἀγωνιστής 1, 3; cf *Protrepticus* (10, 236; 1.78.16–17) where the Word 'acted the drama of salvation,' τὸ σωτήριον δρᾶμα ... ὑπεκρίνετο and is γνήσιος ἀγωνιστής.

8 Lampe *Patristic Lexicon* sv στεφανόω

9 *Odyssey* 4.221

10 πτηνὰ μὲν τοὺς κούφους αὐτῶν, ἑρπετὰ δὲ τοὺς ἀπατεῶνας, καὶ λέοντας μὲν τοὺς θυμικούς, σύας δὲ τοὺς ἡδονικούς, λύκους δὲ τοὺς ἁρπακτικούς (1.8; 1.5.8–10).

11 *LSJ* sv κόσμος. Most Greek philosophers were convinced of this order: D.R. Dicks *Early Greek Astronomy* (London and New York 1970) 63; G.E.R. Lloyd *Early Greek Science* (London 1970) 27; W.K.C. Guthrie *The Greeks and Their Gods* (London 1950) 198.

12 Lloyd *Early Greek Science*; Dicks *Early Greek Astronomy* 71; Aristotle *De caelo* 290b12f

13 σὺ γὰρ εἶ κιθάρα καὶ αὐλὸς καὶ ναὸς ἐμοί, κιθάρα διὰ τὴν ἁρμονίαν, αὐλὸς διὰ τὸ πνεῦμα, ναὸς διὰ τὸν λόγον, ἵν' ἡ μὲν κρέκῃ, τὸ δὲ ἐμπνέῃ, ὃ δὲ χωρήσῃ τὸν κύριον (1, 12; 1.6.15–18).

14 *Legatio* 9.1. Not much is known of Athenagoras: Philip of Side, a fifth-century Christian historian, says he was the head of the school in Alexandria and teacher of Clement, author of *Stromateis*, but this is not confirmed by, and is hard to reconcile with, other sources. He was active in the time of M. Aurelius and was therefore Clement's contemporary. Cf W.R. Schoedel *Athenagoras* (Oxford 1972) ix. Cf also the 'pipe of my lips' in G. Vermès *Dead Sea Scrolls in English* (London 1962) 89.

15 Epiphanius *Heresies* 48.4.1–3

16 On the world as God's instrument, a favourite theme of Athanasius (eg *De incarnatione* 42.22) and Eusebius (*Praise of Constantine* chapters 11 and 12). Cf also Athenagoras *Legatio* 16.3 and Clement *Stromateis* 6.11.1–5.

17 οὐ δάφνης πετάλων καὶ ταινιῶν τινων ἐρίῳ καὶ πορφύρα πεποικιλμένων, δικαιοσύνην δὲ ἀναδησάμενος καὶ τῆς ἐγκρατείας τὰ πέταλα περιθέμενος (1, 26; 1.10.10–12).

18 W.K.C. Guthrie *The Greeks and Their Gods* (London 1950) 192–3

19 W.K.C. Guthrie *Orpheus and Greek Religion* (London 1935) 198

20 P. Bersuire *Metamorphosis Ovidiana moraliter explanata*, quoted by Friedman, *Orpheus in the Middle Ages* 127

21 As in the Apostles' Creed; cf also Ephesians 4:8 and 1 Peter 3:19.

22 In *Post-Nicene Fathers* vol 13 tr J. Gwynn (Oxford and New York 1898) 196–7, Nisibene Hymns 36 stanzas 5 and 11; Ephraim wrote AD 350–78.

23 We might note in contrast *Ovide moralisé* 8.264: 'by Orpheus ... we must understand the person of Our Lord Jesus Christ ... who played his harp so melodiously that he drew from Hell the sainted souls of the holy fathers who had descended there through the sin of Adam and Eve' (see Friedman *Orpheus in the Middle Ages* 125–6) and the sequence 'Morte Christi celebrata' in A. Mai *Nova patrum bibliotheca* (Rome 1852) vol 1 part 2, 208 (a thirteenth-century hymn): 'Sponsam suam ab inferno / Regno locans in superno / Noster traxit Orpheus.'

24 Eusebius *Werke* 1 ed I.A. Heikel (Leipzig 1902) 242; the text, from chapter 14, reads: οἷά τις μουσικὸς ἀνὴρ διὰ τῆς λύρας τὴν σοφίαν δεικνύμενος ... παντοῖα γένη θηρίων θέλγειν τῇ ᾠδῇ ἐξημεροῦν τε τῶν ἀγρίων τοὺς θυμούς, ἐν ὀργάνῳ πλήκτρῳ κρουομένων χορδῶν ... πάνσοφος καὶ παναρμόνιος ... ᾠδὰς καὶ ἐπῳδὰς ... ἀνήμερον Ἑλλήνων τε καὶ βαρβάρων πάθη τε ἄγρια καὶ θηριώδη ψυχῶν.

25 For the figure of Christ–Orpheus in art, cf F. Cabrol and H. Leclerq *Diction-*

naire d'archéologie chrétienne et de liturgie (Paris 1936) vol 12 part 2 sv 'Orphée.'

26 Eusebius *In Praise of Constantine*, chapters 11 and 12

27 See note 12 above and Athenagoras *Legatio* 16; Tertullian *Ad nationes* 2.5.9.

28 *Damasi Epigrammata* ed M. Ihm (Leipzig 1895) 66: 'virtus regit omnia Christi / qui varias iunxit uno sub carmine linguas / ut pecudes volucresque deum cognoscere possint.' (Kern *Testimonia* 156).

29 A. Heussner *Die altchristlichen Orpheusdarstellungen* (Leipzig 1893) 8–9; cf Irenaeus *Adversus haereses* 5.8 and Cassiodorus on Psalm 49.10 (Migne *Patrologia Latina* 70.352).

30 On the use of Old Testament and pagan symbolism in early Christian art, see M. Gough *The Origin of Christian Art* (London 1973) and Friedman *Orpheus in the Middle Ages* 38–85.

31 For discussions see H. Stern 'The Orpheus in the Synagogue of Dura-Europos' *Journal of the Warburg and Courtauld Institutes* 21 (1958) 1–6; A. Graber *Christian Iconography: A Study of Its Origins* (London 1969) 24; E.R. Goodenough *Jewish Symbols in the Greco-Roman Period* 5 (New York 1956) 103–11 and 9 (New York 1964) 89–104.

32 Goodenough *Jewish Symbols* 5, vii–x and 105

33 Cf Tertullian *De carne Christi* 20.3 where the author says that through David's Psalms, Christ sings of himself ('per quem se cecinit ipse Christus'). On the 'new' song, cf F.A. Brigham 'The concept of 'New Song' in Clement of Alexandria's exhortation to the Greeks' in *Classical Folia* 16 (1962) 9–13 and R.A. Harrisville *The Concept of Newness in the New Testament* (Minneapolis, Minn 1960) 18–20 and 96–9.

34 Stern 'The Orpheus in the Synagogue' 4, also compares a secular picture of 'friendship' – five pairs of wild and domestic animals – found at Daphni near Antioch, entitled φιλία. See also M. Gough *The Origin of Christian Art* 73–7.

PATRICIA VICARI

Sparagmos:
Orpheus among the Christians

AS IT SURVIVED in the Middle Ages, the myth of Orpheus developed new forms characteristic of medieval culture. Some of these may, in fact, have been current in Western folk traditions since pre-Latin times. The complex of motifs, themes, and fables we call 'the Orpheus myth' is, apparently, of very ancient origin and almost universal diffusion. Even among the American Indians are many tales of the Orphic type, or various Orphic types.[1] Some Celtic folk-tales that entered Latin culture in the Middle Ages bear the stamp of the same ideas and experiences that are expressed in the classical versions of the Orpheus myth, either because the Celts were originally close neighbours of the Thracians in central Europe[2] or because the experiences themselves are basic to humanity. In any case, the classical form of the myth seems to have joined with and been revivified by some native Celtic 'Orpheus' legends along the Atlantic coast, producing a strand of stories that emphasize certain features of the familiar one and add or alter others. That may explain why the twelfth- and thirteenth-century Orpheus in the lost Breton *Lai d'Orfée* and the anonymous *Sir Orfeo*, as well as Henryson's *Orpheus and Eurydice* and some early Scottish ballads, is strikingly different from the classical Orpheus.[3]

At this point it will be useful to divide the 'classical' tale (the Latin form, as defined by Virgil and Ovid) into two aspects or phases. The first and oldest presents Orpheus as a shaman-theologian, musician of supernatural powers, and Great Initiator. The love-story involving Eurydice is either absent or unimportant. In its second, later and latinate phase, Orpheus is a suffering and heroic human being of genius and everything in the story is subsumed by the theme of love. As it floats down the Hebrus the severed head of the lover, according to Virgil, continues to murmur 'Eurydice!' In the preceding chapter Professor Irwin has shown that the first phase was developed in

Byzantine culture and assimilated into Christianity by the early Fathers until Orpheus became a sort of metaphor for or type of Christ. Although the men of the Middle Ages never forgot the magical musician with his entourage of beasts and trees, that aspect was put in abeyance in pictorial art and narrative literature and had to bide its time until the Renaissance, and the medieval Orpheus was primarily the lover of Eurydice who descended into Hades to win her back. This story of sexual love became the fictional base upon which allegories that compared Orpheus to Christ were constructed.

Of the medieval treatment of myth in general Jean Seznec has shown that it took three main forms: myths could be explained as distorted accounts of historical facts (or a garbled version of Hebrew history and theology), as veiled descriptions of the various powers (natural principles, elements, or demons) that rule the physical universe, or as rhetorical devices for teaching morality or theology allegorically.[4] In any case, the 'form' of the myth got separated from its 'content' of meaning and was made to bear a new meaning relevant to and compatible with the new culture. Thus, Venus became Eve, and Orpheus, as we have seen, Christ. In the mystical, pantheistic, and theosophic atmosphere that prevailed in late antiquity, pagan gods and heroes became identified with the astral divinities that ruled the cosmos. Astrology dominated all the natural sciences in the Middle Ages and Renaissance, and even the Church had to compromise with superstition. To this deification of the natural world was added the doctrine of number. Number was the key to *scientia universalis*, and numerical 'correspondences' between things of every class – seven planets, seven metals, seven virtues, seven sins, seven gifts of the Holy Spirit, seven joys of Mary, seven liberal arts, and so on – were supplemented by the idea of melothesia, the correspondence of the microcosm and macrocosm, especially the planets. The theory of numerical correspondences was also part and parcel of the Neopythagorean and Neoplatonic philosophies, both of which flourished at the beginning of the Middle Ages, and taught that the universe is made according to geometric forms, abstract relations, and proportions which can be expressed numerically. Each of these proportions corresponds to a musical interval, and altogether, therefore, the universe is a harmony. This idea was usually expressed in the image of the music of the spheres, but all things, not only the spheres, harmonize (or ought to) with everything else. The soul of man is a harmony – this Platonic idea is familiar – and so is his body. Moreover, both body and soul are a harmony corresponding to the cosmic harmony. That, in turn, corresponds to or reveals the nature of God. Here we are reminded that it was in the Middle Ages that the rhetorical device of allegory was developed into the quasi-religious doctrine of sacramental Nature, according to which every object in the universe is a symbol of a spiritual truth. The cosmos is a 'book,' whose symbols, which must be 'read,' are made of plant fibres, starlight, fur, and feathers. Whoever can interpret it aright penetrates the veil of nature to the Holy of Holies.

Orpheus, or any other figure out of pagan mythology, could thus be interpreted indiscriminately (and even simultaneously) as a historical figure of great antiquity, who invented the art of poetry, as God, organizing the harmony of the cosmos, or as human rationality, since all truths are at one in the Truth, and what we take as different levels of reality or different logical categories were then seen as all part of the óne reality. It did not even matter if different interpretations of the same myth on different planes did not seem to agree – if Orpheus was a 'good' or Christ-like figure in one interpretation and a 'bad' or Adamic figure in another. Both interpretations could be accepted as true and no effort had to be made to rationalize the contradiction.

Françoise Joukovsky in her monograph *Orphée et ses disciples dans la poésie française et néo-latine du XVIe siècle* finds three main traditional uses of the Orpheus myth in the Middle Ages: Orpheus as a figure for the Divine Word, as a symbol of the harmony of the world, and Orpheus and Eurydice as *nous* and *epithumia* in the Neoplatonic psychomachia of Boethius. John Friedman distinguishes rather between successive phases of the transformational process undergone by myth from the fifth to the fourteenth century; first, it was medievalized and Christianized, and then gradually secularized again until the emphasis came on Orpheus' human feelings, as he was inevitably linked with Eurydice.[5] The process of medievalizing involved first extracting edifying doctrine from the story and later making Orpheus into the prototype of the model lover and courteous knight. In most medieval accounts the centre of attention is the relationship of Orpheus and Eurydice. Eurydice becomes Orpheus' better or worse side; she is the concupiscent nature that draws him down to hell or the Good which eludes him; or else the lovers together symbolize the art of oratory or music and its subject matter or theory. In any case the relationship between them becomes the *moralitas*, and after the fifth or sixth century Orpheus scarcely seems to have been thought of without Eurydice, except by the minstrels, for whom he was a professional archetype.

Friedman's account of the evolution of this myth agrees with Seznec's observations on the three ways of treating pagan myth in the Middle Ages that have already been alluded to, the historical, the physical, and the moral traditions. In the historical or euhemerist tradition, Orpheus is treated as a real, historical man who made an outstanding contribution to culture. The contribution varied. He might be a prophet or religious teacher and innovator, a law-giver or civilizer, a philosopher, an inventor (of poetry, of the alphabet, of the principles of music or harmony). His contribution was not always viewed in a favourable light. In the early centuries of the Christian era, the Fathers of the Church, embattled against paganism, decried Orpheus as a barbarian who taught the Greeks the accursed heathen mysteries (Tatian), a coward and deceiver (Theodoret), to whom was granted a revelation of the monotheistic truth, as his poem *The Testament of Orpheus* witnesses, and who yet turned back to his heathenish polytheism and compounded his sins by transmitting 'the infamous orgies of Dionysus' to the Greeks. According to St Augustine, Orpheus spoke the truth in spite of himself and made no attempt to live up to it. Rather, he regressed to teaching demon-worship to his fellow countrymen. Not all the patristic evaluations were that hostile, however, and Orpheus fared well, compared with other pagan heroes, because he was the author of the *Testament*. Even if his version of monotheism was rather strange and muddled, said Theophilus, it showed that God was present in the inspirations of the Greeks, as well as in those of the Hebrew prophets, though to a lesser degree. The doctrine of monotheism, however adulterated, was still a step forward. Clement of Alexandria was quite hostile towards pagan culture in general and Orpheus in particular, yet even he enlisted Orpheus in the 'philosophical family' of whom Dante speaks in the *Inferno*, where he is associated with the great 'master souls' of all time, such as Socrates and Plato. With Linus, he is found in the lighted tower, the only place in hell where there is any light. Thus the way was paved for Orpheus' becoming again for Christians what he was for Horace, 'sacer interpresque deorum' (*Ars poetica* 391).

No matter in what context Orpheus was mentioned, or whether he appeared in conjunction with Eurydice or not, he was always the enchanting musician with power to charm animals, trees, and even sticks and stones. This aspect of the myth may have been pushed into the background but it never disappeared, and it conditioned whatever form the fable took. Whether the enticing song was interpreted as oratory, philosophical discourse, or music itself, the animals and trees were regularly regarded as representing barbarous or irrational elements, so that (after the Patristic period) whatever else might be said of him, Orpheus always represented a civilizing or humanizing force. A branch of the historical tradition that began with Fulgentius and ran right through the Middle Ages, though somewhat neglected in the central part of the period, came back into prominence at the end and in the Renaissance. In it, Orpheus was taken as a culture hero and his story was an allegory of the *artes humanes*. In his *Mitologiae* Fulgentius etymologizes 'Orpheus' from *oraia phone*, 'best voice,' and 'Eurydice' from *eur dike*, 'profound judgment,' and says these two symbolize the two aspects of song: the power of the words to move the listener and the more mysterious power of the harmony of the tones. From this account sprang the later treatments of the myth in which Orpheus is the champion of music or eloquence, sometimes the greatest of minstrels, sometimes the persuasive courtly lover par excellence. In Remigius of Auxerre's commentary on the *Marriage of Mercury and Philology* of Martianus Capella, Eurydice is 'the very art of music in its most profound principles.' Orpheus neglects his art and so loses Eurydice and has to go to the lower world of deep study. When through such study he can arrange the notes of music by the rules of art he reascends. 'But when [Eurydice] compares the corporeal and transitory notes [sung by his voice] to the profound theory of music she – that is thought itself – flees again into her deep knowledge because she cannot appear in notes and Orpheus remains sad, having the mere sound of music without possessing the underlying principles.'[6] Eurydice here stands for thought and Orpheus for the sensuous or emotional vehicle of thought, whether it be music or words. The interpretation indicates the divorce between form and content in the arts in medieval aesthetic theory which goes back to classical antiquity and was formulated by St Augustine in an influential passage in *De doctrina Christiana*. The Angelic Doctor warned against the potentially dangerous and seductive power of eloquent language; wisdom is always to be preferred before mere eloquence or beauty of form, although it is best that the two be joined. Orpheus thus became for some a symbol of specious or merely sensuous art, incapable of attaining to Wisdom, as represented by Eurydice.

When this tradition was taken up again by later writers such as William of Conches, Bernardus Silvestris, and Nicholas Trivet, a less negative view was presented of Orpheus: his lyre for William symbolized wisdom joined with eloquence. For Bernardus, Orpheus meant wisdom and eloquence and his lyre the rhetoric of the orator. Nicholas Trivet calls Orpheus the intellect and his beautiful music sweet eloquence joined to wisdom. He was the poet-singer beloved of the gods and pre-eminent by his own achievements. Thomas of Walsingham, writing in the early fifteenth century, says in his *Archana deorum* that Orpheus discovered the tonal intervals of the seven spheres and their harmony. He was a very eloquent man and a theologian, a civilizer. By 'skilful modulation of his voice' he obtained Eurydice or 'loftiness of knowledge,' which, however, can never be permanently possessed by means of any art, and so she stole away to the Underworld. For Boccaccio, Orpheus' lyre was the faculty of oratory and its seven strings the seven kinds of oratorical discourse. Orpheus ('best voice') was the wisest and most eloquent of men, for only wise men with beautiful voices can achieve the pinnacles of oratorical art. Orpheus thus became the prototype of the humanist's artistic genius. And again in Boccaccio, after centuries of silence on the subject, we hear of the severed head that continued to sing and the lyre that played on after death (Boccaccio may also have been alluding to the story of the stellification of the lyre); the head and lyre symbolize fame – a new preoccupation that signals the end of the Middle Ages — 'a famous man lives on [after his death] by his fame.' By the fifteenth century Orpheus was regularly taken as the archetype of the poet or artist: in the lowest zone of the bas reliefs of the Campanile in Florence we see him placed among Daedalus, Euclid, Pythagoras, and Hercules as one of the inventors of the arts. In the *Florentine Picture Chronicle* attributed to Maso Finiguerra, all the great figures of the past, Jew or Gentile, are grouped in a series of thematic drawings illustrating the growth of culture and civilization. In the group that includes Apollo as Physician we find also Hostanes, Zoroaster, Hermes Trismegistus, Linus, Orpheus, and Musaeus – 'all the esoteric wisdom of Persia, Egypt and Greece.'[7]

Let us return to our medieval Orpheus and the third of Jean Seznec's 'traditions,' the moral tradition, in which myth is a code language whose deciphered meanings are ethical or theologico-moral precepts. There is no break in this tradition – the most fertile of the three – between the Middle Ages and the Renaissance. In it Eurydice is essential to the story, and interpretation turns upon what happened when Orpheus went down to Hades in search of her. The two most important sources are the account by Boethius in *The Consolation of Philosophy* (Book 3, Metre 12), and the *Ovide Moralisé* of the thirteenth century. The way for Boethius' interpretation was probably paved by the use made of the Orpheus icon in pagan and Christian funerary art. There, as we have seen, the pagan icon of Orpheus among the animals (often sheep) was used by artisans to represent Christ, the Good Shepherd, or the Deliverer of Souls. But it would appear from at least one notable example of this kind of art (the 'Jerusalem mosaic') that Orpheus also came to be used to symbolize Reason (*nous*), in opposition to passion and carnal lust (*epithumia*). The tamed animals among which he was shown are replaced in the Jerusalem mosaic by a centaur and Pan. Orpheus overcomes with his reason (music) the animals that stand in opposition to him as symbols of the carnal lusts. Boethius retained the idea of Orpheus as a representative of the higher powers of the soul, but replaced the animals, as symbols of the earth-bound passions, with Eurydice. It was Boethius' version, along with the elaborations developed in the glosses, that held sway from the sixth to the ninth century. In the *Consolation of Philosophy* Orpheus is the seeker after truth or spiritual enlightenment who, when he has almost gained his goal, looks backward to material concerns and so loses all the good he has gained.

Boethius apparently associates Eurydice contradictorily first with the truth being sought and then with the 'heavy bonds of earth' which entrap Orpheus and frustrate his quest. As is the case generally in the *Consolation*, there is nothing in this 'moral' that is particularly Christian, but later commentators remedied that. John Friedman traces the progress of the interpretation from Boethius through Remigius of Auxerre (c 904), Notker Labeo (who added the biblical text the story supposedly exemplified: 'No man, having put his hand to the plough and looking back, is fit for the Kingdom of Heaven'[8]), and William of Conches (early twelfth century), for whom Eurydice was natural concupiscence and Aristaeus, somewhat startlingly, virtue. Eurydice flees from him into a meadow symbolizing pleasure, and there is bitten by the snake and dies. (Aristaeus, who was missing in Boethius, found his way back into the story in Notker.) Orpheus descends 'to the knowledge of earthly things' but is unable to free his desires from them, and so is frustrated. William's account is Platonic, rather than Christian, but Nicholas Trivet, writing some time near the end of the thirteenth century, set the stage for later Christian interpretations by reintroducing the serpent as the cause of the loss of the concupiscent wife.

Ovid did not really get 'revived' until the twelfth century. The glosses and commentaries which then proliferated as ancillary to the *Metamorphoses* stressed certain points in the legend which Boethius had overpassed in silence. Much wit was exercised in trying to 'moralise' the serpent that bit Eurydice and Orpheus' conversion to homosexuality. In general the Ovidian commentators were more ingenious and more Christian than their Boethian predecessors. One of the more remarkable features of their interpretations is that the loss of Eurydice becomes a paradoxical blessing: it is a fortunate loss, more a renunciation than a loss. Whereas the Boethian commentators treated Orpheus as a would-be-philosopher who simply did not have the will-power to give up the world, the flesh, and the devil (all incarnate in the hapless Eurydice) the Ovidian crew turned him into an ascetic – even, in the case of Giovanni del Vergilio (*Allegorie*, c 1325), a monk – and his bereavement into an edifying conversion. The backward glance still spells disaster: it means, as it did for Boethius, succumbing again to vice, or the temptations of the world and the flesh, and as such it is roundly condemned: Orpheus returned 'as a dog to his vomit,' but now it is usually no more than a temporary lapse. Orpheus regains his equilibrium and 'renounces hell' (Giovanni del Vergilio), for good, this time, and ascends into the mountains of virtue (Arnulf of Orleans), or of Scripture and religion (Pierre Bersuire, *Reductorium Morale*, c 1325–37) and civilizes the savages with his 'preaching.' By shunning women, these writers reassure us, is meant nothing more than that Orpheus shook off all effeminacy and lewd company (for women are notoriously lewd); the 'boys' to whom he transferred his love are those who behave in a manly way (Arnulf), or even, according to Giovanni del Vergilio, God himself. (One often finds innocent blasphemies in these allegorizers.) The serpent is vice of a sensual sort, connected with pleasure (Eurydice was illegitimately wandering in the fields of delight, which were off bounds). The serpent changes from being 'the poison of earthly delight' into the devil (Giovanni del Vergilio, *Ovide Moralisé*, Bersuire). In an illustrated mythographic handbook of the fourteenth century based upon Bersuire's *Metamorphosis Ovidiana*, Orpheus is shown with a dragon and a unicorn, symbols of Satan and Christ. The dragon, or draconopede, in this and other illustrations of the myth in the same period, is of the same outward shape as the serpent in Eden. Two demons are visible, one emerging from hell-mouth and one holding Eurydice.

What is going on here is perfectly obvious. The (by now) exotic myth of Orpheus is being assimilated to the more familiar one of Adam-Christus. The anonymous *Ovide Moralisé* of the end of the thirteenth century is the first commentary to identify Eurydice plainly with Eve; its writer will go to any lengths, moreover, to Christianize every detail of the story. The marriage of Orpheus and Eurydice was apparently the Incarnation, in which the godhead (Orpheus) was joined to human nature (Eurydice). The serpent was the one that tempted Eve and caused the death of the human race. But Christ (Orpheus) descended to hell to save his own from death. Who, then, looked back and spoiled everything? Clearly, it could not logically be Christ (Orpheus) himself; at this point – a difficult one – the text becomes rather obscure: the subject of the sentences shifts from a singular to a plural: it is no longer Christ (Orpheus) that is acting, but a hypothetical 'they' – hardened sinners who cannot be won away from sin even by Christ:

> Ceulz qu'il trouva presentement
> Des siens en traist tout cuitement,
> Et cil qui descendre i deüssent
> Pour l'enleüre qu'il eüssent
> Dou mors dont li premier morurent
> Par lui cuite de delivre furent
> S'il se tenissent vraiement
> En l'amour de lor vrai ament,
> Et s'il emprez lor delivrance
> Tenissent la droite creance
> De Dieu, sans resorter arriere,

Jusqu'il fussent fors de l'orniere
D'enfer et dou monde passez.   (10.486–98)[9]

After he harrowed Hell, Orpheus-Christ went up to the 'high, ever-green plain,' but he had not yet peopled it with saved souls. There, with the sweetness of his song (the gospel) he drew to him the accommodating boys who symbolize his apostles, preachers, and other followers, on the high mountain of Holy Church. Each of the strings of his lyre symbolizes a point of Christian dogma, a sacrament, and a Christian virtue. A summary of the moralizing of the second string alone may suffice to give the reader an idea of this writer's method and the mental atmosphere of such work. Each of the strings is firmly pegged on a double peg. The pegs of the second string are Christ's circumcision, which was a proof of his great love and condescension, and the sacrament of ordination. The string itself symbolizes charity, and it is tuned by the finger of *sainte pitié*. This string sings 'Blessed are the meek for they shall inherit the earth.' The harp is the very one that David (that is, God) used to comfort Saul (the human race) when he was sick with mortal sin. The bow is the mouth of the Son of God and also the tongues of the doctors, teachers, and preachers who have illuminated the Holy Church; by their singing (preaching the gospel) they have filled the mountain top (Holy Church) with trees, birds, and beasts (people of all nations; more specifically, holy hermits, monks, and pious laymen, all symbolized by the trees which bear fruits of good works). Even the trees are catalogued and interpreted: the pine, ivy, and laurel are evergreens, that is, perpetual virgins, and the broom plant mealy-mouthed hypocrites and flatterers.

The rout of Thracian women is the Jews, soft and effeminate when it comes to doing good, but cruel and savage otherwise. The writer is by no means dogmatic in offering only one interpretation. The book is full of such phrases as 'but another meaning may be read into the fable' as prefaces to further suggested meanings. They were not taken to be mutually exclusive. The author suggests an alternative meaning for Orpheus on the mountain: he might stand as a symbol for all Christ's evangelists, preachers, prophets, and believers. Bersuire similarly offers various interpretations: following the *Ovide Moralisé*, he says that Orpheus on Pangaeus represents the saints and doctors of the early Church, and the Thracian women the cruel tyrants who martyred the early Christians. Bersuire refers to both versions of the Orpheus-and-Eurydice story, the happy and the unhappy. In the latter, the Orpheus who looks backward and so loses his soul forever symbolizes 'many' who look back again to *temporalia* and so lose their souls after being converted to Christianity. But in another place he equates the leading of Eurydice back into the light with Christ's successful harrowing of hell, and in this account Orpheus as Christ cannot fail, but emerges triumphantly from hell-mouth saying, 'Rise up, my love, my fair one, and come away.' As Friedman points out, neither the *Ovide Moralisé* author nor Bersuire was concerned with making a pagan story understood: rather, they used the story as a ground to launch lessons that would profit the Christian reader.

In his zeal to leave no stone unturned that might hide a moral, the French writer seizes upon some details of the story seemingly forgotten since classical times, such as the serpent that menaced the severed head of Orpheus (*Metamorphoses* 11.56–60), and the anger of Bacchus, who turned the Thracian women into trees and went off in a sulk to take up his abode in Phrygia with Midas and Silenus (67–88). But while more and more of the classical story is recovered, the commentator gets further and further away from the spirit of it. In two earlier commentators, Peter of Paris (who could claim that Orpheus killed Eurydice because she nagged at him) and Arnulf of Orleans, little sense is to be found of the narrative integrity of the story. This distortion is more extreme in the *Ovide Moralisé*. It exemplifies the developed state of Jean Seznec's 'divorce of form from content' in the medieval treatment of classical mythology. So far were the men of the thirteenth and fourteenth centuries from the classical meaning of the myth that Proserpina in it, the 'Pure One' of ancient times, becomes for Thomas of Walsingham 'the greatest of the vices,'[10] and the second (most heart-breaking) loss of Eurydice becomes for John of Garland and others, Orpheus' triumphant renunciation of her! Yet this subversion of old myth coincides with the apogee of the medieval art of story-telling. It is in the romance-like treatments of the story that we find the greatest 'blurring of the classical outlines' and, at the same time, the most consummate Gothic artistry. With the romantic treatments we have yet to deal, but they do not belong under the heading of allegory. They present essentially an irrational, magical view of the world and in them Orpheus is a magician.

The magical tradition is the third medieval way of treating the Orpheus myth. Seznec calls it the 'physical,' but for the purpose of examining the treatment of the Orpheus myth it will be less misleading to call it 'magical' or 'occult.' Here the personages of classical fable are astral divinities who rule the universe. That means that they are ultimate natural principles that might be spoken of also as angels, demons (or daimons), or 'archons' (rulers of the celestial spheres). Such a view of nature and myth is embedded in primitive animism, a dateless way of thinking which comes to the fore whenever rational conceptions of the universe lose their power over men's minds and people revert to older, instinctual explanations of nature. Probably the oldest myth about Orpheus is that he was a mighty magician, and it kept recurring in antiquity, in the Middle Ages, and in the Renaissance. It is the view of Orpheus powerfully presented in the pseudo-Orphic *Argonautica*, where Orpheus as theurgist-priest presides over some rather thrilling rites outside the grove of Ares in Colchis. Over the gate to the grove sits the deity Hecate-Mounichee whom he propitiates by digging a triple ditch and preparing a fire of magical kinds of wood – juniper, cedar, buckthorn, and poplar. Offerings of barley cakes, three black dogs' blood and entrails, and magical herbs and odours are made, and Orpheus beats upon the 'hostile brass,' whose sound is associated with the moon and Hecate. He invokes the goddess and also Alecto, Tisiphone, and Megara, who hear and appear with torches. The ditch catches fire, and in the black smoke appear the infernal Pandora with an iron body, 'the indestructible monster with three heads,' that is, Hecate, with a horse's head, bitch's head, and human head in the middle, and other hellish spirits called Expiations. The torches fall from the hands of the guardian goddess and the silver bolts of the gates in the iron, steel, brass, bronze, and golden walls withdraw of themselves. After entering, Orpheus sings the dragon to sleep.

In the magical tradition, three ideas about Orpheus are emphasized. First, he is a psychopomp and controls the afterlife of the soul because he is allied with or knows how to manipulate celestial or chthonic powers or both. Secondly, his lyre is the clue to his power. Its seven strings symbolize the seven planets, seven heavens, seven archons, and the divine cosmic harmony. It is not merely symbolic of harmony, however, but magically able to induce it, for a symbol, to the magically minded, is never a mere representation, but also a means of producing an effect. Thirdly, Orpheus is often called a healer, which is to say in a different way, a master of natural forces and producer of effects.

Strabo describes Orpheus as a wizard and soothsayer, a priest of mystical orgiastic rites and a professional musician. In keeping with the last-named, rather disreputable profession, he is a somewhat contemptible fellow who gets illusions of grandeur and uses his power to rabble-rouse (such the moving of trees and beasts becomes), until he is killed by a rival faction. Usually the taming of animals, and moving of trees and of the gods of Hades were taken as proof of his magical (as much as musical) prowess. The figure of Orpheus as magician continues more or less in the background, eclipsed by the portrait of him as a lover in the high Middle Ages, right down to the fourteenth and fifteenth centuries. Ristoro d'Arezzo confused Orpheus with one 'Artephius,' a great magician supposed to have understood the secret of animals' language; in that art, claims Ristoro, Orpheus made use of a magical stone called *liparaios*.

As a psychopomp, Orpheus would naturally be of funerary interest, and indeed the picture of Orpheus among the animals furnished pagan and Christian artisans with a model for some of their tomb decorations in the period from the second to the fifth centuries. The story of his having won over the ruler of the Underworld and led souls from Hades back to life was apparently taken as a way of saying that his magical music could propitiate the archons and smooth the path to the celestial sphere for a departing soul. In Christian tombs the icon of Orpheus first appears as representative of Christ the Deliverer of Souls, or Good Shepherd (as a herder of animals Orpheus was also a kind of shepherd), along with other (pagan) symbols of immortality such as eagles, peacocks, and doves. The lyre, even apart from Orpheus, was supposed to be able by the sound of its music to help the soul return to its celestial home, for it imitates (or encapsulates) the music of the spheres and puts the soul in tune with the celestial orders through which it must ascend if it is to escape from the earth. It is not surprising, therefore, that Orpheus came to be compared and then conflated with Christ, another 'magician' who promised his followers a secure path to heaven. An Orpheus-Christus figure plays a prominent part in the theurgy of late antiquity, which was aimed at modifying astral fate. Representations of this figure often show him with the sun, moon, and stars, symbols of the astral realm where it was hoped the soul might go after death. In all magical thought it was believed that each of the 'archons' or planetary rulers of the 'seven heavens' had to be propitiated in turn by the soul as it travelled upward, on its way to rejoin God, by means of magical invocations and formulae and images carved on stones and worn as amulets. Christianity took over these quite heathenish notions, and made God the Ruler of the Archons, while Christ,[11] as psychopomp, was supposed to be able to bear the soul past them.

The association of Orpheus with magic reappears in a different guise in *Sir Orfeo*, an English poem of the fourteenth century based upon a Breton lay. The story is Celtic and the Orpheus in it is in some ways scarcely recognizable.[12] He is a king, a lover, and a musician who has to contend with the magical powers of a demon-king. The latter, in the manner of his kind, lusts after mortal women, and carries them off if they are so imprudent as to enter the charmed precincts of a tree or bush, particularly at the witching-hour of twelve. Eurydice (now called Queen Heurodis) does so, and is borne off to the Celtic fairyland, a place of threatening beauty, or *glamour*. Sir Orfeo delivers her by a combination of trickery and musical skill.

The whole atmosphere of *Sir Orfeo* seems to me quite Celtic and the treatment of the story entirely pagan, but Friedman conjectures that the unknown author's characterization of Orpheus and Eurydice was influenced by the Christian allegorical tradition that began with Boethius. Here

Eurydice, as a woman, was associated with Eve and the concupiscence of the flesh and was, therefore, only too likely to be carried off by Satan, whether in the form of a serpent or a fairy king. Such reasoning, however, jars with the tone of the poem. There is a considerable difference between the Christian Serpent-Satan and the Fairy King of Celtic tales. The hero, too, seems to come almost intact from Celtic tradition, like the Orpheus of certain Shetland ballads (and in some ways like Henryson's Orpheus, although he is a more complicated mixture). He probably owes something to the cult of 'the All-Knowing God,' who in Norse is called Oðinn or Wotana, and in Irish, Lug-Find. Those, in turn, may be the Germanic and Celtic versions of the Thracian myth of Orpheus. Heinrich Wagner has pointed out, in discussing the etymology of 'Orpheus,' that it derives from an Indo-European root meaning 'skilful,' or artful.' It is a cognate of *ṛbhu*, the Sanskrit word for 'skilful,' according to Saussure.[13] Another cognate is the Irish Gaelic word 'rivros,' a name for the god 'Mercurius-Lugu-,' who corresponds in many ways to Mercury-Apollo and means 'All-Knowing One.' Thracian Orpheus, too, is connected with both Mercury (Hermes) and Apollo: according to some versions of his story he was the son of Apollo, and in any case Apollo certainly taught him to play upon his lyre. The lyre supplies a link with Hermes, another patron of knowledge and artful utterance: he first invented it and later traded it to Apollo. In Norse mythology Oðinn is the god of poetry, music, and wisdom, and the inventor of runic magic. Wagner conjectures that his cult probably originated in Asia Minor and from there spread to the Thracians, the Celts, and the Germans. This same scholar does not mention *Sir Orfeo* or the Breton *Lai d'Orfée*, but it does not seem entirely far-fetched to suggest that the Celtic Orpheus who figures there might have sprung from an association of the native equivalent of Oðinn (or the heroes deriving from him and sharing his qualities) with the foreign name of Orpheus, which we may imagine coming into contact with the Celtic tradition at some point. There was already an ancient racial affinity between them. The Orpheus in *Sir Orfeo* is entirely Celticized, and, as a hero, seems to belong to a well-established Celtic tradition. The existence of a Celtic hero of the Orpheus type from which he derives would account for his presence in this story, and would explain why the story itself has elements quite foreign to the medieval Latin traditions about Orpheus, elements which give Friedman difficulty to reconcile with that tradition. I am referring to the peculiarly Celtic blend, in the descriptions of the Otherworld, of the attractive and the menacing. Although Satan, the King of the Underworld in Christian mythology, is certainly evil, the fairy king of Celtic literature who rules over the Otherworld and certain precincts of this one is not evil, precisely, although he is not good, either, He belongs to a pantheistic universe that predates good and evil; he is a force of nature, at times benign, at times destructive, but in any case strange, fascinating, and incomprehensible in human, ethical terms. This is the character of the Fairy King (Pluto) in *Sir Orfeo*.

Nor can the character of Heurodis make sense in terms of the Boethian allegorized Eurydice. Her fate is a common one for the heroines in Celtic stories, in which no special motive seems to be needed to account for the behaviour of the fairy king. Fairies are always carrying off whatever mortals they can get their hands on. Nor is that done as a punishment for bad or lustful mortals. Heurodis is neither bad nor particularly sensual: she is simply unfortunate.

Henryson's fifteenth-century *Orpheus and Eurydice* stands between the Celtic and medieval Latin versions of the story. The author was obviously a man of classical learning, well acquainted also with Neoplatonism and the allegorical interpretations of ancient fable. He was interested in defining or explaining the art or 'wisdom' which won over Pluto; he could not be content to leave it as simply a miraculous *datum* in the story. Orpheus in his version, begins his quest for 'Erudices' unconventionally in the celestial region, descending through all the spheres and finding her in none of them. However, he does learn the secrets of the harmony of the spheres and it is with this knowledge that he is able to play the celestial music that charms Cerberus, Rhodomantus, and Proserpina, along with a small audience of other notables. Henryson's story is quite romantic – Eurydice is the Queen of Thrace and falls in love with Orpheus' reputation for beauty and courtesy. But Henryson is very much concerned with moralizing his tale, and the deliberately imparted lessons echo Trivet's and are quite Christian. There are hints, however, of a pre-Christian tradition. As Orpheus descends a very dark, slippery way where an odious stink guides him to the house of hell, he encounters various classical figures (Hector, Priam, Alexander, Antiochus, and others) as well as biblical (Herod, Pilate, Pharoah, Saul, Jacob, Jezebel), although the description of hell is definitely Christian. When he sees Erudices, he marvels at her changed looks, and asks her why she seems so ill. She dares not say, but Pluto replies, 'Though she looks like an elf, she fares as well as any in fairyland, but she is languishing. If she could go back home to her country in Thrace, she would soon be well again.' These would be strange words, indeed, if they were spoken either by the classical Pluto or the Christian Satan. We note that hell has become 'fairyland.' Orpheus has been more or less challenged to try to take her back. Here we find that we have slipped over into a Celtic universe, and the relationship between Orpheus and

Pluto is that strangely half-co-operative, half-antagonistic one of mortals with fairies in Celtic legend.

Connected with Orpheus as theurgist, master of the archons, is the idea of Orpheus as healer. In the pseudo-Orphic *Argonautica* it is Jason, not Orpheus, who is the healer and has knowledge of herbs learned from Chiron the centaur. But the power of Orpheus' music over the stars at a time when medicine was a branch of astrology would imply that he also had healing powers. From the earliest times music has been thought to have virtues, particularly in mental diseases. Comparisons were often made in this connection between David's harp and Orpheus' lyre. David drove an unclean spirit out of Saul and Orpheus counteracted the madness caused by the Sirens' music with his more powerful song. Theodulus compared David's healing song to Orpheus' enchantment of Pluto. John Tzetzes, a twelfth-century writer, probably influenced by the myth that music will cure a tarantula bite, believed that Orpheus' music was an antidote for snakebite, and interpreted the story of Eurydice's deliverance from hell as a metaphor for her cure by music and other magical spells.[14] Constantine Africanus (1015–87), in his treatise on the disease of *hereos* ('eros,' or 'the loveres maladye of hereos,' as Chaucer phrased it), mentions Orpheus as a magical minstrel, implying that his music was a cure for the affliction he was describing. John Lydgate and Adam of Fulda, writing in the fifteenth century, refer to Orpheus' music as having power to allay the passions of the soul, relax tension, dispel lethargy, and cure melancholy. Finally, in that compendium of ancient, medieval, and Renaissance medicine the *Anatomy of Melancholy* (1621), Robert Burton sums up the whole tradition, explaining that music works upon the mind by causing the vital spirits about the heart to vibrate in a certain way, or else, 'as some suppose,' the mind is roused by music because it is 'harmonically composed.' Hercules Gallus, Amphion, and Orpheus were therefore 'felices animas' who with their music could interfere with the processes of nature.[15]

Now, in our tracing of the vicissitudes of the myth of Orpheus in the Middle Ages we come to the point where the physical or magical tradition intersects with the romantic literary tradition in which Orpheus is the courteous knight and noble lover. There is a connection between Neoplatonic magic and the medieval doctrine of love. Both presuppose an animistic universe shot through with 'correspondences,' occult qualities and secret identifications of this with that. A magician is one who has power over nature and can produce 'mighty effects.' A lover exemplifies and co-operates with the processes of nature. Indeed, he perfects them – like the alchemist but in a different way. That same Boethius, for whom Orpheus' backward glance was the lamentable result of sensuality, also partially excused him and hinted at another interpretation by invoking the irresistible power of Amor: 'But who can give a law to lovers?' (*Consolation* 3, Metre 12). In the Neoplatonic tradition Amor is not base sensuality but a glorious natural principle holding the elements of the cosmos together in their beautiful order. Without him chaos would immediately be restored. That same Amor who in the physical world joins the atoms which constitute all things is the bond of society among men; it is the first law of God's own operation, the natural basis of the law of charity, and a personal raison d'être to each individual. Here are Boethius' ideas expressed in Chaucer's words:

'Love, that of erthe and se hath governaunce,
Love, that his hestes hath in hevenes hye,
Love, that with an holsom alliaunce
Halt peples joyned, as hym lest hem gye,
Love, that knetteth lawe of compaignie,
And couples doth in vertu for to dwelle,
Bynd this acord, that I have told and telle.

'That that the world with feith, which that is stable,
Diverseth so his stowndes concordynge,
That elementz that ben so discordable
Holden a bond perpetuely durynge,
That Phebus mote his rosy day forth brynge,
And that the mone hath lordshipe over the nyghtes, –
Al this doth Love, ay heried [praised] be his myghte!

'That that the se, that gredy is to flowen,
Constreyneth to a certeyn ende so
His flodes that so fiersly they ne growen
To drenchen erthe and al for evere mo;
And if that Love aught lete his bridel go,
Al that now loveth asondre sholde lepe,
And lost were al that Love halt now to-hepe.

'So wolde God, that auctour is of kynde [nature],
That with his bond Love of his vertu liste
To cerclen hertes alle, and faste bynde
That from his bond no wight the wey out wiste;
And hertes colde, hem wolde I that he twiste
To make hem love, and that hem liste ay rewe
On hertes sore, and kepe hem that ben trewe!'

(*Troilus and Criseyde* 3.1744–71)

This is Troilus' hymn to Love, based on *The Consolation of Philosophy* 2, Metre 8. No doubt the reason why the secular religion of Cupid was a serious rival to the otherworldly religion of Christ in the thirteenth and fourteenth centuries was that that cult found its roots in Neoplatonic metaphysics and cosmology. Neoplatonic theories of love took on new vigour in the Renaissance and survived till nearly the end of the seventeenth century, if not later. Boethius and Chaucer show us how the force of Love, as 'the law of kynde,' may be both deplored and celebrated by the same man almost in the same breath. Later writers were generally not so ambivalent: they hailed Orpheus as an eloquent example of the divine power of Amor.[16] Boethius did not forget that Orpheus had written poetry about the ordering of the cosmos and he probably found a peculiar irony in the fact that Orpheus himself succumbed to the very force he had hailed as irresistible.

The later writers of romance altered Orpheus' image as a magician, philosopher, sage, or prophet to something more suave and secular – a minstrel, knight, or, more commonly, a king or noble – in any case, a contemporary courtly lover and very much a man of the world. He is both king and knight to Henryson, 'King schir Orpheouss,' as remarkable for his good looks and gentle breeding as for his skill in song – perhaps more remarkable, since it is the former that wins the heart of Eurydice. They also, in keeping with the demands of the romance as a genre, focused much attention on Orpheus' human feelings, with emphasis, naturally, upon the passions of grief and love. A new *topos* developed from a hint in Ovid – that of Orpheus' love-sickness *before* he married Eurydice and his wooing of her. As early as the tenth century, Reginus of Prüm, a musicologist, said that Orpheus used his skill as a singer to win Eurydice in the first place. By the time we get to Monteverdi this episode has grown in size and importance until it parallels the second 'winning of Eurydice' in Hades. Yet this naturalizing, humanizing, and socializing of Orpheus remains tied to a theoretical proposition: Orpheus *illustrates* the power of Love, or the power of Love and Music combined, or the power of Love and Eloquence combined.

At the end of the medieval period we find Boccaccio's *Genealogia deorum gentilium* and Coluccio Salutati's *De laboribus Herculis*. Although they lived in the fourteenth century, these men were humanists in the Renaissance sense of the word. They were concerned with the art of poetry and had the historian's intellectual interest in the ancients and their pagan religious practices. Their remarks on Orpheus have a new emphasis and flavour, that of the Renaissance. Orpheus is dislodged from his medieval courtly setting and is placed back firmly in antiquity, but now with a sense of the space of historic time that separates him and his beliefs from us. If he retains his significance for moderns, it is by virtue of his extraordinary gifts as an artist (musician or orator) which make him an exemplar, but not of virtue or vice. Boccaccio says nothing of the tradition that Orpheus was an early monotheist; for him Orpheus is the gifted artist rather than the inspired prophet. He does indeed retail the medieval historical and moral interpretations, but his interest in the story is that of a philologist. He brings together almost every detail from the classical accounts, including the voyage of the *Argo* and the fate of the severed head. The latter, as we have seen, is treated as an allegory of the fame of the artist. The serpent which tried to bite it on the Lesbian shore until Apollo intervened becomes Time. Boccaccio comments, 'Nothing stands in the way of time and the serpent could not have gone hungry, save to this extent, that a famous man lives on by his lyre ...'[17] (For Pope, the severed head is poetry itself and the serpent, by a logical but witty extension, bad poets and carping critics.[18])

Salutati is still concerned with allegories of virtues and vices, though he reveals new interests and attitudes prophetic of the Renaissance; even more prophetic, however, is his method, and the confidence with which he presents his own, new interpretation. Whereas for the medieval man the search for truth would involve consulting the *auctors*, collating them and squeezing and pulling them until they all fitted together, a new, critical spirit makes itself felt in Salutati. He does a comparative study of this myth (and others), collating sources, accepting some, rejecting others. He notes where sources agree and where they do not, and dares to say that the most revered of them 'agree on few points.' He says he knows the earlier interpretations of the Orpheus myth, but has his own interpretation. His ethical interests are entirely humanist and secular. Instead of finding Christian morals in the tale, he sees Orpheus as symbolic of Epicureanism, with its emphasis on pleasure, while Hercules represents the Stoics, who follow virtue. Salutati accepts Hyginus' rather odd version of the story of Orpheus' death (that is, that in Hades, Orpheus praised all the gods except Liber, who thereupon, understandably piqued, instigated his followers to murder the rashly neglectful singer), and even more oddly interprets it to mean that Orpheus was a voluptuary who unwisely gave himself up to the work of Venus rather than the worship of Liber and quite deservedly died in 'Pangaeus' ('All-Earth'), a suitable haunt for such an earthy spirit. Salutati's condemnation of Orpheus, however, is closer in spirit to Boethius' than to those of the later medieval Christian commentators on Boethius: as Friedman says, he removes Orpheus and Eurydice from the Christian allegorical hell and makes them again citizens of the secular world.

The title of this chapter is, of course, intended to be a gentle joke at the expense of those purist classical scholars of the latter age who regarded any deviation from or distortion of classical language or mythology as a sort of blasphemy, or unpardonable barbarism. They would, no doubt, find much to feed their righteous indignation in this account of the fate of the Orpheus myth at the hands of the Gentiles. Surely it is a piece of academic *naïveté* to be amused at the spectacle of what the men of any age do to their inherited culture to make it conformable to their needs. Rather, it is a testimony to human ingenuity and to the genius of those long-gone generations who could forge a symbol so perdurable because so eloquent in expressing what is fundamental to human striving and frustration. The striving and frustration are endlessly repeated; only the forms they take vary. Partly owing to historical accident, the myth of Orpheus was particularly well calculated to endure the rigours of the Middle Ages: Orpheus was believed to be a real, historical character, not just a fiction that could be outmoded or explained away. There is more classical erudition, more variety, and more personal idiosyncracy in the ways the myth is handled in the Renaissance, but not, I think, more intelligence. It would be well, while remembering the logical schematizing of the *nous-epithumia* gloss, not to forget the haunting beauty of Boethius' sad cadences, the pure glamour of 'King schir Orpheouss' in the land of the fairy king.

NOTES

1 In the Stith-Thompson Motif-Index analogues are noted from various mythologies for the motif of a culture hero who teaches some art or other and does not quite die. Culture heroes often go off by water and are often expected to return or said to have been resuscitated or to be alive still in a hidden place (mountain, tree, island, sky, the end of the world). Corresponding perhaps to the trees that followed Orpheus is an African myth of a magic song that caused chips from a tree to move (D 1565.1.1). There are Irish, Icelandic, Jewish, and Indian analogues for the story of a head that retains life after being separated from the body (E 783), an Irish analogue for the singing of a severed head (D 1615.7), Finnish, Indian, and African analogues for the magical musical instrument that can call animals together, not to mention a quite vast number of polyethnic stories of magical music in general (D 1275) and music attractive to animals in particular (B 767). Especially striking is the diffusion of the Eurydice motif among early Amerindian peoples in North America. See John MacCulloch *The Mythology of All Races* (Boston 1932) IX 118–20.

2 See Heinrich Wagner *Studies in the Origins of the Celts and of Early Celtic Civilisation* (Belfast 1971).

3 The Celtic Orpheus is linked with Hermes and Apollo, for instance, rather than

with Dionysos. However, the Celtic counterpart of Dionysos, Lug, is a sun-god, like Apollo. See below p 75.

4 *The Survival of the Pagan Gods* tr Barbara Sessions (New York 1961)

5 F. Joukovsky (Geneva 1970) chapter 1 and J. Friedman, *Orpheus in the Middle Ages* (Cambridge, Mass. 1970) 'Introduction' and 155–69. In preparing this essay I have been much indebted to Friedman's lucid and scholarly work for background information generally. I have been concerned to examine the myth as it appears in the later vernacular literature of the Middle Ages, especially in English, and have found reason respectfully to differ from him in his interpretation of the treatment of the myth at some points.

6 Translated and quoted in ibid 101.

7 Seznec *Survival* 29

8 Luke 9:62. Oddly, no one seems to have thought of Lot's wife in connection with Orpheus.

9 'Ovide Moralisé': *Poème du commencement du quatorzième siècle publié d'après tous les manuscrits connus*, ed C. de Boer, in *Verhandelingen der Koninklijke Akademie van Wetenschappen te Amsterdam*, N.R., Deel 37, 22–3.

10 Quoted by Friedman *Orpheus in the Middle Ages* 134.

11 The early Fathers – Clement and Eusebius, for instance – contrasted or compared Christ with Orpheus in such a way as to suggest that Orpheus was a prefiguration or imperfect pagan foreshadowing of Christ. Christ's and Orpheus' activities in the Underworld were compared, to show that what Orpheus began Christ finished (Friedman ibid 57–8). See above, Chapter 3.

12 It is hard to draw exact parallels between Celtic and Greco-Roman heroes and divinities since each of the Celtic personages seems to be a conflation of almost all the rest. For drawing my attention to the relevance of the Celtic materials, and for offering advice on what I have written here, I am indebted to Dr Ann Dooley of the Department of Celtic Studies, St Michael's College, Toronto.

13 Wagner *Studies in the Origins of the Celts* 56

14 Friedman *Orpheus in the Middle Ages* 149 and 156

15 *Anatomy of Melancholy* 2.2.6.3

16 Boethius' language in *Consolation* 2 Metre 8 is reminiscent of the Orphic hymns. Eros plays a conspicuous part in Orphic cosmology, a feature of Orphic thought that was taken over by the Neoplatonists. See the discussion of love in connection with the Florentine humanists of the fifteenth century, below, in the next chapter and pp 208ff. Love is always called an irresistible force, and it would have been absurd if that irresistible force could fail. So we find that the story of Orpheus is often refurbished with happy endings.

17 *Genealogia deorum gentilium libri* 11 5 Vincenzo Romano (Bari 1951) 246

18 The epigraph to the second version of the *Dunciad* consists of the Ovidian lines

Tandam Phoebus adest, morsusque inferre parantem
Congelent, et patulos, ut erant, indurat hiatus.

But Sandys, in his seventeenth-century *Ovid's Metamorphoses Englished*, had
already interpreted the serpent as 'detraction and envy,' a sort of Blatant Beast;
ed Karl K. Hulley and S.T. Vandersall (Lincoln, Nebraska 1970) 519.

JOHN WARDEN

Orpheus and Ficino

THIS CHAPTER and those that follow describe something of the career of the myth of Orpheus during the Renaissance. It should come as no surprise that there is no sudden or easily perceptible change in the treatment of the myth; allegorization, euhemerization, the encyclopedic treatment of mythology – all these go on apace. What is new is not easy to define. For Jean Seznec in his *Survival of the Pagan Gods*,[1] there is a 'reintegration' of the figures of pagan mythology, that is, they are divested of their medieval accretions and restored to classical form. This, however, is a brief moment of glory that belongs to the early Renaissance (the end of the fifteenth century) and soon fades. C.S. Osgood in his *Boccaccio on Poetry* remarks, 'The Renaissance, with its advance in classical scholarship, knew more and more about mythology, but took it less and less seriously. With the increase of knowledge the conviction of reality declines, at least in artistic use, and the old myths tend to become mere playthings, material of applied ornament and superficial decoration.'[2] The truth of both these comments can, I believe, be seen in the treatment of mythology by the Florentine Neoplatonists. Though their fanciful and antiquarian treatment of myth leads to trivialization by less earnest minds, the figures of myth themselves do for a brief moment recover in their hands something of their classical brilliance and their integrity. This is especially true of Orpheus.[3]

In his poem *Altercazione*, Lorenzo de' Medici takes a rest from his civic duties to wander among the fields and hills and muse on the virtues of the pastoral life. He encounters a philosophical and somewhat cynical shepherd, who tries to convince him that life in the country is tough and hard, and that those aspects of city life that disgust Lorenzo – ambition, acquisitiveness, and so on – are present in the country too. The polemic is stilled by the sound of a lyre:

... una nuova voce a sé gli trasse
da più dolci armonia legati e presi.
Pensai che Orfeo al mondo ritornasse ... [4]

(A new voice drew them towards itself, bound and taken captive by its sweeter harmony. I thought that Orpheus had returned to the world.)

It is Marsilio Ficino, who for the next five Cantos expounds in terms very close to his own *De voluptate* the nature of true happiness.

The identification of Ficino and Orpheus might be dismissed as a mere literary compliment appropriate to the contrived pastoral setting, if it did not recur with such frequency in a wide variety of literary forms and contexts. A poem of Naldo Naldi for instance traces the career of Orpheus' soul from Homer to Ficino.[5] Each recipient inherits some aspect of Orpheus' gifts: song for Homer ('cantavit numeros novos'), ethical teaching for Pythagoras ('mores edocuisse proprios'), piety for Ennius. After the death of Ennius the soul of Orpheus must wait 1600 years for its next incarnation:

Marsilius donec divina e sorte daretur
indueret cuius membra pudica libens.
Hinc rigidas cythara quercus et carmine mulcet
atque feris iterum mollia corda facit.

(Until Marsilius should be granted by divine fate, whose chaste limbs he may willingly put on. Hence he soothes the unyielding oaks with his lyre and his song and softens once more the hearts of wild beasts.)

The conclusion echoes the opening ('mulcentur silvae'), and this together with the syntax (it is the soul of Orpheus that is the subject of 'mulcet') and the 'iterum' (once again) suggests that it is Ficino and he alone in whom Orpheus truly lives again. For him alone is reserved the privilege of inheriting the whole of Orpheus.

Andrea Ferucci's bust of Ficino which stands in the church of Santa Maria dei Fiori makes the same point in stone. Ficino is represented in the guise of the mythical lyre-player, his face alight and his mouth half-open to sing, and between his hands he holds, like a lyre, a volume of Plato.[6] Poliziano puts it slightly differently: 'his lyre ... far more successful than the lyre of Thracian Orpheus, has brought back from the underworld what is, if I am not mistaken, the true Eurydice, that is Platonic wisdom with its broad judgment' ('longe felicior quam Thracensis Orphei ... veram ni fallor Eurydicen hoc est amplissimi iudicii Platonicam sapientiam revocavit ab inferis'[7]).

But Orpheus' voice and lyre are not only a metaphor to describe Ficino's teaching. They are meant literally too. As Corsi tells us in his biography, 'He set forth the hymns of Orpheus and sang them to the lyre in the ancient manner with incredible sweetness, so people say.' ('Orphei hymnos exposuit, miraque ut ferunt dulcedine ad lyram antiquo more cecinit.'[8]) Johannes Pannonius says much the same: 'You restored to the light the ancient sound of the lyre and the style of singing and the Orphic songs which had previously been consigned to oblivion.' ('Antiquum cytharae sonum et cantum et carmina Orphica oblivioni prius tradita luci restituisses.'[9]) Cosimo de' Medici finishes a letter of invitation with the words: 'Farewell. And do not forget your Orphic lyre when you come.' ('Vale et veni non absque Orphica lyra.'[10]) Naldi wrote a pair of couplets to the image of Orpheus painted on Ficino's lyre: 'I am that Orpheus who moved the woods with his song.' ('Orpheus hic ego sum, movi qui carmine silvas ... '[11]) Philippe Callimaque accompanies the gift of a shirt from Poland with some verses:

> Orphea sed verum faciet te barbara vestis
>   cum tibi sit cantus illius atque lyra.[12]

(This foreign costume will make you a true Orpheus, since you already have his singing and his lyre.)

There can be no doubt then that Ficino played an 'Orphic' lyre, emblazoned with a picture of Orpheus; and that as he played he sang 'antiquo more' the Hymns of Orpheus. What is more difficult to decide is how seriously all this should be taken. Is it an important ingredient in Ficino's philosophy, or is it mere metaphor and play? Poliziano we will remember is nicknamed Hercules by Ficino for his skill at slaying the monsters of textual corruption. Landino is Amphion. It is hard to re-create the atmosphere of the Academy at Careggi, but the intense interest in and concern about man's soul and destiny was accompanied by a large ingredient of make-believe. The aesthetic and imaginative qualities of classical mythology provided a sense of 'detachment and joy'; but at the same time, as we shall see below, the content of the myths was treated seriously not simply as allegory, but as a set of symbols which if correctly read offered an understanding of higher levels of reality. So too the festivals and hymn-singing – on one side a 'jeu erudit,' on the other a seriously intended religious ritual. So that our question was wrongly formulated – metaphor and play were taken very seriously by the Florentine Neoplatonists. At the most profound level the activities of the Academy were 'a game of symbols and forms.'[13]

Ficino's epistolary, with its gently bantering tone and its delight in puns and word-play, gives us some insight into this closely meshed world of communication where the line between metaphysics and good manners cannot always be determined. Two appropriate examples. First, Ficino writes a letter to Cavalcanti complaining that the latter will not visit him; he has tried in vain the lyre of Orpheus; but Cavalcanti is made not of stone or wood, but of iron.[14] Second, Ficino writes to Cosimo de' Medici a letter accompanying a translation of the Orphic Ὕμνος Οὐρανοῦ, the *Hymnus ad Cosmum*, in which he says that he was singing the hymn, 'ritu Orphico,' to relax his mind, when the news arrived of Cosimo's offer of financial support. The last line of Ficino's translation of the hymn runs: 'Hear my prayer, Cosimo, grant a quiet life to a reverent young man.' ('Exaudi nostras, Cosme, preces vitamque quietam pio iuveni tribue;' there are subtle changes from the Greek – κλῦθ᾿ ἐπάγων ζωὴν ὁσιάν μύστῃ νεοφάντῃ – especially 'quietam,' 'tribue,' and the direct address to Cosimo.) Ficino continues: 'By some instinct of divine inspiration you seem to have heard at that very moment at which I sang the hymn, and to have granted me the very things that the prayer was asking for.' ('Tu autem celesti quodam afflatus instinctu exaudisse videris eo ipso tempore, quo a nobis relatus est hymnus, atque eadem que vota obsecrant tradidisse.'[15]) Do we take this as gratitude for patronage expressed in an elegant pun, or an assertion of the power of the Orphic hymns?[16]

We have evidence from a hostile witness, Luigi Pulci, not only that Ficino was well known, indeed notorious, for his singing and chanting, but also that they were an integral part of his philosophizing. In his Sonnet 90 he describes Ficino as 'lo dio delle cicale,' and in Sonnet 145 he speaks of those who:

Aristotil allegano e Platone
e vogliono ch'ella in pace requiesca
fra suoni e canti e fannosi una tresca
che t'empie il capo di confusione.[17]

Finally, if we need further evidence that Ficino himself took his singing and playing seriously, the following well-known passage is conclusive: 'This age, like a golden age, has brought back to the light those liberal disciplines that were practically extinguished, grammar, poetry, oratory, painting, sculpture, architecture, music, and the ancient singing of songs to the Orphic lyre.' ('Hoc enim seculum tanquam aureum liberales disciplinas ferme iam exstinctas reduxit in lucem, grammaticam, poesim, oratoriam, picturam, sculpturam, architecturam, musicam, antiquum ad Orphicam Lyram carminum cantum.'[18]) The climax of the list of achievements that mark the dawn of a new golden age is 'the ancient singing of songs to the Orphic lyre.'

Why was Orpheus so important to Ficino? Before attempting an answer we must be sure what we are trying to account for. The presence of references to and quotations from Orphic teaching in Ficino should occasion no surprise. One important ingredient in the unique hotchpotch that makes up Ficino's philosophy is of course the writings of the Greek Neoplatonists in general and Proclus in particular. It became an orthodoxy to the Neoplatonists that Plato was drawing on Orpheus in developing his own philosophy. 'In every respect Plato imitates the teaching of Orpheus,'[19] says Olympiodorus; or in the words of Proclus: 'All Greek theology is the offspring of the Orphic mystical doctrine.'[20] We shall have occasion to discuss below the significance of Orpheus the *poeta theologus* for Ficino and his contemporaries. My purpose now is merely to show that we should rather remark the absence than the presence of Orphic quotations in the followers of the Greek Neoplatonists.

But it is the whole figure of Orpheus, three-dimensional and real, not just his theoretical teaching, that is drawn into Ficino's thought. And this I believe is something one does not find in Proclus or in the later eastern Neoplatonic tradition. For the Byzantine artist the image is justified in that it raises the mind to God; for the Renaissance artist the image is also enjoyed and explored for its own sake.[21] Myth grows from allegory into symbol, and as it grows it puts on flesh. One can see the process occurring by comparing the abstract moral allegorizing of Landino with the concreteness and plasticity of Poliziano, for whom the illustrative moment has its own autonomy, its own right to exist and be cherished.[22] One can only guess how much is owed to Gemisto Pletho who brought his baggage of Byzantine Neoplatonism to Italy by way of Islam and Zoroastrianism, giving it a new exoticism and a new paganism.[23] The gods of antiquity acquire again a significance as powers within the universe; nothing perhaps that was not already present in the Henads of Proclus, but introduced afresh into a Christian context. More important, however, is the continuity of the iconographic tradition through the western Middle Ages and its meeting with the rediscovery of ancient art. However much he is sucked bloodless by the allegory that spreads from Boethius and Fulgentius, Orpheus remains a person in the illustration of the manuscripts of the *De consolatione* or of *Ovide moralisé*.[24] Pletho's use of pagan mythology, like his hymn-singing, is self-conscious and intellectual: for Ficino and his companions at Careggi it is rather a mixture of aesthetic delight and simple piety.

Perhaps the most familiar image of Orpheus to the Italian Renaissance is that of Orpheus the civilizer. The *locus classicus* is Horace *Ars Poetica* 391ff: Orpheus the first poet is the first to soften the hearts of the 'stony and beastly people' and set them on the path to civilization.[25] His instrument is his eloquence (for Boccaccio the lyre is 'oratoria facultas'[26]). Since Fulgentius[27] Orpheus has been allegorically interpreted as *Oraia phone* – beautiful voice; in William of Conches and Nicholas Trivet he is that divine eloquence which the Christian must aim to combine with true wisdom.[28] For Clement and the early apologists Orpheus prefigures the *logos*, which leads men to the truth and announces the coming of the New Jerusalem.[29] These elements interwoven provide a key concept for the Renaissance, what Buck calls 'die spezifische Bildungsidee.'[30] Humanism represents the moral action of the word fashioning the raw materials of primitive man into a civilized member of a community. As Boccaccio puts it: 'He makes wild beasts gentle, that is to say bloody and rapacious men whom eloquence often recalls to gentleness and humanity.' ('Feras mites facit, id est homines sanguinis rapacesque, quos saepissime eloquentia revocat in mansuetudinem et humanitatem.'[31]) And Landino describes how 'loquenzia' leads men, who are like wild beasts dwelling in the woods without laws or customs, to live together in a community and submit themselves to justice: 'and this is precisely what the poets meant when they said that Orpheus could make the wild beasts tame with his lyre, make the rocks and woods move and halt streams in their courses; that he could with his sweet speech bring to civilization men who were insensitive to virtue as though made of stone and who were crazed and maddened by the pleasures of the body.'[32]

This is a social and political programme. Orpheus is the statesman or legislator who with his *dolce parlare* brings men to live together in communities. This civil life is the essence of *humanitas* – man is a political being. In Ficino the emphasis is rather metaphysical and moral. The skilful speaker is replaced by the artist, who looks within himself to discover the harmony of the cosmos, and by artistry leads others to an understanding and beyond. Indeed the artist not only reflects, he creates; he is 'costruttore de sé.'

> sic species terris, vitae sua forma, suusque
> dis honor, ipsa sibi tandem sic reddita mens est.[33]

(Thus the earth is given its beauty, life its shape, the gods their honour and mind itself at last becomes itself.)

The artist by fashioning our perceptions of the sensible world and by his privileged access to its secrets is able to act on it and change it; those magical powers which Orpheus lost in Horace's euhemeristic interpretation are, as we shall see, returned to him with interest.[34]

And there is a corresponding deepening in the concept of *humanitas*. It is that by which man is defined and it consists in the capacity for love. 'Venus [significat] humanitatem.'[35] Humanity is the love that extends throughout the universe as manifested in man. Thus, the effect of Orpheus' song is to lead man to love.

What is the song he sings? Not far behind Orpheus the civilizer comes Orpheus the theologian. Here we are dealing with a figure of a different order, not a mythical hero, redefined by allegory, but a historical personage (for such he undoubtedly was to the *quattrocento*), religious teacher, and author of a number of works (especially the *Rhapsodic Theogony*, the *Argonautica*, and the *Hymns*) which had a great influence on the period in general and on Ficino in particular.[36] We have seen that to the early Neoplatonists he was the theologian par excellence. Already for Porphyry he is 'the oldest and foremost of all theologians.'[37] He is the ἐξηγητής, the interpreter of reality, who speaks ἐνθέῳ στόματι, inspired of God.[38] Christian and pagan vie for his adherence. Orpheus, says Augustine, is said 'to have predicted or spoken truth of the Son of God or the Father' ('De Filio dei aut Patre vera praedixisse seu dixisse perhibetur'[39]). So too in the early Renaissance he is the *theologus poeta* to Petrarch, Boccaccio, and Salutati.[40] Indeed by this time Orpheus has become one in a chain of poets and teachers who represent the unbroken tradition of the *prisca theologia*. There are various different versions of the line of descent, but the chief recurrent figures are Abraham, Moses, Zoroaster, Hermes Trismegistus, Orpheus, Pythagoras, Plato. Orpheus holds a key position as the first of the Greeks to belong to the *theologi* and as the teacher of Pythagoras and Plato. Plato for Numenius is nothing else than Moses speaking Greek.[41] Orpheus is the go-between in the liaison between Hebrew and Greek. The results of this doctrine are far-reaching: pagan religion is not something to be shunned and feared, but a source of truth, a partial evolution. Religion is treated not as a revelation, but as a natural evolutionary phenomenon depending for its development on a few individuals of superior knowledge and will-power. Christianity is a continuation of ancient theological thought. Whether it marks the end-point is a question never fully answered.[42]

It would be a vain task to enumerate all the doctrinal elements in Ficino that can be traced to Orphic influence. The Neoplatonists had demonstrated that given the will and the ingenuity anything can be shown to be Orphic, and thus they emptied the exercise of much of its meaning. But several examples should be given, both for their intrinsic importance, and also as examples of method. It is as cosmologist that Orpheus is most familiar. In the *Argonautica* of Apollonius Rhodius as later in the 'Orphic' *Argonautica* he sings to the heroes of the Creation of the World, how Chaos came before the world and the other gods, and how love came to being in the bosom of Chaos.[43] The primacy of love in Orphism is one of the most important things that Ficino learned from it. 'Omnia enim ex te sunt' (for all things come from thee), says the Orphic *Hymn to Venus* in Ficino's translation. In *Convivium* 1.3 Ficino quotes 'Orpheus': love is 'antiquissimum, se ipso perfectum, consultissimumque' (very ancient, perfect in itself and very wise), and then offers the following exegesis. He starts by outlining the levels of reality: God, Angelic Mind, the World Soul, the World Body. Of the worlds created by God, each was a *chaos*, so an unformed world, before it became a *mundus*. Let us follow the creation of Mind. In the first place God creates its substance or essence. At the first moment of creation this is shapeless and dark. As it is born of God, it turns towards God, its origin, through some inborn appetite. And once turned it is lit up by the rays of God's light. Its appetite is inflamed by that brightness. So it devotes itself entirely to God ('totus inhaeret'); and thus it is fashioned. So before the *mundus* (cosmos), there is *chaos*; the turning to God is the beginning of love; which in turn leads to the fashioning and shaping of the cosmos. Orpheus is thus right in saying that love is 'antiquissimum'; it is 'se ipso perfectum' (which Ficino interprets as meaning 'se ipsum perficientem' or self-perfecting) since the object created completes its own creation by turning in its love towards its creator – the importance of this idea will become apparent when it is applied to man the artist; and it is 'consultissimum' because all wisdom is the result of the love that turns the mind to God so that it shines with God's brightness. The passage as a whole provides an instructive example of the way in which Ficino adapts an Orphic passage to his own peculiar brand of Christian Neoplatonism – the three hypostases, the triad of procession, rapture, and reversion, and the overwhelming emphasis on the love of God.

Another important doctrine associated with Orphism is the insistence on the unity and singleness of the *cosmos*. This issue is one that is fundamental to all Greek philosophy and religious thought. It has been called the problem of the One and the Many: 'how shall all be one, yet each thing apart?'[44] This is expressed philosophically in words ascribed to Orpheus' pupil Musaeus: ἐξ ἑνὸς τὰ πάντα γίνεσθαι, καὶ εἰς ταὐτὸν ἀναλύεσθαι (everything comes to be out of one and is resolved into one);[45] and mythologically in the so-called κατάποσις Φάνητος: Zeus according to the myth swallowed down Phanes the first-born and the whole of his creation.[46] 'Here was a system which, on the side of doctrine, taught of the absorption of everything, gods included, into one god, and their rebirth from him again, and on the side of active religion taught the complementary idea of the worship of one god above all others.'[47] Zeus, in the words of a hymn which in some form dates back to

Plato, is beginning, middle, and end.[48] Or, as Ficino puts it translating an Orphic Hymn,[49] Jupiter, the sky, is 'omniparens principium omnium omniumque finis.' Jupiter contains within himself all the other gods; they are his powers. Orpheus 'deos omnes in uno collocat Jove.'[50] For the Neoplatonist such teachings could be used to support the emanation from and return to the One. 'A bono in bonum omnia diriguntur' (everything is directed from the Good to the Good), read one of the mottoes on the walls of the villa at Careggi. For the Christian they might seem to offer support to monotheism and the doctrine of the Trinity.[51] They provide some standing room for the Christian Neoplatonist, a justification for accepting the multiple gods of paganism while remaining within the confines of Christian orthodoxy.

Orpheus, of course, is not just *theologus* but *theologus poeta*. He is the first poet to celebrate the mysterious principles that underlie the universe. It is because he is a poet, because he has skill and inspiration, that he is able to understand and is privileged to tell of these mysteries. He sings ἐνθέῳ στόματι; he is possessed with the *furor divinus*. He is an artist and this world, this 'bel tempio,' is a work of art; he has privileged access to its secrets and to the mind of its architect. Here myth and pseudo-history come together; the singer with his lyre is the one who understands cosmic secrets:

> Hor se la tua lyra havessi Orpheo
> Canterei come et gli elementi et il mondo
> Diterminò e infinito il signor feo
> In numero creò misura et pondo
> Tempio si bel che tre persone sembra
> Nume divino mirabile et profondo.[52]

(Now if I had your lyre Orpheus, I would sing how the infinite Lord established and made the elements and the world, created in number, measure and weight a temple so beautiful that it resembles three persons, a divine godhead, marvellous and profound.)

The lyre, given, as Gafurio tells us,[53] to Orpheus by Mercury and by Orpheus to Pythagoras, confers the divine right, like the sceptre of Agamemnon. It represents the harmony of the spheres, its seven strings standing for the seven planets.[54] And it is more than a symbol; mathematically the intervals of the Orphic lyre are the structural basis of the entire visible universe[55] and of the human soul.[56] It offers an assurance on the relationship between microcosm and macrocosm. Man by exploring his own interior space finds a structure in the microcosm identical with that of the macrocosm.[57] He finds the lyre within himself and 'explicates' it, as Cusanus put it.

'Neque ex aliquo extrinseco, sed ex propria mente' (and not from something outside himself but from his own mind).[58] The lyre makes explicit the assumption that underlies all Platonic 'realism' that the route to the truth lies through introspection, that the structure of the mind is identical with the structure of reality: 'Begin by considering thyself and better still, end with that.'[59]

For Ficino there are two types of music. First there is the divine music, which is itself divisible into two – the music in the mind of God and the music of the spheres. And then there are the *imagines* of the divine music in the human soul. This reflection of the divine music is expressed in various forms and at various levels – as reason, imagination, discourse, song, instrumental playing, and dance.[60] 'We see then that the music of the soul gradually spreads to all the limbs of the body. And it is this that orators, poets, painters, sculptors and architects express in their works.' ('Videmus igitur animae musicam gradatim ad omnia corporis membra deduci. Quam etiam oratores, poetae, pictores, sculptores, architecti in suis operibus imitant.') It is not only the musicians in the narrow sense but all the artists who express this divine music of the soul.

God granted us these two types of music 'so that through the former [ie, the divine] we might imitate God himself in our thought and feelings [music is thus a paradigm of the mind of God], and through the latter we should celebrate the name of God for ever with hymns and instrumental music.' ('Ut per illam quidem deum ipsum cogitationibus affectibusque imitaremur per hanc vero Dei nomen hymnis sonisque semper celebraremus.'[61])

This then is the most obvious explanation for Ficino's own hymn-singing. But if we examine his analysis of the physical basis of music we can begin to understand what he thought was the precise effect of these hymns of praise. In his letter *De musica* to Canisianus he describes how singing and instrumental music start from the mind, the imagination, and the heart (of the player) and are translated into movements and controlled disturbances of the air; these impulses strike the *spiritus* of the listener, being itself composed of air. The *spiritus* is the *nodus* of soul and body – the meeting-point of the physical and the psychological. Thus the impulses can easily be translated back into psychological terms and reach the imagination, heart, and innermost mind of the listener. ('Nam cum cantus sonusque ex cogitatione mentis et impetu phantasiae cordisque affectu proficiscatur, atque una cum aere fracto et temperata aereum audientis spiritum pulset, qui animae corporisque nodus est, facile phantasiam movet, afficitque cor et intima mentis penetralia penetrat.'[62])

What exactly is the *spiritus*? The simplest answer is found at *Convivium* 6.6. We consist of three parts, *anima*, *spiritus*, and *corpus*. *Anima* and *corpus* being very different in nature are held together by *spiritus*, which is 'a very fine and transparent vapour, generated from the subtlest part of the blood through the heat of the heart' ('Vapor ... tenuissimus et perlucidus, per cordis calorem ex subtilissima parte sanguinis genitus'). It acts as a go-between transmitting the *animae vires* to the body, and transforming sense-experience into the purer perceptions of the imagination. As it is 'an airy vapour from the blood' ('aereus sanguinis vapor') it is tempered and nourished 'by scents and sounds and songs that consist of air' ('aereis ... odoribus sonisque et cantibus'[63]).

What we have been talking of so far is the *spiritus humanus*, that which links the human body and soul. But there is also a *spiritus mundanus*, which 'interconnects the sublunary world with the translunary.'[64] *Spiritus* in its fullest sense is 'a divine influx, flowing from God, penetrating through the heavens, descending through the elements and finishing up in lower nature' ('Divinus influxus, ex Deo manans, per coelos penetrans, descendens per elementa, in inferiorem naturam desinens'[65]). It is 'an uninterrupted current of supernatural energy [which] flows from above to below and reverts from below to above, thus forming a *"circuitus spiritualis."*'[66]

The musician plugs into this current. The aim of his hymns is to bring the *spiritus* of man into accord with the *spiritus mundi*; or more particularly to make man accessible to the *influence* of the *spiritus* of a particular astral body. This is brought about in the first instance by our own predisposition, by an act of love; and only then by the magical techniques of song, light, and scent. It is important that the music, perfume, etc be appropriate to the deity being invoked. 'Our *spiritus* is in conformity with the rays of the heavenly *spiritus*, which penetrates everything either secretly or obviously. It shows a far greater kinship when we have a strong desire for that life and are seeking a benefit that is consistent with it, and thus transfer our own *spiritus* into its rays by means of love, particularly if we make use of song and light and the perfume appropriate to the deity like the hymns that Orpheus consecrated to the cosmic deities ...' Ficino then gives a list of deities and the appropriate scents. 'For the *spiritus*, once it has been made more akin to the deity by emotional disposition, song, perfume, and light, draws a richer influence from it.' ('Spiritus noster radiis illius [ie, spiritus caelestis] tam occultis quam manifestis omnia penetrantibus [est conformis]. Evadit etiam longe cognatior, quando erga vitam illam [caelestem] vehementer afficimur, consentaneum illi beneficium exoptantes, atque ita spiritum nostrum in illius radios transferentes amore: praesertim si cantum et lumen adhibemus, odoremque numini consentaneum quales Orpheos hymnos mundanis numinibus consecravit ... Spiritus enim per affectum, cantum, odorem, lumen, cognatior affectus numini, uberiorem haurit illinc influxum.'[67])

Ficino in his hymn-singing is in part drawing on a Neoplatonic tradition.

Plotinus tells us that it was possible to provoke astral influences εὐχαῖς ἢ ἁπλαῖς ἢ τέχνῃ ᾀδομέναις – by prayers either delivered in a simple straightforward way or *technêi*, artistically, with special skill.[68] Proclus, we are told, studied and sang the Orphic hymns and practised Orphic ritual.[69] Whether they were the same hymns that Ficino translated and sang, we cannot be sure. Each of the latter as they have come down to us is prefaced by instructions on the appropriate perfume to burn during performance, and the whole collection is prefaced by an address from Orpheus to Musaeus in which he promises to teach him θυηπολία – the proper way to perform sacrificial rites. Most scholars are agreed that the hymns are of relatively late composition (third to fourth century AD), and that they did in fact serve as a hymnal for an eclectic pagan sect that described itself as Orphic (although there is little evidence of specifically Orphic doctrine in the hymns' content).[70] Gemisto Pletho recurs as an important but shadowy figure in the handing down of this tradition. He does not in his surviving works mention either Orpheus or the Orphic writings. But we know that hymn-singing played a large part in his reconstructed paganism, and that he devoted a chapter of his *Nomoi* to 'Hymns to the Gods' and another to 'The Arrangement of the Hymns.' We have evidence also that he copied out fourteen of the Orphic Hymns. It may be that it was Pletho's appearance at the Council of Florence in 1438 that awakened in the West an interest in this ritual practice. There are, however, significant differences in the motives underlying the hymn-singing of Pletho and that of Ficino. As Walker tells us[71] Pletho saw the effect of the hymn-singing as subjective rather than objective. It did not actually reach the gods, but prepared or 'moulded' our imaginations. Ficino's motives are more direct and straightforward, and closer to the theurgic tradition of Iamblichus and Proclus. The singing of hymns can prepare man's *spiritus* to receive the influx of *spiritus* from a particular astral body. Music recovers its powers of magic, its ability to exploit and turn to advantage the forces of the phenomenal world. 'Nothing is more effective in natural magic,' says Pico, 'than the hymns of Orpheus, if the proper music, mental concentration and other circumstances which the wise are aware of be applied.' ('Nihil efficacius hymnis Orphei in naturali magia, si debita musica, animi intentio et caeterae circumstantiae, quas norunt sapientes, fuerint adhibitae.'[72])

The astral deity most frequently invoked is the sun. Ficino, like Orpheus on Mt Pangaeus, is 'Apollinei modulator carminis'[73] (he tunes Apollo's song). Here he is consciously following the tradition of the *Platonici*: 'Julian and Iamblichus composed orations to the sun. Plato called the sun the offspring and visible image of God; Socrates as he greeted the rising sun often experienced a state of ecstasy; the Pythagoreans sang hymns to the sun on their lyres ... God indeed has set his tabernacle in the sun.'[74] The sun is the leader of the heavenly bodies; they dance to his tune: 'This troupe of Muses sings and dances without stopping, as Orpheus says, shaping their tune to the command of Apollo.' ('Haec Musarum chorea cantat saltatque perpetuo, ut ait Orpheus, musicis modulis ad Apollinis ipsius imperium.'[75]) As the tabernacle of God, or the son and visible image of the highest deity, the sun in some way represents that deity within the sensible world. 'Light is so to speak a sort of divinity in this temple of the world bearing a likeness to God.' ('Lumen est quasi numen quoddam in mundano hoc templo Dei similitudinem referens.'[76]) The invocation to the sun then is something more than an attempt to exert a magical control over the forces contained within phenomena; it is an attempt to lead the soul to an understanding of God.

The sun stands as a symbol for God. Each level of reality has its appropriate mode of perception – sense-perception, discursive reason, intuitive reason – and the objects of perception take the appropriate form: 'Among angels examples and ideas; among souls reasons and concepts; in the physical world shapes and images.' ('In angelis exemplaria et ideae; in animis rationes et notiones; in orbis materia formae atque imagines.'[77]) The relationship between the images of the sensible world and the ideas of the angelic is one of identity at different levels or reality. This world is the 'tertius dei vultus' – the third face of God. Nature is seen not as a chain of causes and effects, but as a set of signs and symbols.[78] 'The world is the book in which God's eternal wisdom has written.'[79] The whole cosmos is held together by obscure links and sympathies both between levels and within levels. To communicate with the world of *anima* (soul), we use science or magic; to communicate with the world of *mens* (mind), we use 'the comparative method,' what Ficino calls *Orphica comparatio*; that is, we pursue the images or symbols of the phenomenal world to their originals (this applies as much to the myths as the physical objects of the world; allegory is reified into symbol). Man being of a double nature cannot proceed direct to the level of the angels. He must first traverse the world of *anima*.[80]

The *Orphica comparatio* is then a kind of symbolic description; at the literal level Ficino is talking about the nature of the sun; but what he is really talking about is the nature of God.[81] The comparison of the sun to God is however something more than an example of method; it also contains for Ficino the essential Orphic mystery, the symbolic explanation of unity in multiplicity: God is 'the eye by which all eyes see, and, according to Orpheus, the eye which sees everything in every object, and truly sees everything in himself.' ('Oculus quo omnes vident oculi, et, ut inquit Orpheus, oculus qui cuncta in singulis inspicit, ac re vera omnia conspicit in se ipso, dum esse se perspicit omnia.'[82]) 'And so the divine mind, as it is infinite, is properly called by the Orphics the infinite eye.' ('Quapropto divina mens cum sit infinita merito nominatur ab Orphicis ἄπειρον ὄμμα, id est oculus infinitus.'[83])

The singer (or artist) performs in an inspired state 'aroused by the Muses' frenzy' ('musarum concitus oestro').[84] 'Then his eyes burn, and he rises up on both feet and he knows how to sing tunes that he has never learnt.' ('Tunc ardent oculi, tunc planta exsurgit utraque, / et quos non didicit comperit ille modos.'[85]) It is this state of God-given frenzy, this *furor divinus*, that enables the mind to perceive and understand the symbolic structure of the universe. It is *divinus* because it comes from God and raises to God. The artist under the influence of this madness is free to range beyond his normal limits, he is lifted to the height of heaven like Ganymede on the back of the divine eagle. The state of inspiration is visible in the rapt expression on the face and the 'Orphic' pose.[86] There are four phases or levels of *furor*, the poetic, the sacerdotal, the prophetic, and the erotic. The first calms the agitation of the soul, the second prepares it for exaltation, the third raises the soul from its own level to the level of the angels, and the fourth unites the soul with God.[87] For Ficino Orpheus is possessed of all four *furores*: he is poet, priest, prophet, and lover. Only he and David have this status; only he among the pagans comes so close to God.

Ficino also speaks of certain conditions which free the soul from everyday concerns and open it to the 'influxus mentium superiorum' (the influence of higher minds). These he calls states of 'vacatio' or 'alienatio': 'When the influence finds our reason unoccupied or devoting itself to the mind, it shows it something of those things which pertain to the universal knowledge of eternal matters or to the governance of the cosmos.' ('Quando mentium ille influxus rationem nostram sortitur ociosam, sive menti vacantem, ipsi aliquid ostendit eorum quae ad universalem aeternarum rerum cognitionem seu mundi gubernationem pertinent.'[88]) Among the seven types that he mentions are sleep and syncope, melancholy and, greatest of all, 'the chastity of a mind devoted to God.' Orpheus 'in the wilds of Thrace' after the second loss of Eurydice lived close to the Gods and learnt to think as they did ('eadem quotidie cogitat, quae caelestia numina cogitant facere'); he abjured the love of women and lived a life of chastity; and he sought solace for his loss in the music of his lyre and in the loneliness of nature. It was a period of introspection, of melancholy self-examination.[89] As Chastel describes it, Ficino regarded melancholy as a physiological condition necessary in order to achieve exceptional mental states; it was a prerequisite for *furor*. It was induced by the planet Saturn, who stands in antithesis to Venus, like the love and strife of Empedocles. Venus joins together and Saturn sets apart. The anguish that comes from self-absorption and loneliness detaches the soul from the world of appearances (Saturn destroys the kingdom of Jupiter), jerks it out of its natural position, so that it is free to move either up or down. The proper remedy for melancholy is sublimation – the *furor divinus* then catches up the dissociated mind and raises it to God.[90]

Orpheus the self-conscious artist. The phrase brings together two themes which are of great importance for Ficino and his time. The notion of the dignity of man, which gets its best-known treatment from Pico della Mirandola, is already familiar to classical antiquity. 'There are many marvels,' says the Chorus of Sophocles' *Antigone*, 'but nothing is more marvellous than man.' And some 600 years later a similar sentiment is expressed in the Chaldaean Oracles: 'O man, invention of nature at her boldest.' ($\tilde{\omega}$ τολμηροτάτης φύσεως ἄνθρωπε τέχνασμα.[91]) In the Hermetic writings there is a significant difference of emphasis. It is not so much man as a creation who is held up for our attention, but man the creator. Man's special status stems from the intermediary position of the human soul which can range from the bestial to the divine. 'Man is a great miracle, a creature fit to be worshipped and honoured. For he crosses over to the nature of a god, as though he were himself a god … God composed him out of both natures, divine and mortal, and thus it was arranged through the will of God that the constitution of man was superior even to that of the gods.' ('Magnum miraculum est homo, animal adorandum atque honorandum. Hoc enim in naturam dei transit, quasi ipse sit deus … [deus] ex utraque natura composuit, divina atque mortali, et sic compositum est per voluntatem dei hominem constitutum esse meliorem et deis.') And his privileges are manifested in his power to create; it is as 'artifex' that he is 'deus in terris.' The startling conclusion is reached that man shows these powers to the highest degree in the creation of the gods, ie, the bringing alive of statues. 'Just as the Lord and Father made the eternal gods so that they should both be like him, so let mankind fashion its gods in the likeness of its own face.' ('Sicut pater ac dominus, ut sui similes essent deos fecit aeternos, ita humanitas deos suos ex sui vultus similitudine figuraret … statuas animatas sensu et spiritu plenas.'[92]) Pico is not the first to present a strange and disconcerting mixture of humanism and occultism. Man's creative powers are shown best in the practice of theurgic magic.

Ficino is clearly drawing directly on this tradition. In Book 14 of the *Theologia Platonica* he cites both the passages from the oracles (Chapter 1) and from the *Asclepius* ('magnum miraculum' in Chapter 3). In Book 13, Chapter 3, where his object is to prove the immortality of the soul by showing the extent of its power, he deals at length with the notion of man the 'artifex.' 'It is a remarkable thing that the human arts fashion on their own whatever nature herself fashions, as though we were not the servants of nature but her rivals.' ('Quod mirabile est humanae artes fabricant per seipsas quaecunque fabricat ipsa natura: quasi non servi simus naturae sed aemuli.') Man controls the elements and the other animals that inhabit the world; in this respect, 'vicem gerit dei' (he stands in for God). But more than this, he creates for the pleasure of creation and for the delight in sense experience. 'Hence proceeds the unspeakable variety of pleasures which bring delight to the five bodily senses, pleasures which we ourselves devise by our own genius.' ('Hinc proficiscitur innarrabilis varietas voluptatum hos quinque sensus corporis oblectantium, quas ipsimet nobis proprio ingenio machinamur.') (This aesthetic delight in the senses is something new that the Florentines gave to Neoplatonism; one cannot imagine Plotinus, for all his sense of beauty, saying anything like this.) This creativity manifests itself in textiles, paintings, sculptures, buildings, artistic activities which may not in themselves be functional or useful, or even pleasant; but they satisfy man's aesthetic need to create. Similarly 'musicae consonantia ... oratorum facundia,' 'poetarum-que furores' are activities we pursue even though they bring no material benefit, but are often hurtful ('sed plurimum noxiae'). We are imitating the activities of God the creator. We are equipped with an 'artifex interior' (the soul) which uses as its instruments the tongue and the hand. We are doing in our own way what God is doing: 'So our mind conceives within itself by thought as many things as God creates in the universe by thought. Just so many things does it express in the air by speaking, does it write with a pen on paper, does it fashion in matter by manufacturing.' ('Ergo tot concipit mens in seipsa intelligendo quot deus intelligendo facit in mundo. Totidem loquendo exprimit et in aere. Totidem calamo scribit in chartis. Totidem fabricando in materia mundi figurat.')

If we ask how this can be so, how the mind can conceive what does not already exist in nature, the answer is that everything that is possible, that has potential existence, already exists in the infinite mind of God. Now the human mind has the capacity to conceive possibilities that do not exist. It can proceed to infinity. 'Quis infinite progreditur? ... mens certe haec facit.'[93] The mind in fact can conceive something 'which, as possible, is already real in God.'[94] Man the artist follows in the footsteps of God the artist. Man 'prolongs the divine act.'[95] The motive in both cases is aesthetic.

Creation starts from within. 'Begin by considering thyself.' This emphasis on the inner life of man, on the importance of the will as a dynamic and creative force, is common in the Renaissance writers who precede Ficino, and of course owes much to St Augustine. For Petrarch 'man's inner life is a continual process of self-creation.'[96] Orpheus-like, man through his studies softens his own spirit and tempers his own wrath ('mollitque animos et temperat iras').[97] We must start from within ourselves, 'abs te itaque ad te occurre,' says Traversari; for within ourselves, 'in ore nostro et in corde nostro,' we will find the divine.[98] 'The soul,' says Ficino, 'on its own through its own activity continually fashions itself and completes itself by the continual exercise of the intellect and the will' ('Per se ipsum operatione sua se format semper et perficit, semper intelligendo atque volendo'). For Poliziano, in his *Nutricia*, man fashions himself through his art.[99] Poetry once again becomes a form of making.

> sic species terris, vitae sua forma, suusque
> dis honor, ipsa sibi tandem sic reddita mens est.

(Thus the earth is given its beauty, life its shape, the gods their honour and mind at last becomes itself.)

Man is the creator and what he creates is himself. 'Ogni dipintore dipigne sè.' What we see is the 'arrangement and shape of his very soul' ('dispositio praeterea et quasi figura quaedam animi ipsius inspicitur').[100] 'For in such works the soul expresses and provides an image of itself, just as the face of man looking in the mirror provides an image of itself in the mirror. Especially in conversations, songs, and instrumental playing the creative soul is brought into the light.' ('Ita enim seipsum animus in operibus istis exprimit et figurat, ut vultus hominis intuentis in speculum seipsum figurat in speculo. Maxime vero in sermonibus, cantibus atque sonis artificiosus animus se depromit in lucem.')

And lastly and above all, Orpheus the lover and prophet of love. Love is of course the overriding concept in the system of Ficino. It explains the relationship between the different levels of reality, between microcosm and macrocosm, between man and his fellows, between man and God. This is not the place for a full exposition of its role. What might be of interest would be to discover how much Ficino owes, or thinks he owes, to the teaching of Orpheus. A partial way of doing this is to examine the most important 'Orphic' quotations in the *Convivium*. We have already discussed the first of these (love is 'antiquissum,' 'se ipso perfectum,' 'consultissimum'), and have seen how it is used as a basis for the Neoplatonic triad of procession, rapture, and reversion, for the nature of creation and of the love of the created for the creator. At the end of 3.2, Ficino quotes a line from the *Hymn to Eros*: μοῦνος λὰρ τουίων πάντων οἰήκα κρατυνέις (You alone control the reins of all these things).[101] Love is the power that produces harmony in all things. This leads into a discussion of love as the master ('magister') and controller ('gubernator') of the arts. What artists or craftsmen in their various crafts seek to achieve is a state of love. Take the example of the doctor who tries to bring about accord between the humours. Or the musician who tries to discover which intervals are harmonious, 'which notes show greater or less love for which notes' ('qui numeri quos numeros aut magis aut minus diligant'). They blend tones and rhythms, 'so that they should become as friendly as possible' ('Ut amici potissimum fiant'). 'Every art indeed is an expression of love, since it is an endeavour to impose order upon formlessness.'[102]

It is thus appropriate that Orpheus should call love (3.3) εὐπάλαμον, διφυῆ, πάντων κληῖδας ἔχοντα (inventive, double-natured, holding the keys of everything).[103] As to its double nature, there is a sacred and a profane Venus, like the two musics of Urania and Polyhymnia. And like the latter, the profane Venus can, if properly used, lead the mind upward to contemplation. That it holds the key to the universe is clear from the fact that everything strives for its own perfection and it is love that unlocks the door and brings that aspiration to the light. 'All the parts of the world, because they are the works of a single creative artist, and, as components of the same construct, are all alike in their essence and manner of existence, are bound together each with each by a sort of mutual affection, so that love can properly be called the perpetual knot or link of the universe.' ('Omnes mundi partes, quia unius artificis opera sunt, eiusdem machinae membra inter se in essendo et vivendo similia, mutua quadam caritate sibi invicem vinciuntur, ut merito dici possit amor nodus perpetuus et copula mundi'.) All the hidden and secret relationships that exist between objects within the sensible world and that permit the practice of Orphic magic, all the symbolic intermeshing of different levels of reality that permits the soul to ascend through *Orphica comparatio*, are evidence of the presence of love in the universe.

In *Convivium* 5.11 Ficino again quotes from two Orphic Hymns, from the *Hymn to Night*: δεινὴ γὰρ ἀνάγκη πάντα κρατύνει ('terrible necessity rules over all'[104]) and from the *Hymn to Venus*: καὶ κρατεέις τρισσῶν μοιρῶν, γεννᾷς δὲ τὰ πάντα ('and you rule over the three fates, and you bring everything to being').[105] Venus is the 'mater necessitatis.'[106] The principle of love is prior to and stronger than the immutable laws of nature. Love can raise man above the limitations of his corporeal state and give him freedom of will.

Ficino's love is a composite of Plato's sublimated sexual love, of Aristotle's 'scala naturae' yearning for the Prime Mover, of Plotinus' lonely relationship with the One, of the Christian love of God for man and man for God. There are important additional ingredients: an emphasis on friendship and the social role of love from Aristotle and the Stoics, an elegiac quality from the Stilnuovisti and Petrarch.[107] Orpheus as civilizer brings about a state of *humanitas*, which is defined as man's love for his fellows; Orpheus as theologian asserts the primacy of love as a cosmic force, as that which brings about creation, and thus acts as a go-between for Christian and Neoplatonist; as musician and artist he brings about a state of love by imposing order and shape; as one who loves and suffers he is privileged to be filled with the *furor amatorius* which leads the mind beyond understanding to the vision of divine beauty and to a state of joy.

> amando, alla sua immensa latitudine
> amplifichiamo e dilatiam la mente:
> questo par sia vera beatitudine.[108]

Orpheus has helped Ficino in many ways: to bridge the gap between pagan and Christian; to rescue Neoplatonic monism and restate it in Christian terms; to redefine the relationship between the first principle and the created world; to combine a sense of delight in the beauty of this world with an aspiration for the beauty that lies beyond;[109] to be aware of both the joys and sadness of existence, its permanence and its evanescence.[110] Above all he enables Ficino to hold the balance between the ordered and stable cosmos of antiquity and the Middle Ages, and the new dynamic concept of man, the restless creator, Proteus and Chameleon,[111] ranging at will and creating his own space. He has contributed to this moment of equilibrium between two worlds.

And what has Ficino done for Orpheus? If the Middle Ages subjected him to *sparagmos*, Ficino has found his heart and brought him back to life – the musician, magician, and hierophant that he was in the beginning.

NOTES

1 Seznec *Survival of the Pagan Gods* tr Barbara Sessions (New York 1961) 184–215
2 *Boccaccio on Poetry* (Princeton 1956) Introduction 23
3 This paper offers no new thesis but a synthesis. It owes a heavy debt to many scholars, especially André Chastel *Marsile Ficin et l'art* (Genève 1954); D.P. Walker 'Orpheus the theologian and Renaissance platonism' *Journal of the Warburg and Courtauld Institutes* 16 (1953) 100–20 and 'Le chant orphique de

Marsile Ficin' in *Musique et poésie au XVIe siècle* 17–33; A. Buck, *Der Orpheus-Mythos in der italienischen Renaissance* (Krefeld, 1961); N.A. Robb *Neoplatonism in the Italian Renaissance* (1935; rpt New York 1968); P.O. Kristeller *The Philosophy of Marsilio Ficino* (New York 1954).

4 Lorenzo de' Medici *Scritti scelti* ed Emilio Bigi (Turin, 1955) 2.2–4

5 *Supplementum Ficinianum* ed P.O. Kristeller (Florence 1937) II 262

6 Chastel *Marsile Ficin* 48

7 Poliziano *Opera* (Basel 1553) 310. The interpretation of Eurydice as 'broad judgment' (εὑρεῖα δίκη) is commonplace in the Middle Ages and goes back to Fulgentius *Mythologies* 3.10.

8 C.G. Corsi *Vita Marsilii Ficini* 6 printed as Appendix 1 in R. Marcel *Marsile Ficin* (Paris 1958)

9 Ficino *Opera* (Basel 1576) 871

10 Ibid 608

11 *Supplementum Ficinianum* II 262: 'Ad Marsilium Ficinum de Orpheo in eius cythara picto'

12 Ibid II 225

13 Chastel *Marsile Ficin* 74; for a discussion see 1of and 48f, and Robb *Neoplatonism* 57 n 1.

14 *Opera* 844 on Ficino's word-play, see Chastel *Marsile Ficin* 45.

15 *Supplementum Ficinianum* II 88

16 For a discussion of this passage and others see A. Buck *Der Orpheus-Mythos* 22f and D.P. Walker 'Orpheus the theologian' 102f.

17 Robb *Neoplatonism* 165; see also *Morgante* 25.156–7 and 27.41. For Pulci's relations with Ficino and the Academy see Luigi Pulci *Il Morgante* ed R. Ramat (Milan 1961) 16f and Robb *Neoplatonism* 163–6.

18 *Opera* 944. Ficino is almost certainly referring to himself: see P.O. Kristeller 'The scholastic background of Marsilio Ficino' *Traditio* 2 (1944) 272 n 84.

19 *In Platonis Phaedonem commentaria* 70c ed W. Norvin (Leipzig 1913) 58; Ficino *Commentarium in Philebum* in *Opera* 1216: 'Orpheus ... cuius theologiam secutus est Plato.'

20 *Theologia Platonica* 1.6

21 See especially Chastel 'Le Platonisme et les arts à la Renaissance' *Actes du congrès de Tours et Poitiers* (Paris 1954) 387ff.

22 Chastel *Marsile Ficin* 144

23 B. Kieszkowski *Studi sul Platonismo del Rinascimento in Italia* (Florence 1936) Chapter 2; Abbé R. Marcel, 'Le Platonisme de Petrarche à Léon l'Hebreu' *Congrès de Tours et Poitiers* 315; M.F. Masai 'Le Platonisme italien et le problème des influences byzantins' ibid 321; Kristeller *The Philosophy of Marsilio Ficino* 15; 'The scholastic background of Marsilio Ficino' 259; Walker 'Orpheus the theologian' 107ff; Chastel 'Le Platonisme et les arts' 392 and *Marsile Ficin* 9f

24 Friedman, *Orpheus in the Middle Ages* (Cambridge 1970) Chapter v passim; Pierre Courcelle, *La Consolation de philosophie dans la tradition littéraire* (Paris 1967) 190f and plates 107 and 108.2; Chastel *Marsile Ficin* 136ff

25   silvestris homines sacer interpresque deorum
caedibus et victu foedo deterruit Orpheus
dictus ob hoc lenire tigris rabidosque leones;
... fuit haec sapientia quondam
publica privatis secernere, sacra profanis,
concubitu prohibere vago, dare iura maritis,
oppida moliri, leges incidere ligno.

26 *De genealogia deorum* 5.12

27 *Mythologies* 3.10; translated in L.G. Whitbread *Fulgentius the Mythographer* (Columbus, Ohio 1971) 96f

28 William of Conches and Nicholas Trivet, in their respective commentaries on Boethius; see Friedman *Orpheus in the Middle Ages* 105ff.

29 Clement of Alexandria *Exhortation to the Greeks* Chapters 1ff. For a discussion see above, Chapter 3 'The new song of Christ.'

30 Buck *Der Orpheus-Mythos* 14

31 *De genealogia deorum* 5.12

32 'Orazione facta quando cominciò a leggere' in 'Studio i sonetti di M. Francesco Petrarca' in *Miscellanea di cose inedite o rare* ed F. Corazzini (Florence 1853) 133; Buck, *Der Orpheus-Mythos* 32 n 47

33 E. Garin 'L'ambiente di Poliziano' *Atti del IV convegno internazionale di studi sul Rinascimento: Il Poliziano e il suo tempo* (Florence 1954) 21

34 A. Poliziano *Nutricia* ed Del Lungo 114–15; see Garin, preceding note, Buck *Der Orpheus-Mythos* 14ff, and Chastel *Marsile Ficin* 176.

35 Ficino *Opera* 805. He continues: '... est enim humanitas ipsa praestanti corpore nympha, coelesti origine nata ... eius anima spiritusque sunt amor et charitas.' For discussion see Kristeller *Philosophy of Marsilio Ficino* 113f.

36 The *Argonautica* and the *Hymns* were among the first 'Platonic' writings translated by Ficino (1462), although he did not publish them. His reasons for this are given in a letter to Martinus Uranius (*Opera* 933): 'Argonautica et hymnos Orphei ... edere nunquam placuit, ne forte lectores ad priscum deorum daemonumque cultum iamdiu merito reprobatum, revocare viderer, quantum enim Pythagoricis quondam curae fuit ne divina in vulgus ederent, tanta mihi semper cura fuit, non divulgare prophana.' The reason given should be taken seriously. Corsi (*Vita Marsilii Ficini* viii) describes the struggle that Ficino went through in reconciling his interest in pagan writings with his Christian conscience: 'cogitavit hoc tempore ... Orphei hymnos ac sacrificia invulgare, sed divino prorsus miraculo, id quo minus efficeret, in dies magis impediebatur, quadam, ut aiebat, spiritus amaritudine distractus ... tandem aperte cognovit

divinitus ea se pati, quod a Christianis plus nimio transfugisset.' But there is another perhaps more important reason implicit in Ficino's reference to the secrecy of the Pythagoreans. As Pico puts it (*Orphicae Conclusiones I* in *Opera* (Basel 1572) 106): 'secretam Magiam a nobis primum ex Orphei hymnis elicitam, fas non est in publicum explicare.' Ficino is in the Neoplatonic tradition in wishing to confine the most sacred writings to the elect. There is a curious similarity between Ficino's divine inhibition, and what Marinus has to tell us about Proclus, in *Procli philosophi platonici opera inedita* ed V. Cousin (rpt Frankfurt 1962) xxvii: for a long time he resisted requests to write a commentary on the Orphic writings, feeling himself κωλυθῆναι ... ἐναργῶς ἐκ τινῶν ἐνυπνίων.

37 Porphyry, cited by Eusebius *Evangelica Praeparatio* 4 (470B); Kern 17
38 Proclus *In Republican Platonis* 1.72, 1; Kern 19
39 *Contra Faustum* 13.15
40 Boccaccio *De Genealogia Deorum* 14.16; Salutati *De laboribus Herculis* 1.1; Petrarch *Invective contra medicum* 3 (he describes Orpheus as 'maxime nobilitatus'); Buck *Der Orpheus-Mythos* 18
41 Walker 'Chant orphique' 22; τί γάρ ἐστι Πλάτων ἤ Μωϋσῆς ἀττικίζων, in Clement of Alexandria *Stromateis* 1.22
42 Kieszkowski *Studi sul Platonismo* 84, 88; for a summary see D.P. Walker *The Ancient Theology* (London 1972) 1ff; Chastel *Marsile Ficin* 157ff; Ficino *Opera* 25 and 871f.
43 Apollonius Rhodius *Argonautica* 1.494ff; [Orpheus], *Argonautica* 419ff. The latter scene is imitated in Poliziano *Manto* 1–30 in *Opera* 288f. The Creation is a regular and appropriate theme for the minstrel, the original imposition of order on chaos. See Virgil *Aeneid* 1.740ff, and *Beowulf* 90–8, with comment by H.R. Ellis Davidson *Gods and Myths of Northern Europe* (London 1964) 198.
44 W.K.C. Guthrie *Orpheus and Greek Religion* (1934; rpt New York 1966) 84
45 Diogenes Laertius 1.3
46 Proclus *In Platonis Timaeum Commentaria* (ed E. Diehl) 28c (Kern 167); See also the Orphic Hymn to Pan 11.1–3 (ed Abel): πανῦ καλῶ κρατερόν, νόμιον, κοσμοίο τὸ σύμπαν / οὐρανὸν ἠδὲ θάλασσαν ἰδὲ χθόνα παμβασίλειαν / καὶ πῦρ ἀθάνατον· τάδε γὰρ μελε' ἐστὶ τὰ Πανός.
47 Guthrie *Orpheus and Greek Religion* 100
48 Kern 168
49 *Orphei Hymni* 4.2
50 *In Platonis Phaedrum, Opera* 1371. Kieszkowski, 'Studi sul Platonismo' 116
51 Walker 'Orpheus the theologian' 115ff
52 Giovanni Nesi *Poema visione* Canto VII 24ff as cited in Robb *Neoplatonism* 51 n 2; Chastel *Marsile Ficin* 57ff
53 *De harmonia musicorum instrumentorum* (Milan 1512) 1.4

54 Ps.–Lucian *De astrologia* 10; Servius in Virgil *Aeneid* 6.645. See Chastel *Marsile Ficin* 54 n 61.

55 Chastel ibid 100. For this reason it guarantees the secret correspondences with the sensible world that afford the artist his magical powers: 'nonne sonante cithara quadam altera reboat?' *De vita* (*Opera* 555). See note 67.

56 See the *Commentarium in Timaeum* in *Opera* 1438ff; the Orphic Hymn to Apollo (quoted in *Theologia Platonica* 2.9 *ad fin*): 'tu sphaeram totam cithara resonante contemperas'; *De divino furore* in *Opera* 614: 'Jupiter ... coelum, quasi citharam quandam ... exagitans, coelestem efficit harmoniam.'

57 *Commentarium in Timaeum* in *Opera* 1453: '[Plato] putat ... animam inde (ie from music) natam musica similiter ratione citharam pulsare coelestem ... anima profecto non possit universam harmoniam diiudicare nisi ipsa harum causas in se haberet ... constat enim anima nostra ex omnibus proportionibus quibus anima mundi.'

58 *De ludo globi* (Paris 1514) II, fol clxv

59 Saint Bernard *De consideratione* 2.3 n 6; see Etienne Gilson *The Spirit of Medieval Philosophy* (London 1936) 209ff; Chastel 'Le Platonisme et les arts' 397

60 *Opera* 651 (letter to Canisianus *De musica*); see R. Marcel in Walker 'Le chant orphique' 30.

61 *Supplementum Ficinianum*, I. 51–6, *De rationibus musicae*, addressed to Domenico Benivieni. Compare the analysis of music in *Convivium*, 5.1, 2, and 6. Beauty is 'the flower of goodness;' it manifests itself in *ratio, visus*, and *auditus* – these are, it is said, the three Graces of whom Orpheus speaks (Hymn 9.3): ἀγλαΐη τε, θάλεια καὶ εὐφροσύνη, πολυόλβε, *Splendor, viriditas, laetitiaque uberrima*. The last of these, *laetitia*, is music, 'sincerum illud et salubre et perpetuum, quod in musica sentimus, oblectamentum.' Through the three Graces, beauty 'animos nostros movet atque delectat, delectando rapit, rapiendo ardenti inflammat amore.'

62 Cf *Commentarium in Timaeum* in *Opera* 1453: 'concentus autem per aeream naturam in motu positam movet corpus; per purificatum aerem concitat spiritum aereum animae corporisque nodum [text has 'notum']; per affectum afficit sensum simul et animum; per significationem agit in mentem. Denique per ipsum, subtilis aeris motum penetrat vehementer; per contemplationem lambit suaviter; per conformem qualitatem mira quadam voluptate perfundit; per naturam, tam spiritalem, quam materialem, totum simul rapit et sibi vendicat hominem.' See also the important page on the power of song in *De vita* 3.21 *Opera* 563.

63 *Opera* 609; for a discussion of *spiritus* see Walker 'Le chant orphique' 18–19 and 'Ficino's *spiritus* and music' *Annales musicologiques* (1953) 131–50; also Kristeller *Philosophy of Marsilio Ficino* 115ff.

64 E. Panofsky *Studies in Iconology* (New York 1939) 136

65 Ficino *Theologia Platonica* 10.7

66 Panofsky *Studies in Iconology* 132

67 Ficino, *Commentarium in Plotinum* 38 in *Opera* 1747. If the magic is effective, the deities will reply 'vel instar Echo, vel sicut corda quaedam in cithara tremens, quoties vibratum altera temperata similiter'; *De vita* 3.21 in *Opera* 563.

68 Plotinus *Enneads* 4.4.38. I am drawing in this section on D.P. Walker 'Le chant orphique', 19–22.

69 Marinus, *Life of Proclus* (for reference see above note 36). The rituals (ἀποτρόπαι, περιρραντήρια, καθαρμοί) and the hymn-singing are mentioned in separate passages (18 and 20). The hymns were sung to cheer them up and allay their anxiety when Proclos was ill. They produced εἰρήνη and ἀταραξία. The passage continues: ἀρχομένων γὰρ ἡμῶν ὑμνεῖν, ἐκεῖνος ἀνεπλήρου τοὺς ὕνους καὶ τῶν Ὀρφικῶν ἐπῶν, τὰ πλεῖστα. καὶ γὰρ ταῦτά ἐστιν ὅτε παρόντες ἀνεγιγνώσκομεν. Walker 'Orpheus the theologian' 101.

70 For a discussion see Guthrie *Orpheus and Greek Religion* 257–61.

71 Pletho περὶ Νόμων ed C. Alexandre (Paris 1858) 150 and 186; Walker 'Orpheus the Theologian' 108 n 6. For references on Pletho see above, note 23.

72 Pico *Orphicae Conclusiones* 2 in *Opera Omnia* 106. See also *Conclusiones* 4: 'sicut hymni David operi Cabalae mirabiliter deserviunt, ita Hymni Orphei vere licitae, et naturalis magiae.'

73 Poliziano in *Supplementum Ficinianum* II 282

74 *Commentarium in Plotinum* in *Opera* 1745; Walker 'Le chant orphique' 19, 21f

75 *Theologia Platonica* 4.1

76 *Liber de lumine* in *Opera* 984

77 *Convivium* 5.4 ed and tr S.R. Jayne *University of Missouri Studies* XIX 1 (1944)

78 E. Cassirer *Dall' umanesimo all' illuminismo* (Florence 1967) 31ff; see also 30–4.

79   Il mondo e il libro, dove il seno eterno
    scrisse i propri concetti, e vivo tempio
    dove pingendo i gesti e'l proprio esempio
    di statue vive orno l'imo e'l superno.

Tommaso Campanella *Poesie* ed G. Gentile (Bari 1915) 16, quoted by Cassirer.

80 See especially E.H. Gombrich 'Icones Symbolicae' *Journal of the Warburg and Courtauld Institutes* 11 (1948) 163–92; Chastel *Marsile Ficin* 71ff, 143ff.

81 Kristeller *Philosophy of Marsilio Ficino* 97f; 'Orphica comparatio solis ad deum' *Opera* 826. 'Quapropter Orphicum mysterium illud si nolumus fateri verum, saltem parumper fingamus quasi verum, ut solem coelestem ita suspiciendo prospiciamus, in eo supercoelestem illum, tanquam in speculo, qui in sole posuit tabernaculum suum.'

82 *Opera* 985; Chastel *Marsile Ficin* 83 and n 9

83 *Theologia Platonica*, 2.10

84 Poliziano *Supplementum Ficinianum* II 283
85 G.A. Campano *Supplementum Ficinianum* II 230; see letter to Ugolino in *Opera* 634: 'furentes canunt ... paulo post defervescente furore ipsimet non satis intel-ligunt, quasi non ipsi pronunciaverint, sed deus per eos ceu tubas clamaverit.'
86 Landino in Dante *Purgatorio* 9.19f; Chastel *Marsile Ficin* 130f
87 Letter to Naldo Naldi *Opera* 830; *Convivium* 7.14; 'De divino furore' *Opera* 612–15; letter to Pietro Dovuzzi *Opera* 927; Buck *Der Orpheus-Mythos* 18f
88 *Theologia Platonica* 13.2
89 For the melancholy Orpheus see the figure on a thirteenth-century MS at Reims representing the harmony of the spheres; illustration and discussion in Ch. de Tolnay 'The Music of the Spheres' *Journal of the Walters Art Gallery* 6 (1943) 86 and 89. Orpheus broods over the universe, his chin on his left hand, his lyre at rest in his right. For a more intensely introspective figure, foreshadowing roman-ticism (and recalling the suffering Christ), see the Teniers copy of Giorgione (discussed and illustrated below pages 136ff and figure 9).
90 De Vita 3.22 in *Opera* 565; letter to Cavalcanti *Opera* 731f; Chastel *Marsile Ficin* 119, 164f
91 Sophocles *Antigone* 332f; *Chaldaean Oracles* Psellus 1136ᵃ; Chastel *Marsile Ficin* 59ff
92 *Asclepius* 6 and 22–4. Cicero is of course another important link in the transmis-sion; see the passages from *De natura deorum* 2.54–60 quoted by Giannozzo Manetti in his *De dignitate et excellentia hominis* ed E. Riley (Cornell University PHD 1964) I.3–12.
93 *Theologia Platonica* 8.16. Here is part of what precedes: '[mens] currit per omnia; per omnia inquam, non modo quae sunt, sed quae fuerunt eruntve. Neque id solum. Sed per illa etiam quae neque sunt, neque fuerunt unquam aut erunt. Multa enim excogitat quae forte esse possent, non tamen fient unquam; et multa quae esse forsitan nunquam possent, ipsa fingit ... Novas quoque semper rerum facies vi propria et quodam ordine fabricat, et rursus innovat alias.'
94 Kristeller *Philosophy of Marsilio Ficino* 55ff; see 53ff.
95 Chastel *Marsile Ficin* 66
96 Cassirer *Dall' umanesimo* 24 comments that Augustine *Soliloquia* 1.7 might serve as the motto of Ficino's *Theologia Platonica*: 'deum et animam scire cupio. Nihilne plus? Nihil omnino.'
97 Petrarch, *Secretum* II in *Opere Latine* ed A Bufano (Turin 1975) I 162, quot-ing Virgil *Aeneid* 1.57; Robb *Neoplatonism* 29
98 A. Traversari, *Epistolae* 13.526 ed Méhus (Florence 1759) II 639; see Robb *Neoplatonism* 41.
99 'Si plasma a se stessa (i.e. l'umanità); e il nascere operoso ... dell uomo costrut-tore di se'; Poliziano *Nutricia* 114–15 in Garin 'L'ambiente di Poliziano' 21.

100 *Theologia Platonica* 10.4; Chastel 'Platonisme et les arts' 396. The preceding quotation is ascribed to Cosimo (Chastel *Marsile Ficin* 66).
101 *Hymn* 58.8
102 Robb *Neoplatonism* 82
103 *Hymn* 58.4
104 Ibid 3.11
105 Ibid 55.5
106 Kieszkowski *Studi sul Platonismo* 55ff, 117
107 Kristeller *Philosophy of Marsilio Ficino* 287
108 Lorenzo de' Medici *Altercazione* 5.52–4
109 It might be added that Orpheus can be seen as representing the magico-scientific (or Promethean) attitude that seeks to change the phenomenal world from the outside, as well as the more strictly 'Orphic' mode which 'proposes to transmute the inner man.' For the terms and a discussion see W. Strauss *Descent and Return* 10f.
110 Robb *Neoplatonism* 111: 'Its [i.e. Neoplatonism's] sincerest followers so loved the beauty of the world and the greatness of the human spirit that they hungered to believe them both divine, and yet were aware of something vaster than either, continually apprehended behind the mutable variety of things, but continually evading their most ardent pursuit.'
111 Pico della Mirandola *De hominum dignitate*; *Opera* 315; Kristeller *Philosophy of Marsilio Ficino* 184

GIUSEPPE SCAVIZZI

The Myth of Orpheus
in Italian Renaissance Art, 1400–1600

THE EARLIEST REPRESENTATIONS of Orpheus in Italian art belong in most respects to the medieval allegorical tradition. An example is the relief in the lower part of the Campanile (or bell-tower) of Florence Cathedral (figure 1). The Campanile decoration – which took nearly a century to complete – included a great variety of subjects of an allegorical nature. In 1437, as a conclusion to the work, the sculptor Luca della Robbia was entrusted with the commission of five reliefs in which the symbols of Music, Grammar, Philosophy, and two sciences had to be represented. Orpheus was chosen to symbolize Music and the relief, hexagonal in form, was completed and put on the wall two years later, in 1439.[1]

The programme, although medieval in nature, demonstrated through the choice of some of the figures representing the Arts a shifting of interest from the biblical to the classical and mythological which is typical of the Early Renaissance. True, in the Cathedral of Chartres the man who represents Music is sometimes interpreted as Pythagoras; however, the common symbol for Music in the Middle Ages was the biblical Tubalcain, who for Vincent of Beauvais had been the inventor of that art. The appearance of Orpheus in this context is probably due to the association between the myth and music which had been re-established – on the basis of a new knowledge of Fulgentius – by Coluccio Salutati.[2] Chastel, after noticing that the introduction of Orpheus into the previous series of the Campanile reliefs is awkward, suggests that his presence does not refer to instrumental music (which was represented by Tubalcain), but rather to the 'superior music,' the 'ideal principle of spiritual life.'[3]

Was the inclusion of Orpheus due to the personal choice of Luca della Robbia? It is impossible to answer; but we can attempt to see how the sculptor envisaged this mythical character. Orpheus is represented playing and singing

Figure 1   Luca della Robbia. Music (Orpheus). Florence,
Campanile of the Cathedral

among lions and swans (known in antiquity for their love of music), who are shown in attitudes of keen interest. His posture is distorted by the intensity of his emotions – his eyes almost closed, his mouth open. He is sitting in a garden surrounded by flowers. The classical aspect of his figure and the late Gothic treatment of the surroundings indicate a tendency toward idealization; this Orpheus is not a historical figure but the poetic and beautifying element in art.

Della Robbia characterized all his other figures in a very poignant way; it seems here that he is giving us the image of the medieval troubadour, modernized under the influence of the new concept of artistic practice and possibly the influence of the new interpretation of Orpheus which would be fully developed in Florence in the years to follow. For at the very time that Luca was working on his reliefs for the Campanile the official introduction of Platonism was taking place; Gemisto Pletho had just arrived in Florence (1438), and it was Pletho who convinced Cosimo de' Medici to found the Platonic Academy, who remained fascinated throughout his life by this supposed 'oriental' wisdom, and to whom Ficino possibly owed his interest in Orpheus.[4]

This new Platonic phase of the myth of Orpheus, which is another myth in itself, was clearly centred on Orpheus as a prophet-philosopher and was exclusively promoted by a small circle of humanists and thinkers all belonging to the so-called Careggi Academy; it was in conflict for some time with the still 'euhemeristic' tendencies of fifteenth-century historiography, which treated the image of Orpheus in a reductive way. For that tradition, still medieval in nature, Orpheus was not the philosopher or the great poet but rather the magician, a historical character, but devoid of any heroic dimension.

These tendencies are particularly visible in those chronicles of world history produced in the late Middle Ages (none of which, though, had been illustrated before our period) in which the histories of the pagan and biblical worlds were given parallel treatment. In one miniature that accompanies a Florentine chronicle probably produced between 1440 and 1450,[5] Orpheus appears in company with Heracles, Theseus, Midas, Gideon, Cadmus, and Proserpina. He is surrounded by birds as a flower is surrounded by bees. A supernatural power emanates from him, but the power is not of daemonic origin – he is quiet and smiling, idealized and beautiful. He is young and wears a fine costume of the time, which gives him a kind of worldly grace.

A second example appearing in a Florentine world history is found in a slightly later codex usually dated between 1455 and 1470 containing drawings attributed to Maso Finiguerra (figure 2).[6] Orpheus appears here as one of the most prominent personages in ancient history, together with Linus, Musaeus, Zoroaster, and Hermes Trismegistus. He is dressed as a Florentine page, singing and playing the lyre to a large number of animals, some of which are fantastic, derived from either classical mythology or medieval bestiaries (harpies, dragons, sirens); the landscape opens into a harbour where ships are quietly sailing. As Colvin and Seznec have pointed out, medieval and popular elements abound here. The only thing one may add is that Orpheus again appears as a youth of great beauty, dressed elegantly in fifteenth-century fashion, and placed in an open landscape (the only one of the series exhibiting a lyrical sense of nature). If we then compare this figure to real magicians, like Hostanes, Zoroaster, and Mercury, or to famous poets like Linus and Musaeus, who are all presented in a dignified manner and clothed in ancient costumes, we have the impression that the author treats Orpheus more as a metaphor than as a historical reality, and that this treatment is more gentle: Orpheus is a symbol of unity with nature, of a lyrical expression of sentiment, and perhaps he even suggests a self-portrait of the artist.[7]

The acceptance of the new myth of Orpheus is however fully revealed in a group of works executed in Florence between 1470 and 1491 by Bertoldo. Bertoldo, a former pupil of Donatello, had a privileged position in the circle of the Medici; he was probably a rather learned man who supervised the collection of Medici antiques, and has at times been considered the founder of an Academy of Fine Arts. What we know for certain is that in the last years of his life, partly because of his knowledge of ancient art, and partly because of the interest of his patrons in antiquity, he revived a large number of classical mythological themes. It had become customary in Florence and Padua to reproduce those themes in little bronze statuettes, plaquettes, or medallions, which imitated the ancient originals to the point of falsification. Since it was a fashion, however, the subjects were in many cases not really important.

There is one example of a little statuette by Bertoldo which could equally well be considered an Apollo, an Orpheus, or an Arion (figure 3). The figure is playing the viola and is in a state of inspiration.[8] It seems that here Bertoldo was trying to revive in a sort of indiscriminate fashion a type of nude in motion, almost dancing under the influence of music or of poetic frenzy. The ancient source might have been an Orpheus, an Apollo, or perhaps simply a Bacchic figure to which a contemporary instrument has been added; it might have been an Etruscan piece, as Chastel suggests,[9] some old image of Orpheus

Figure 2, opposite   Maso Finiguerra (?). Orpheus (detail). Illustration in the *Florentine Chronicle*, 1460–70. London, British Museum

Figure 3   Bertoldo. Orpheus (?). Florence, Bargello

like the one still existing today in Florence,[10] or perhaps a combination of both. If Bertoldo had really meant to represent Orpheus here, this would be one of the oldest examples of the type of Orpheus-Apollo, of which more will be said later; but there cannot be any certainty of this.

On other occasions Bertoldo treated the subject with a more precise characterization of the story. Three of his plaquettes show stories from the life of Orpheus: Orpheus playing to the animals, Orpheus in the underworld, Orpheus killed by the Maenads.[11] The choice is significant. Although the focus of the myth has been diffused by the interpretations of philosophers, it is narrated here from a purely 'poetic' view of the hero. All three stories refer in fact to the tragic side of Orpheus – his loss of Eurydice, his grief, his attempt to rescue his love, his death. The theme is Orpheus as the sad champion of unhappy love.

Unfortunately the date of execution of these three plaquettes is not known. It would be very interesting to know if, by any chance, Bertoldo was inspired by Poliziano's verses. The date of Poliziano's *Favola d'Orfeo*, however, is also not precisely known; although usually set around 1480, an earlier date of execution is sometimes suggested. According to Marrone, it was in 1471 that Poliziano, then only seventeen, was invited by Cardinal Francesco Gonzaga of Mantua during his visit to Florence to compose some poetry to celebrate the wedding of Galeazzo Sforza and Bona of Savoy; and it was in the period immediately following that the 'Homeric youth' composed his poem.[12]

Poliziano's *Favola* is derived from Virgil and Ovid. It is a lyrical piece centred on the theme of love with a melancholy and pastoral quality. His view of Orpheus is human and poetic just as Ficino's is symbolic and philosophical. Bertoldo's reliefs were executed in the spirit of Poliziano. The Poliziano-Bertoldo connection acquires a rather mysterious quality when we consider that in the same period of time three scenes from the myth of Orpheus – the very same scenes that Bertoldo had represented – were painted in fresco by Mantegna in one of the rooms of the Gonzaga residence in Mantua (the so-called Bridal room). Cardinal Gonzaga, who had been in touch with Poliziano earlier and whom Mantegna portrays in the Bridal room, might then have had some part in the commission. It was also in Mantua, in 1480, that Poliziano gave final shape to his *Favola*. Furthermore, after 1474 Bertoldo was active for long periods of time in the Veneto, where direct contact with Mantegna in these years is well within the realm of possibility.

The occasion for the decoration of the Bridal room is not known; nor is it known when it was started although the execution seems to have been completed by 1474. We do not know precisely whether the decoration of the room followed a specific programme. Mantegna decorated the lower part of the room with compositions referring to events that occurred in real life, but he covered the upper part with a series of images which apparently bear little relationship to each other: busts of Roman emperors, stories from the lives of Hercules, Periander, Arion, and Orpheus. For Ilse Blum, these subjects have an allegorical meaning and symbolize Christian marriage;[13] however, the idea is not convincing. Instead, it seems that Mantegna followed his fantasy freely and collected a number of images in a rather loose way, in order to establish an atmosphere of classical learning with antiquarian overtones. The *putti* and the Caesars are copied from classical models but cannot have any specific meaning except, perhaps, a reference to Ludovico Gonzaga's passion for ancient objects and medals. The only section of the room where a meaning could be reasonably assumed is the spandrels. The connection between Orpheus and Arion seems of course rather obvious: both are musicians, both go through difficult vicissitudes because of the exceptional nature of their lives and talents; Orpheus dies, but Arion survives through the protection of Periander. Also clear is the relationship of Periander and Hercules, both champions of virtue. (The former was king of Corinth, one of the seven wise men, and a protector of the arts.) May we see symbolized in these two pairs of characters the artist and his protector? If so, then these marginalia of the decoration might be seen as a very personal note by Mantegna trying to ingratiate himself to his patron through a celebrative and encomiastic touch: a panegyric played softly in veiled symbols, a declaration of gratitude to the master. It would also follow that Mantegna saw in Orpheus the tragic part of his own story as an artist from two possible points of view. As the counterpart of Arion, Orpheus can symbolize either the tragic and unsuccessful side of poetic activity in general, or the lack of success which leads in time to recognition (Periander and Arion). In the first case Mantegna would use the symbol to point to immutable values in the creativity of the artist, whereas in the second he would simply use Orpheus in an autobiographical vein, as the unrecognized model of his own artistry. Thus in both cases, Mantegna would see Orpheus as the image of himself as a painter and obviously as a tragic symbol.

It has been mentioned already that the three stories of Orpheus appearing in Mantua are those that Bertoldo had treated in his plaquettes. One should add that Mantegna's compositions show some similarities to Bertoldo's: the positions of several figures are so close in all three scenes that it seems difficult to conceive that they could be wholly independent of each other. Were Bertoldo's reliefs already executed when Mantegna painted the *Camera degli Sposi*, and were they known to him? Or are we rather to suppose an influence of Mantegna on Bertoldo? It is generally believed that it was Mantegna who

Figure 4   Anonymous Ferrarese. Death of Orpheus

introduced Bertoldo to antiquity.[14] Mantegna played a key role in the early Renaissance as a mediator between antiquity and contemporary artists, and it is quite probable that he was the one who interested Bertoldo in the subject.

The above hypothesis is strengthened by the fact that Mantegna demonstrated in later times a great interest in Orpheus, whom he represented in at least two more works, none of which is extant.[15] We know that in 1494, three years after Poliziano's *Favola d'Orfeo* had been publicly performed in Mantua, Mantegna was busy painting some stories of Orpheus in Marmirolo. These frescoes are unfortunately lost.

But another image of Orpheus can be traced back to Mantegna: Orpheus beaten and killed by the women in Thrace. That such a composition originated in one of Mantegna's engravings or drawings is only a matter of supposition but the odds are strongly in favour of it. In fact three works still exist today – one engraving and two drawings – all with a similar composition and all, in one way or another, traditionally associated with Mantegna. One is a drawing by Marco Zoppo;[16] if the style and the composition are only in a general sense Mantegnesque, the figure of Orpheus appears identical with the Orpheus of an anonymous engraving of the same subject which is much more obviously derived from Mantegna (figure 4).[17] This engraving, furthermore, is identical with the well-known drawing in the Museum of Hamburg signed by Dürer and dated 1494, the Mantegnesque origin of which has never been questioned.[18]

If there is little doubt that a drawing by Mantegna (or even better an engraving by him – which would explain the diffusion of the motif) is at the origin of the three works, it is much more difficult to guess what exactly the original might have looked like, and in what spirit it was executed. Edgar Wind decided that Dürer's drawing had been done in a mock-heroic mood; but Wind did not consider at all the relationship of this drawing with the lost Mantegna, and his interpretation has appeared unsatisfactory to some.[19] So the problem remains: how and with what symbolism did Mantegna choose to depict Orpheus in his original?

It seems to me that the anonymous engraving, although of rather modest quality – or perhaps because of it – reflects Mantegna's style rather well. The landscape is purely Mantegnesque, with a broad and open view over rocky, stratified, stony terrain that resembles the master's early style; the town in the centre is as close as it could be to the townscapes painted by Mantegna in the sixties. The story speaks for itself. The presence of a child makes the point that Orpheus has turned away from the love of women; this detail is there simply to underline the reason for his punishment but does not seem to suggest a negative attitude towards homosexuality.

As to the meaning of the composition we are much more in the dark. It is possible that Mantegna could have copied from an ancient piece simply for the pleasure of it; his engravings with sea-gods or with Dionysian subjects demonstrate his purely antiquarian taste. Yet we should not discard a priori other interpretations. A satirical representation is not likely. All derivations from Mantegna maintain a serious and almost heroic sense of grandeur. In Zoppos's drawing the child is present but not as obviously so as in Dürer; in later derivations from this composition (from the 1497 woodcut to Boscoli) the child disappears completely. The Italian Renaissance did not attach any openly sexual, much less negative, significance even to the myth of Ganymede. Mantegna as well as his followers saw Orpheus as the victim of the fact that he was different from others. His death could be interpreted as a consequence of his manliness, of his sense of religion, of his discovery of Amor as a powerful and idealistic force, or simply because of his being ἄγαμος. All these interpretations were already well established in the medieval tradition. The other thing which set Orpheus apart was his artistic creativity, the gift that made him immortal; and here we might put forward the hypothesis that in Orpheus Mantegna saw the symbol of Poetry.[20]

The most notable difference between the drawings by Mantegna and Dürer is the introduction in Dürer's work of an open book and a scroll containing the words 'Orpheus the first homosexual' ('Orpheus der erst puseran'). The presence of the book in the drawing is essential, and Wind has wrongly overlooked this detail for which – as he himself points out – so many readings have been given. I think it is safe to assume that the most obvious interpretation of the presence of both lyre and book is that the artist wanted to represent Poetry. Poetry appears commonly in that way, as we can see in Raphael's *Stanze* (ceiling of the *Stanza della Segnatura*), and Ripa's *Iconologia.*[21] Orpheus as symbol of Poetry appears in another work, which is contemporary to or perhaps older than Dürer's: a Florentine drawing at the British Museum where similarly book and lyre have both become attributes of Orpheus.[22] Indeed the ideas of harmony symbolized by the lyre and of learning symbolized by the book are central to the Renaissance concept of poetic activity, and are possibly its two single most important elements.

If Mantegna's Orpheus represented Poetry, or the Poet, then perhaps he was punished because his highly idealistic and creative qualities clashed with the triviality and materialism of a world not ready to accept him; thus he was doomed to a defeat which was also, in a way, a martyrdom.

If Dürer's drawing helps to clarify the meaning of Mantegna's work, the group of Italian works related to the lost Mantegna also helps us to understand Dürer's ideas. There is little doubt that the German painter here made fun of a *puseran*, as has been recognized by many who have analysed his work. One might, however, suggest that he had a very special type of homosexual in mind: the poet who, under the impact of the *furor melancholicus*, turns away from the world and loses his capacity for creating according to the laws of nature. This reading of the drawing would correspond with some of the interpretations provided for the 'Melencolia,' especially those which tend to see in the etching a representation of the artist.

To return to Mantegna, one may conclude, first, that his original must have been very close to the engraving just considered and, secondly, that this episode from the life of Orpheus was seen by him not necessarily in the spirit in which Wind has interpreted the similar drawing by Dürer. Mantegna apparently viewed Orpheus in a rather eclectic fashion, using the myth in a highly instrumental way in the Mantuan frescoes, and with a possibly deeper meaning in the lost original. In all cases however Orpheus is the symbol of artistic creativity in its most noble and sublime aspects.

Thus we have seen that the figure of Orpheus was of increasing popularity beginning around 1470 and that Mantegna was the moving force behind this popularity. As I suggested earlier, it was probably Mantegna's frescoes that provided Bertoldo with ideas for his plaquettes. Not even Poliziano seems to have had any influence on Mantegna from this particular point of view.[23] But

Figure 5   J. del Sellaio. Aristaeus and Eurydice. Rotterdam,
Boymans–van Beuningen Museum

since Mantegna, alone among the great masters of the early Renaissance, dealt
with the subject, we are left wondering about the reasons that he revived the
myth of Orpheus. Mantegna represents the best example of an attitude of
extreme curiosity about the classical world, which at times borders on
antiquarianism. Since Mantegna treated myth eclectically, it would seem that
he did not attach the importance to its content that Dürer did later. This was
the time when artists plagiarized ancient works without any scruple, and
Mantegna happened to be the artist most keenly interested in ancient art. His
education had taken place in Squarcione's workshop among ancient works of
art, either original or casts, and among fervent discussions on antiquity. Even
before the Mantuan frescoes he had travelled extensively in Tuscany and had
probably been to Rome. It is possible that among the reasons behind
Mantegna's images of Orpheus was a direct knowledge and study of ancient
works in which the myth was represented.[24]

The image of Orpheus singing and playing among animals was very
common in Roman floor mosaics, and some fifty odd examples, mostly from
suburban villas, still survive. The non-dramatic quality of the subject lent
itself to pastoral scenes, landscapes, and pictures of animals. We can suppose
that the subject was viewed in a similar way to the equally popular 'nilotic'
landscapes. It is quite likely that these scenes were known in the fifteenth
century. Although not as common, the image of Orpheus as a single figure,
singing passionately, could also have been known: for example, the statue in
the Palazzo dei Conservatori, which comes from the *Monument of the
Tibicini*. Examples of Orpheus in the company of Thracians and satyrs, and of
Orpheus playing in Hades in front of Pluto, survive to this day. Some
examples of satyrical treatment of Orpheus' death also existed in antiquity;
and the image of Orpheus on funerary steles must have been known in Italy,
since so many ancient copies are still extant today. The image of Orpheus
appeared also on funerary frescoes, on Etruscan mirrors, and on a large

Figure 6   J. del Sellaio. Orpheus and the animals. Vienna,
Lanckoronski collection

number of coins from Thrace. Finally, the death of Orpheus was frequently
found on Greek and Apulian vases – a motif which would have comple-
mented their funerary function – and Greek vases could be found easily in the
tombs of the rich Etruscans which the Florentines had started exploring in the
second half of the fifteenth century.

It is likely that some of these works were known in Mantegna's time.
Bertoldo's depiction of Orpheus playing in front of Pluto has a similarity to
ancient reliefs, as does the Orpheus playing in Thrace by Mantegna;[25] but
most striking is the near-identity between the death of Orpheus as represented in the lost work by Mantegna and the later work by Dürer, and the
compositions on Greek vases. Ziegler has already pointed out this similarity
and suggests that the source of the figure of Orpheus in the scene of his death
was an Attic vase in the Museo Gregoriano in Rome.[26] This is very possible,
although it could be added that it is really hard to specify the exact source of
Mantegna's figure since the representation of Orpheus' death found on the
Vatican vase is common on Greek vases (and may ultimately derive from the
famous fresco by Polygnotus).

The revived interest in Orpheus (who now begins to appear in classical
poses and draperies) proceeded hand in hand with the enthusiastic rediscovery of the visual and literary heritage of antiquity. It is this element that
characterizes the artists of Mantegna's generation and, more then anybody
else, Mantegna himself.

The only other artist of the fifteenth century – besides Bertoldo and
Mantegna – to narrate a series of episodes from the story of Orpheus was the
Florentine Jacopo del Sellaio. Jacopo had dealt on other occasions with
cyclical translations of literary works into painting (viz his *cassone* with the
story of Cupid and Psyche taken from Boccaccio's *De genealogia deorum*). In
three *cassone* panels he represented Aristaeus following Eurydice (figure 5),
Orpheus playing in front of the animals (figure 6), and Orpheus in front of

Pluto.[27] His interpretation of the story is most original and curious – not to say obscure: Orpheus appears as an oriental philosopher, aged and imposing, establishing order in a chaotic world still not free from its animal inheritance. The panel with Orpheus and the animals, with the musician set in opposition to the violence breaking out in the background, shows obvious dependence on Leonardo's *Adoration of the Magi* and suggests that Jacopo saw in Orpheus a counterpart of the religious Christian order. The presence, however, of griffins, dragons, centaurs, and other mythical creatures appears to indicate that this counterpart of Christ lived at the dawn of history, in remote times and places which for the painter coincided with the classical world. Orpheus here is also the counterpart of Prometheus, whose myth was being illustrated in those same years in Florence by Piero di Cosimo[28] – but with this difference: while Prometheus brought order and civilization among humans, Orpheus seems here concerned with the realm of nature: no human being in fact is shown in any of the three panels by Jacopo.

There are representations of Orpheus during the fifteenth century which refer to other aspects of the myth, or which introduce him only in a marginal way. The most common association is with the Argonauts. Two *cassone* panels of Pesellino's school show (1) Orpheus with Jason, Chiron, and Hylas leaving Pelias, and Orpheus with Jason, Mercury, and Medea after landing and taking the Golden Fleece;[29] and (2) Medea performing magic acts. It is difficult to say whether the stories are intended to deal with magic or esoteric wisdom. In both cases, however, Orpheus is inactive and confined to a relatively secondary role. One should of course remember that in many other instances where the romantic and popular story of the Argonauts was treated Orpheus does not appear. He was certainly part of the mysterious atmosphere surrounding Medea, but he had no central role in it.[30]

Apart from the few examples just mentioned, it appears that toward the end of the fifteenth century Orpheus was primarily associated with the idea of artistic activity as a whole, that universal form of poetry which becomes music when it touches the sublime. So, if in della Robbia's relief Orpheus was still seen essentially as a musician, now he has assumed a wider meaning. It is rather characteristic that when music alone had to be symbolized, other images were chosen: two medals done by the Venetian artist Giovanni Boldù to celebrate the musicians Filippo Maserano and Nicola Schlifer carry on the reverse the figures of Arion and Apollo; later in the sixteenth century David will be chosen to fill a similar role.[31]

Orpheus' increased importance as an esoteric symbol of the arts was certainly due to the influence of Neoplatonism, and we have to assume that it is for the same reason that immediately after 1500 he enjoys a new wave of popularity. During the High Renaissance, especially in the Veneto, the image

Figure 7   Francesco di Giorgio. Orpheus (?) among the animals. Siena,
S Domenico

of the painter and the poet overlapped constantly with that of the musician –
who in a way came to summarize the other two. Raphael paints his Poetry
holding a lyre. Giorgione deals in a number of instances with musicians in the
countryside, shown in romantic attitudes, lost in their reverie; so do Palma,
Cariani, Mancini, Giulio and Domenico Campagnola. Music for all these
painters is not the art of producing sounds but a state of mind and a way of
being which coincides with Poetry. The harmony of celestial happiness is of
course also symbolized by music, and in the late fifteenth century the image of
heaven is rendered more and more commonly through angels playing various
instruments and singing.[32]

Orpheus belongs to this symbolism, as the Renaissance substitute for
Apollo Citharedos. It is the phase of the idealized Orpheus, a symbolic figure
seen outside history, time, and space. These images of Orpheus in a landscape
express the idea of Music within the framework of an arcadian and pastoral
view of nature, such as we find in Sannazaro's poetry. Orpheus is always
depicted – according to this iconography – in a solitary, peaceful setting, in

Figure 9   D. Teniers (from Giorgione). Orpheus. New York, formerly
Suida collection

Figure 8, opposite   Francesco del Cossa (?). Orpheus. Florence, Uffizi

Figure 10   Titian. Eurydice. Bergamo, Accademia Carrara

complete happiness, and in total harmony with his surroundings. This vision, which attained its greatest popularity between 1480 and 1520, conforms to the spirit of the High Renaissance, one of serene grace and avoidance of the tragic. Although it declined after 1520, it was still present at times during the sixteenth century.

The idealized Orpheus-Apollo, an updated version of the Della Robbia example, can be seen in a drawing (figure 8) attributed to Francesco del Cossa (died 1477).[33] Two niello prints of a later period, attributed to Francia and to Pellegrino da Cesena,[34] might have derived from this drawing. Francia's print in turn seems to have influenced two prints by Nicoletto, who in fact showed a great dependence on Francia himself. These two prints are particularly beautiful.

Nicoletto da Modena – active between 1500 and 1510 – took part in the great revival of ancient mythology that immediately followed the activity of Mantegna. His works can be related to those of *L'Antico*: the choice of themes seems at times indiscriminate: Heracles, various gods, satyrs, tritons, Leda. He deals with Orpheus in two instances: in one engraving he shows the hero naked, singing as he plays a primitive type of violin. Here Orpheus is young,

Figure 11   Cima da Conegliano. Orpheus. Florence, Uffizi

idealized, living in harmony with his surroundings (a quiet open landscape) without any trace of his passion.[35] In a second engraving Orpheus, crowned like a poet (as in the ancient statue from the *Monument of the Tibicini* quoted above), plays but does not sing; he sits – as in Sellaio's painting – under an arch formed by rocks which opens onto a landscape with a veiw of a port. He is watching a monkey on the left, who might be interpreted as a symbol of the imitative arts. (The arch in the centre might also be interpreted in a symbolic way: Orpheus as the key figure in a transition from the purely natural to a civilized society. A comparison with other works by Nicoletto, however,

Figure 12   Anonymous Venetian. Marriage of Orpheus and other scenes from his life. Woodcut, from Ovid *Metamorphoses* (1509)

Figure 13   Anonymous Venetian. Orpheus playing before the animals. Woodcut, from Ovid *Metamorphoses* (1509)

Figure 14   Anonymous Venetian. Death of Orpheus. Woodcut, from Ovid
Metamorphoses (1509)

convinces us that the same image was used over and over again in the most
different compositions and that it must be devoid of any meaning.[36]) Hind
noticed that in both these engravings Nicoletto substituted a fantastic
instrument for the traditional lute which appeared in older prints.[37]

The beautified Orpheus in a landscape will disappear with time, yet many
examples testify that the image survived for some decades.[38] The Orpheus-
Apollo figure can be seen again in the pageantry organized in Florence for the
marriage of Francesco de' Medici and Giovanna of Austria. This included a
series of triumphal carriages decorated according to a complicated symbolism
related to the marriage. A figure of Orpheus, representing the sun, rode on
the fourth carriage.[39] Here Orpheus is nothing more than an alternative to the
more common figure of Apollo, and all the more interesting aspects of his
story are forgotten. Another instance of this type of easy transference between Orpheus and Apollo can be found in Vasari. This very knowledgeable
writer, who had been unable to identify Orpheus on the Campanile of
Florence Cathedral (where Orpheus did not bear any resemblance to Apollo),
made a drawing of Orpheus simply writing on the margin: 'Orpheus, son of
Apollo.'[40] Finally, it can be mentioned that in contemporary theatrical pieces
in Florence it was common to associate Orpheus with Apollo, and that this
association continued well into the early history of opera.[41]

At the close of the High Renaissance the myth of Orpheus took two

Figure 15   B. Carrari. Aristaeus and Eurydice. Paris, Spiridon collection (ex)

distinctly different paths. One is followed in the Roman milieu by artists like Peruzzi or Giulio Romano: it is of a literary nature, dealing essentially with the illustration of a literary source in a comprehensive way. Orpheus is a hero-figure; but he is one of many cardboard heroes used in large decorations primarily for decorative purposes. The other path is followed by the Venetian artists (Giorgione, Titian) and by those who were influenced by them, like Baldassare Carrari. This second trend follows the more serious interpretation of Orpheus that we associate with Mantegna and turns the story into a symbol of tragic significance and grandeur; but at the same time it moves away from Orpheus himself and becomes increasingly interested in Eurydice, who more fully embodies the tragic side of the story. In one case Orpheus and Eurydice are fairy-tale characters as real as pagan gods could be in the sixteenth century; in the other they are personages of eternal grandeur and their tragedy acquires an existential quality.

Baldassarre Peruzzi, the learned architect and painter from Siena, was the first in Rome to create a large decorative ensemble based on an ancient literary work. His interest in antiquity was intense and not restricted to visual remains; around 1509–10, in one little room of the elegant villa which had just been built for Agostino Chigi, he painted a long continuous frieze illustrating Ovid's *Metamorphoses*. The story of Orpheus is told in three scenes unified by the same nocturnal landscape (figure 17). In one Orpheus is sitting and playing his viola beside a little pond, in front of some animals; in the next Orpheus is standing, still playing his instrument, and so absorbed in his music that he hardly throws a glance at the desperate Eurydice as she is dragged down by a demon (or Pluto?) into the darkness of the earth; in the third, Orpheus is being beaten by the Maenads. They are basically the same three

Figure 16   Moderno. Death of Orpheus. Florence, Bargello

stories narrated by Mantegna and Bertoldo. Especially in the first two scenes
Orpheus is beautiful, idealized like Apollo, crowned with flowers. His aspect
is divine. He is beyond emotions, quite unconcerned with Eurydice's
suffering. All the emotions instead are on Eurydice's side: she extends her
arms toward him, unable to reach him, and doomed to disappear forever. The
obvious contrast aims at glorifying Orpheus and suggests that he represents
the ideal of divine beauty which is beyond human reach, and that Eurydice is
somehow at fault for being unable to stay with Orpheus. (Indeed, in the
fresco it is not Orpheus who causes the tragedy; he turns his head simply to
watch the tragic fate of his wife.)

Figure 17   B. Peruzzi. Orpheus and the animals; Orpheus and Eurydice. Rome, Farnesina, Sala del fregio

This reversal of events, with the consequent strong idealization of Orpheus' role, was not new. During the Middle Ages the story had been changed in this way on several occasions when the myth was used to symbolize the relationship between Christ (Orpheus) and the soul (Eurydice); however, it seems unlikely that Peruzzi was trying to give such a spiritual meaning to his frieze at the Farnesina. Given the general characteristics of the frieze and the choice of subjects, it has been suggested that what Peruzzi had in mind in the Farnesina was a representation of the four elements or spheres (earth, gods, sea gods, gods of death).[42] If this is true then Orpheus here would show on the one hand the sublime power of poetry, and on the other the relativity and frailty of the physical existence of the poet. The poet then shares some elements of the divine and yet is subject to the laws of life and death. As long as he is alive, though, Orpheus is all-powerful, and his relationship to Eurydice shows an opposition between divine and earthly beauty which can be compared to the symbolism expressed by another popular myth of the time, that of Apollo and Marsyas.

In its conception as an illustration of a literary work, Peruzzi's decoration set an example followed by Raphael in the same Farnesina, and later by some of Raphael's pupils, such as Perino del Vaga and Giulio Romano.[43] The frescoes finally realized the dream of Alberti and other theoreticians of the Renaissance: the concept that painting should be as learned as poetry, a theme derived from the Horatian *ut pictura poesis*. Giulio Romano borrowed the ideal of representing the stories from the *Metamorphoses* in his Sala di Ovidio (or Sala delle Metamorfosi) in Mantua, Palazzo del Te.[44] There, among other

Figure 18   Marcantonio. Orpheus and the animals

subjects, we find Orpheus playing in Hades before Pluto and Proserpina; the most sombre part of the story has been chosen, with the accent still placed on Orpheus as the conqueror of gods of the underworld.

A similar representation of Orpheus can be found in two plates done by the most popular engraver of the time. Marcantonio Raimondi dealt in a very original way with the myth, centring in both cases on one very dramatic instant: the moment when Orpheus has won Eurydice from Hades and is taking her back to the upper world. It is the moment that precedes the tragedy, yet the tragedy itself is ignored and Orpheus is again presented as the hero who succeeds in an impossible task. In the first engraving Orpheus is playing the viola, crowned as a poet; Eurydice confidently puts her left hand under his right arm, a kind of touching and expressive *coniunctio dextrarum* symbolizing the final reunion and the triumph of love (figure 19).[45] In the second engraving the artist again shows Orpheus leading Eurydice out of Hades (figure 20).[46] There is a sense of great peace in the action here, with both figures moving quietly forward to the light of the world; Orpheus' determination is absolute, and as a matter of fact the scene reminds us of the iconography of Christ leading the souls out of Limbo. Was Marcantonio aware of the similarity between the two scenes? Did he see Orpheus as the symbol of Christ, as in the early Christian tradition? We can certainly say that the artist more or less consciously transferred a sense of certainty which formerly belonged to the Divinity into an aesthetic sphere, stating by means of his image his confidence in the absolute power of art and poetry.[47]

A different way of looking at Orpheus developed in Venice, where the 'Olympian' view of the hero became rapidly obsolete. It is not surprising that the change took place with Giorgione, whose attitude towards his subjects and towards traditional iconography was so radically new. Nor is it surprising that Giorgione was interested in Orpheus: several of his compositions dealt with musicians in a pastoral, arcadian setting (the traditional iconography of Orpheus). He was constantly attracted by the image of the poet in the solitude of the countryside and often created landscapes whose atmospheres suggested a state of melancholia and, in some cases, a protoromantic idea of passion.[48]

Giorgione's original painting of Orpheus is now lost, but it is known to us through an engraving by Vosterman and through David Tenier's copy (figure 9).[49] The moon appears among the clouds, dramatically revealing Eurydice with Orpheus following, searching for her; in the foreground Orpheus looks at the spectator in anguish. If my interpretation is correct, Orpheus is represented twice in the painting: in the foreground remembering his loss and in the background[50] at the moment when his loss occurs. The background

Figure 19   Marcantonio. Orpheus and Eurydice

Figure 20   Marcantonio. Orpheus and Eurydice

Figure 21   Agostino Veneziano. Orpheus in Hades

Figure 22   L. Cambiaso. Orpheus (?). Florence, Uffizi

Figure 23   F. Salviati. Orpheus. Florence, Uffizi

would thus form a dream or fantasy which Orpheus communicates to the spectator. It must be noticed that Orpheus is still the protagonist of the scene, but that the attention has shifted to the emotional side of the story, and to Orpheus' suffering. The similarity of this figure with the famous *Christ on the Way to Calvary*, formerly in S Rocco and now in the Scuola Grande, is striking, and suggests that Giorgione too saw in Orpheus a sort of profane counterpart of Christ – a counterpart in the sense that just as the passion of Christ is necessary for the moral salvation of man, so the passion of Orpheus is necessary for man's search for beauty. The relationship assumes a special meaning if we consider the strongly autobiographical quality of all of Giorgione's works, and remember that Giorgione was himself a musician.[51]

Figure 24   G. Stradano (?). Orpheus. Florence, Uffizi

This Orpheus–Christ is like a confession: Orpheus dresses in a contemporary costume, holds a violin whose shape is unmistakeably contemporary, holds his right hand on his breast as if unable to control his emotions (a gesture appropriate to a singer like Giorgione himself; it is also the gesture of his *Passionate Singer* of the Borghese Gallery). Finally Orpheus, as we have found in two earlier examples, is crowned as a laureate poet, or as an Apollo.[52]

From these observations it follows that Giorgione too sees in Orpheus Poetry *tout court* but he substitutes Orpheus for Apollo because the latter, with his aura of divine superiority, does not reflect the passionate state of the poet: a passionate state which is not simply one way of being for the poet but the quintessence of poetry. Earlier, art had chosen a quiet image of Orpheus, but now it prefers the tragic one. Inspiration for Giorgione means suffering, and his idea of artistic activity is one of pain and melancholy, an unhappy and almost sinister inner turmoil.

Giorgione's *Orpheus* is a turning-point. It is in conflict with the traditional iconography of music which at that time still implied a state of grace with the world and the harmony of the spheres. Now there is no longer a universal harmony and the universe is no longer peaceful. Perhaps because of the traditional equation of the musical instrument with a sense of joy, Orpheus' violin disappears under his mantle.

Giorgione painted an Apollo and Daphne, which is now also lost.[53] We do

Figure 25   Anonymous Venetian. Orpheus and the animals

not know whether the two paintings were related in any way to each other. Probably they were not, since the format was different. We do not even know what the lost *cassone* looked like. Yet the two themes were probably related in Giorgione's mind and in the mind of his contemporaries. In fact a later painter heavily dependent on Giorgione, Dosso Dossi, represented his Apollo and Daphne in a way which is strongly reminiscent of Giorgione's *Orpheus*: it seems that the two themes were seen as close enough to be iconographically almost overlapping, and that the younger painter found the story of Apollo and Daphne a more suitable one in which to convey the meaning of the tragic in the pursuit of beauty.

The autonomy of Giorgione's vision had a lasting effect on painting[54] and first of all on Titian, which would be expected from Giorgione's spiritual heir. The little painting in Bergamo, done by Titian in his early years, shows Eurydice twice: once, in the foreground, bitten by the snake (which is a dragon here); a second time in the background as she follows Orpheus out of Hades, and is lost again when Orpheus turns back (figure 10). The story has now turned away completely from the musician and centres on the sad fate of the woman. The sense of fatality implicit in the story has increased dramatically, but the rendering of it has become objective and, in a way, detached, without losing its obviously tragic quality.[55]

From Titian's work we evince that to the younger painter Orpheus ceases

Figure 26 F. Bassano. Orpheus. Rome, Galleria Doria

to be an interesting character, or at least that Eurydice is more interesting to him. Titian abandons the emotionalism and subjectivity of Giorgione while maintaining the tragic sense of the story. The tragedy however is no longer within the artist but in the world outside him. Hades and the dragon contrast sharply with the beauty of the Venetian landscape and of Eurydice herself; they are the hidden perils and sad fate of human life, to which beauty is a consolation, but no remedy. Orpheus is powerless and can only recognize his own inadequacy and weakness. He withdraws quietly, still the artist, but an artist who remains outside and motionless as he contemplates the loss of his wife.

The two paintings by Giorgione and Titian were very important factors in bringing about a change in attitude toward the myth. The first exploded the conventional arcadian and positive view of Orpheus and probably caused a certain decline of his popularity. The second was even more significant, as it focused attention on Eurydice rather than Orpheus for the first time in the modern era. The two scenes have in common a 'negative' view of the myth. Whether as symbol of the artist or of man in general, Orpheus is an

Figure 27   F. Bassano. Orpheus. Florence, Uffizi

acknowledgment of man's frailty, his inability to reach and to hold; and the treatment of Eurydice, whether as a woman in her own right or as a symbol of beauty and nature (that is, whether as subject or object) also implies a wretched destiny for man.

This change corresponded of course to a much wider change in the customs and mental habits of the time which we might refer to as to the age of Mannerism, an age characterized by a growing sense of pessimism and scepticism about human life and its limitations. As for the myth of Orpheus and Eurydice, it appears that, when the two protagonists are combined, they are seen more and more in the same light as Apollo and Daphne.[56] As the myths came closer together, Orpheus and Eurydice were doomed. For the myth of Apollo and Daphne was more appealing, as it could concentrate the whole content of the story in one single image; and it was more reassuring, since it granted the protagonist a somewhat less miserable fate.

As the implications of the myth grew deeper, involving descriptions of characters, and lyrical or melodramatic situations, the visual arts yielded to literature in the treatment of the theme. While losing their popularity in the arts, Orpheus and Eurydice were appearing more and more frequently in literature and in drama. In France during the sixteenth century there was a blossoming of poetry about Orpheus that culminated in the long poem by Guidon Lefèvre de la Boderie.[57] In Italy during the same century Poliziano's *Favola* gave birth to a number of stage representations which marked the resumption of a classical dramatic genre – tragedy.[58] At the turn of the century Ottavio Rinuccini and Alessandro Striggio developed an introspective study of characters that led to the appearance of the first operas with the same subject, by Peri, Giulio Caccini, and Monteverdi. These are discussed more fully in the following chapter.

In the visual arts it was the 'Venetian' view with its emphasis on Eurydice that established itself in the sixteenth century. Baldassarre Carrari the Younger, in two panels now in Dublin and Paris (figure 15),[59] dealt only with the tragic story of Eurydice. Nicolò dell'Abate, in the *Aristaeus and Eurydice* of the National Gallery in London,[60] again focused on the motifs of the violence that Eurydice undergoes, and Aristaeus' inability to grasp the object of his desires. It is significant that the panel was probably conceived, originally, as a pendant to a *Rape of Proserpina*; and since among Nicolò's favourite subjects were also the *Rape of Anymone* and the *Rape of Helen*, it would seem that in the London work the painter was dealing primarily with an act of sexual violence. This type of topic would have been suitable to the erotomania of the French patrons for whom the painting was done; it also would have been in keeping with Fontainebleau imagery and taste which were contained in Nicolò's art. The composition is very theatrical (although, in truth, not very dramatic): the action takes place in an open and beautiful landscape which here may actually be the protagonist of the story.

The last example I shall deal with, important because its period is chronologically and ideally at the crossroad of Renaissance and Baroque, also fits into this category. It is the medallion painted in fresco by Annibale Carracci in the Farnese Gallery in Rome, around 1600 (figure 28). The theme is the loss of Eurydice. The figures are almost dancing, or rather running, in a state of wild agitation. The iconographic similarity with *Apollo and Daphne* is striking. It is the passionate element in Orpheus that makes him lose Eurydice.[61] Thus Eurydice becomes the symbol of an intangible reality which cannot be grasped on the level of nature. It is rather interesting that this is the way the myth will be seen in seventeenth-century art. Although Rubens never represented the myth, in one instance he referred to it; to make the point that he could not grasp the appearance of ancient painting, he compared himself

Figure 28   A. Carracci. Orpheus and Eurydice. Rome, Farnese Palace

with Orpheus trying to catch Eurydice – something obviously impossible. Rubens refers to the same part of the story that Annibale had painted in the Galleria – a work he knew very well – and sees it the same way. So Orpheus and Eurydice have become another Apollo and Daphne.

In summation, we have seen that in less than two hundred years Orpheus went through various metamorphoses, like a new Proteus. The troubadour, the magician, the philosopher-theologian,[62] the discoverer of Amor, the melancholic or tragic poet, the alter-Apollo, the winner and the loser, and of course the musician. All these facets were treated, leaving us at times in doubt as to what Renaissance people really thought of this *favola antica*. We can only cite some associations to explain his presence in the imagery of the time and the importance that the myth had in the panorama of the Renaissance classical revival.

First of all there is the association with music. The Renaissance was still influenced by the Pythagorean-Platonic concept of a universe based on harmony and numbers. Music was the best expression of this harmony and Orpheus was thought to be the best musician of all times. [63] Secondly, there is the association with Apollo from whom Orpheus received his lyre. He was also associated with Marsyas. The divine origin of his art gave him a quality of prophet-seer which the Neoplatonists of Florence associated with artistic genius. Thirdly, there is the idea of superiority of art over nature (actually, the *power* of art over nature) which was also part of the humanistic doctrine of art established by Alberti and which continued well into Baroque times.[64]

However, whether or not we agree with Symonds's statement that 'Orpheus was the proper hero of Renaissance Italy' – a statement made in the context of a study on Italian literature[65] – we have to say that the image of Orpheus in the *art* of the Renaissance was blurred. Too many associations made him lose that sharpness of contour which is necessary for a myth to succeed. As a symbol of the tragic passion of the artist, the myth of Marsyas was more pregnant; as a symbol of the impossibility of grasping reality or beauty, the story of Apollo and Daphne was also more clearly self-explanatory; and as for Eurydice, the myth of Proserpina was by far more poetic and rich.

So it happened that Orpheus was treated only for general associations (and therefore in a very subjective fashion), and despite his frequent presence in painting, especially between 1480 and 1520, he was not really popular. Considering that this age revived ancient mythology in a programmatic way, and that the story of Orpheus could be found in two of the most widely read classics, the *Georgics* and the *Metamorphoses*, we are surprised to find that so few of the great artists of the time dealt with him. Even among the engravers of the sixteenth century, who popularized practically every one of the old fables, Orpheus is not commonly found. Not one plate is devoted to him by Caraglio, Bonasone, or Vico. The myth was too complex and lent itself to too many interpretations.

From the late sixteenth century on the myth became more clear and its figuration more limited in scope. Some implications of the story were left out: the Baroque period, for instance, preferred to synthesize the concept of poetic activity with other images like the Blind Homer or Narcissus. As in Nicolò dell'Abate and Annibale Carracci (or in the words of Rubens) the myth became simply an alternative to Apollo and Daphne, the usual representation being Aristaeus following Eurydice, or Eurydice escaping from Orpheus' hands. The appeal had been lost in the change, and the myth was reduced to something almost unrecognizable.

The visual arts have a need to symbolize more than other arts, since they can only represent exterior events, and one scene chosen out of an endless series of moments. It appears that the myth of Orpheus could not be reduced to that one moment without becoming obscure or meaningless. The Renaissance revived a general interest in various facets of the story, but it was left to the poets and the musicians of the following century to provide a fully three-dimensional and more profound representation of the myth.

NOTES

1 The identity of the historical figures symbolizing the Arts has been variously interpreted. See eg Vasari *Life of L. della Robbia* and, among the moderns, M. Reymond *Les Della Robbia* (Florence 1897); P. Schubring *L. della Robbia und seine Familie* (Leipzig 1905); J. Seznec *The Survival of the Pagan Gods* (New York 1961). Although Orpheus is today the only figure identified without any hesitation, Vasari recognized all the figures but Orpheus, who was for him just 'a figure playing the lute.' For J. von Schlosser 'Giusto's Fresken in Padua ...', *Jahrbuch der Kunsthistorischen Sammlungen des allerhöchsten Kaiserhauses* 17 (1896) 73, Orpheus here symbolizes not Music, but Poetry. The same identification of the Arts is subject to different interpretations. Music and Grammar have always been identified as such, but Dialectic is sometimes referred to as Philosophy and the remaining two figures as, among other things, Astronomy, Arithmetic, Geometry, or Harmony. For the history of the construction and the decoration of the Campanile during the fourteenth century, see M. Trachtenberg, *The Campanile of Florence Cathedral* (New York 1971).

2 C. Salutati *De laboribus Herculis*: 'I am not ignorant that Fulgentius has assigned this fable to the art of Music' (quoted by J.B. Friedman *Orpheus in the Middle Ages* [Cambridge, Mass, 1970] p 144). Salutati is also the one who takes Orpheus out of the Christian frame of reference common to medieval allegory.

3 Although of a later period, the floor of the Cathedral of Siena had representations of Hermes Trismegistos and Socrates, and a similar mixture of pagan and Christian motifs occurred in Bergamo, Pavia, and Florence. In the exterior decoration of the Tribuna of Florence Cathedral a statue of Hercules was included as part of a programme sometimes attributed to Brunelleschi and Donatello and possibly going back to 1414; C. Seymour *Michelangelo's David* (Pittsburgh 1967). For another representation of Orpheus in a religious building, see below, note 38. For the continuity with the Middle Ages in the use of pagan symbols, and the 1437 reliefs in the Campanile, see Seznec *Survival of the Pagan Gods*, and for an opposite point of view, A. Chastel *Art et humanisme au temps de Laurent le Magnifique* (Paris 1959) 191ff.

4 For references see above, the essay 'Orpheus and Ficino' n 23.

5 Collection of S.C. Cockerell; Seznec *Survival* figure 2. The miniature executed c 1435–42 by Leonardo da Besozzo formerly in the Norbio coll., sold in Berlin in 1885 (H. Brockhaus, *Festgabe A. Springer* [Berlin 1885]) was very similar: see S. Colvin, *A Florentine Picture-chronicle* (London 1898; rpt New York 1970) 9, figure 6. The miniature by Leonardo da Besozzo was probably the original from which the other one derived. The origin of Leonardo's miniature was instead a cycle of fescoes of the late fourteenth century (Seznec *Survival*, 29 n 43).

6 Colvin *A Florentine Picture-chronicle* pl XXVIII–XXIX p 6ff, attributes the series to Maso Finiguerra and suggests the date 1455–65. For A.E. Popham and P. Pouncey *Italian Drawings … in the British Museum* (London 1950) 173ff n 274, the attribution can only be accepted as a hypothesis, and the date has to be slightly advanced to 1460–70. See also Seznec *Survival* 29.

7 Colvin finds in the figure, particularly in the expression of the face, an element of great naturalism. I would describe the expression rather as conventional, since it refers to the type of the 'singing' Orpheus. Note the similarity with L. della Robbia's relief, which obviously the author of this drawing had in mind.

8 A. Venturi *Storia dell' arte italiana* (Milan 1908) 514, Orpheus or Arion; W. Bode *Florentiner Bildauer der Renaissance* (Berlin 1911) 255, Arion; W. Bode *Bertoldo und Lorenzo dei Medici* (Freiburg im B. 1925) 92, Apollo; G. Galassi *La scultura fiorentina del Quattrocento* (Milan 1949) 143, Orpheus. It should be noted that there is a certain affinity between Orpheus and Apollo in Ficino's work (Chastel *Art et humanisme* 278 note). Contemporary instruments were intentionally put in the hands of Orpheus and Apollo as a demonstration that

that was the real model; on cases of artistic 'reminiscence' see E. Winternitz 'A *Lira da braccio* in Giovanni Bellini's *The Feast of the Gods' Art Bulletin* 28 (1946) 114 ff, and Chastel *Art et humanisme* 265.

9 Chastel ibid 71 n 5

10 See *Enciclopedia dell' arte antica sv* 'Orfeo.'

11 Chastel *Art et humanisme* 82. The group used to be attributed to an anonymous master who drew his name from it. (The Master of the Orpheus Legend; see E. Molinier, *Les Plaquettes de bronze de la Renaissance* 2 v [Paris 1886] who considered this master a Paduan active at the close of the fifteenth century.) Full bibliography in J. Pope-Hennessy, *Renaissance Bronzes from the Samuel H. Kress Collection* (London 1965) 38ff n 120–2.

12 L. Marrone 'Il mito di Orfeo nella Drammatica Italiana' *Studi di letteratura italiana* 12 (1922) 119ff. For a full assessment of the problems of Poliziano chronology, see N. Pirrotta *Li due Orfei* 6ff.

13 I. Blum *Andrea Mantegna und die Antike* (Strasbourg 1936) 57. P. Kristeller *Andrea Mantegna* (Berlin-Leipzig 1902) 250, suggests that the stories of Arion and Orpheus are an allusion to Ludovico's love for music.

14 K. Rohwaldt *Bertoldo* (Berlin 1896) 32. Rohwaldt also refers to Semrau's studies on Bertoldo.

15 One of the figures in Mantegna's 'Parnassus' (Paris, Louvre, executed c 1497) used to be considered, on the basis of an inventory of 1542, an Orpheus, but is now generally believed to represent Apollo. For a brief summary of the various hypotheses and bibliography, see E. Tietze-Conrat, *Mantegna* (New York 1955) 195, and more recently, P.W. Lehmann and K. Lehmann *Samothracian Reflections* (Princeton 1973) 59ff. Cases of confusion between Orpheus and Apollo in ancient and modern literature are common: see for instance the frescoes in Città di Castello of around 1545; A. Ronen, 'Palazzo Vitelli alla Cannoniera ...' *Commentari* 26 (1975) 56. On this, see also above, note 8.

16 Popham and Pouncey *Italian Drawings*, n 260 162ff. It is part of a series of 25 (Rosebery coll) engraved by F. Novelli in 1795 as Mantegna's originals. C. Dodgson *A Book of Drawings Formerly Ascribed to Mantegna* (London 1923) xxi, connected them to M. Zoppo. Others have suggested a date between 1465 and the early seventies. The drawing is reproduced in C. Ephrussi 'Quelques remarques à propos de l'influence italienne dans une œuvre de Dürer' *Gazette des Beaux Arts* (1878) 447.

17 A.M. Hind *Early Italian Engraving* (London 1938) 1 257 pl 409, considered by the author as a Ferrarese and dated c 1470–80. As Hind notices, the central figure of the drawing appears on reverse in the engraving, so that the engraving can be considered as adapted from the drawing, or possibly from another very similar original. Hind also notices that a woodcut with the same subject (repro-

duced in H. Delaborde *La Gravure en Italie avant Marc Antoine 1452–1505* (Paris 1883) 243, probably derived from this engraving, appeared in an edition of Ovid's *Metamorphoses* (Venice: G. Rosso for L. Giunta 1497) f 91ᵛ; and that the woodcut was probably a source of inspiration for a dish in majolica at the Museo Civico in Venice (reproduced in *Gazette des Beaux Arts* 10 (1861) 356). The engraving was erroneously considered a Florentine work by J.D. Passavant *Le Peintre-graveur* (Leipzig 1860–4) v 47 n 120. C. Ephrussi *A. Dürer et ses dessins* (Paris 1882) 19ff also adds to the list of works derived from the original engraving a woodcut in Ovid's *Metamorphoses* (Venice: G. de Rusconibus 1509).

18 See especially Ephrussi *Quelques remarques* 444ff; A. Warburg *Der Tod des Orpheus; Dürer und die Italienische Antike* (Hamburg 1905).

19 E. Wind ' "Hercules" and "Orpheus": two mock-heroic designs' *Journal of the Warburg and Courtauld Institutes* 2 (1939) 206ff

20 Orpheus had been identified with Poetry as early as the thirteenth century; Buck *Der Orpheus-mythos*. See also above, note 1.

21 The symbols of lyre and book appear in the descriptions of both Poesia and Furore Poetico.

22 Popham and Pouncey *Italian Drawings*, 207 n 348, not reproduced. The drawing is attributed to a Florentine master dependent on Botticelli and working in the third quarter of the fifteenth century.

23 For the chronology of Poliziano, see above note 12. It is possible that Orpheus could have been a subject of conversation between Poliziano and Mantegna; in 1471–2 Mantegna was working at his Mantuan frescoes when Federico brought Alberti and Poliziano from Florence. Although the execution of the *Favola d'Orfeo* is probably later, its conception could go back to those very days. To my knowledge it has never been suggested that Mantegna had any relationship with the writing of the *Favola*, yet it could be pointed out that the three episodes of which the *Favola* is composed – bucolic, heroic, bacchic (Pirrotta *Li due Orfei* 19) – are basically the same as the three episodes of Mantegna's frescoes.

24 On Mantegna and antiquity, see especially L. Blum *A. Mantegna und die Antike*, and on images of Orpheus in the classical world F.W. Schoeller *Darstellung des Orpheus in der Antike* (Freiburg 1969) and *Enciclopedia dell' arte antica*, 'Orfeo.'

25 See for example the Ince Blundell Hall relief (Schoeller *Darstellung des Orpheus* 66).

26 K. Ziegler 'Orpheus in Renaissance und Neuzeit' *Form und Inhalt* (Festschrift O. Schmitt) (Stuttgart 1950) 240

27 P. Schubring *Cassoni* (Leipzig 1915) no 357–9

28 O. Raggio 'The Myth of Prometheus' *Journal of the Warburg and Courtauld*

Institutes 21 (1958) 44ff; M. Bacci *P. di Cosimo* (Milan 1966). On the similarity between the myth of Orpheus and those of Hercules and Prometheus during the Renaissance, see Buck *Der Orpheus-Mythos* 14.

29 S. Reinach 'Essai sur la mythologie ...' *Revue Archéologique* 1 (1915) 136. Acquired in 1900 by the Pierpont Morgan and exhibited at the Metropolitan Museum in New York; *Bulletin* (December 1909) 223ff. Schubring *Cassoni* n 296–7.

30 Orpheus occasionally appears in the company of other pagan heroes and gods, as in Lorenzo Costa's panel in the Louvre (n 1262; Reinach 'Essai' 108, Orpheus with Apollo, Mercury, and others). In these cases there is often nothing particularly 'Orphic' about his position, and he is combined with figures who do not belong to his myth. Orpheus and Eurydice, attributed to the school of Perugino, appeared on the market in Paris in 1903 (sale Ravaisson–Mollien, 23 November 1903; Reinach 'Essai' 177). The title would indicate a novel treatment of the subject, but not having been able to trace the panel, I refrain from any comment on it.

31 G.F. Hill *Renaissance Medals from the Samuel H. Kress Collection* (London 1967) nos 139–40. As an example of a David in the sixteenth century, see the medals for Federico II; A Magnaguti *Le medaglie dei Gonzaga* (Rome 1965) no 33. For Orpheus as a symbol of Music and Poetry in the Renaissance, Buck *Der Orpheus-Mythos* 18.

32 On music as an all-pervading symbol in Renaissance life, see E. Winternitz *Musical Instruments and Their Symbolism in Western Art* (London 1967) 204ff. For Orpheus and music in the Middle Ages, see Friedman *Orpheus in the Middle Ages* 142.

33 Drawing in Florence, Uffizi, no 1394E. *Catalogo dell' esposizione di pittura ferrarese* (Ferrara 1933) no 231; Hind *Early Italian Engravings* II 116; *Mostra degli strumenti musicali* Catalogue by L. Marcucci (Florence 1952) 30 n 6. The attribution to Cossa is by Giglioli; for Longhi it is the work of a Ferrarese c 1475.

34 Passavant *Le Peintre-graveur* I 280 and V 200; Hind, *Early Italian Engravings* II 116

35 Ibid II 116 pl 644; the engraving is signed.

36 Ibid with bibliography

37 Ibid 118 pl 652

38 For examples see Appendix A, Numbers 39, 41, 46, 47, 56, 65, 66, 67, 68, 69, 72, 74.

Two strange and rather obscure images of Orpheus, both executed toward the end of the fifteenth century, are those attributed to Francesco di Giorgio Martini and Giovanni Bellini. The first one is incised in the pavement of the chapel of S Caterina in S Domenico at Siena (figure 7). The figure, naked and seated on a rock, is surrounded by a number of animals, some of which are of an unreal nature, like the unicorn. In between the trees, the sun and the moon appear. But the supposed Orpheus is not playing the lyre; he contemplates himself in a mirror. The figure was first believed by Cust to be Esculapius, then later by the same author, to be Orpheus; H. Cust, *The Pavement Masters of Siena, 1369–1562* (London 1901) 147 and 'On some overlooked Masterpieces' *Burlington Magazine* 4 (1904) 256ff. Hartlaub thinks he is the Adam of the Kabbala; G.F. Hartlaub 'Ein unbekanntes Kunstwerk des Francesco di Giorgio Martini' *Pantheon* 31 (1943) 174–81. Cust (1904) describes the figure as 'the mystic intermediary between the seen and the unseen; the mystic teacher, with attributes akin in many points to both the Esculapius and the Bacchus of classical fables,' and sexless, 'a twofold nature – while his mirror is the type of the imperfection of mere human intellect this side of the grave.' According to Cust all animals here have their own symbolic meaning; the river indicates the mysterious world between present and future life; finally, all virtues could apply to S Catherine, to whom the chapel is dedicated.

The symbol of the mirror appears in both religious and profane iconography; the 'cantarus' with water, the sun and the moon, the eagle could all carry eschatological meaning (for the images of sun, moon, and eagle in association with Orpheus in early Christian times, see Friedman *Orpheus in the Middle Ages* 50–1 and 59ff). But although the composition could be related to Christian imagery – the good shepherd – with a possible association with ancient mosaics of Orpheus among animals, the symbolism of the composition remains unclear. Before being given to Francesco di Giorgio the work was attributed to Beccafumi and G.B. Sozzini. Besides Cust and Hartlaub, see also Chastel *Art et humanisme* 274 and A. Buck *Der Orpheus-Mythos* 28.

The second painting is possibly even more intriguing, also because so much has been written and so many different conclusions have been reached on it. It is the Widener Orpheus of the National Gallery of Washington, which has been variously attributed to G. Bellini, A. Previtali, and Giorgione or his circle. W. Sheard, who has recently provided an extensive analysis of the painting ('The Widener Orpheus: attribution, type, invention' in W. Sheard and J.T. Paoletti *Collaboration in Italian Renaissance Art* [New Haven and London 1978] 189–219, which includes all the important bibliography on the painting), gives us the most satisfactory interpretation to date of the various figures. According to her, the couple Pan-Venus on the left indicates a dualistic principle of reproduction whereas the couple Pan-Orpheus points to another dualistic principle of nature, that of unity and multiplicity. Both pairs of figures are examples of *discordia concors*. The couple Orpheus-Circe, on the contrary, represents irreconcilable opposites (naturally versus black magic, good versus evil, etc) which are historically related to Pico's idea of man's 'freedom.' If it is so, and I tend to agree with this interpretation, then Orpheus represents here the type of philosopher-artist-magician created by the Florentine Platonists, a type which – as we have seen – is neither new nor original. Judging from a purely stylistic point of view, however, I cannot resolve to attribute this painting to Giorgione and I still prefer the vague but proper collocation of the work in the 'circle' of Giovanni Bellini.

39 Winternitz *Musical Instruments* 268

40 'Orfeo figliuolo di Apollo,' Florence, Uffizi, no 2722f; Parigi *I disegni musicali* no 1171

41 Pirrotta *Li due Orfei* 302

42 C.L. Frommel *B. Peruzzi als Maler und Zeichner* (Vienna and Munich 1965) 61ff. The frieze contains: Hercules' deeds (Earth); Jupiter's loves (Gods); figures of Sea Gods; Marsyas, Meleager, and Orpheus (Death). Frommel notes that the sequence of the three scenes does not express Orpheus' story well; but he does not realize the obvious connection between Peruzzi's frescoes and what we might call the tradition of Mantegna.

43 Peruzzi's fresco probably also had an influence on the later iconography of Orpheus. The plaque by Moderno, for instance, seems to derive some elements from Peruzzi.

44 F. Hartt *Giulio Romano* (New Haven 1958) I 111; E. Verheyen 'Die Sala di Ovidio im Palazzo del Te' *Römische Jahrbuch für Kunstgeschichte* 12 (1969) 161–70. The only other stories recognizable in the frieze refer to Apollo and Marsyas and the Judgment of Paris.

45 A. Bartsch, *Le Peintre Graveur* XIV (Leipzig 1867) n 282. The composition of this etching has also been attributed to Francia. It is probably earlier than 1506. Like all the other prints listed in the fourteenth volume of *Le Peintre Graveur* these engravings are reproduced in *The Illustrated Bartsch* v 26 ed K. Oberhuber (New York 1978).

46 Bartsch *Le Peintre Graveur* XIV 295. For Hirth, the author of this engraving is Peruzzi; for Passavant instead the composition is by Sodoma: see A. Oberheide *Der Einfluss M. Raimondis auf die nordische Kunst des 16. Jahrhunderts* (dissertation; Hamburg 1933) 62f. The date of the work is likely to be around 1507–8.

47 Oberheide notices a similarity between the figure of Eurydice in this print and representations of Eve by the same Marcantonio. A third engraving by Marcantonio with Orpheus – probably the oldest in time, still similar to the current image of Orpheus in Venice and with stylistic elements from Dürer (figure 18) – is more traditional and shows Orpheus playing in front of the

animals (Bartsch *Le Peintre Graveur* XIV 314). Also traditional is the treatment of Orpheus and Eurydice in two other engravings of Marcantonio's circle: the Eurydice, probably by Marco da Ravenna (Ibid 262) and the Orpheus by Agostino Veneziano (figure 21) date 1528 (Ibid 259). On Marcantonio see: H. Delaborde *M.A. Raimondi* (Paris 1888) 175ff; A.M. Hind (ed *Great Engravers. Marcantonio and Italian Engravers ... of the* XVI *Century* (London 1912) passim. For the influence of Marcantonio's Orpheus on Northern art, see A. Oberheide *Der Einfluss*; Marcantonio's Orpheus was particularly followed by Aldegrever and Altdorfer (ibid 62ff); the image of Eurydice in the Orpheus (Bartsch XIV no 295) had a stylistic influence on Baldung Grien and Cranach the Elder.

48 On Giorgione's image of the poet, see H. von Einem *Giorgione. Der Maler als Dichter* (Mainz 1972).

49 W. Suida 'Spigolature giorgionesche' *Arte Veneta* 8 (1954) 159f; and T. Pignatti *Giorgione* (Venice [1970]) figure 50. The painting was in the collection of the Archduke Leopold William (inventory 1659, no 290), catalogued as an original Giorgione and reproduced as such in the *Theatrum Pictorium* by Teniers (1658, no 15) for which Vosterman's copy was made. Teniers' own copy, formerly in the Suida Collection, was recently in the Finch College Museum of Art, New York. Other interpretations of this painting are reported in G. Tschmelitsch *Zorzo, genannt Giorgione* (Vienna 1975) 263.

50 My interpretation of the subject differs here from the traditional one. I think the scene in the background originally represented not Eurydice pursued by Aristeus but the exit from Hades. In fact, the presence of three figures cannot be explained unless we think that Tenier added one figure between Orpheus (at the extreme right, turning his head backwards) and Eurydice (who raises her hand in discomfort). Perhaps the painting by Giorgione was darkened, or in bad condition, and Tenier misunderstood the composition. This is the only way to explain the building in the background, obviously Hades as in Titan's painting at Bergamo (which is based on Giorgione's work) and Marcantonio's contemporary engraving.

51 Vasari says in the life of Giorgione (*Le Vite* ed G. Milanesi (Florence 1879) IV 92): '... e piacqueli il suono del liuto mirabilmente e tanto, che egli sonava e cantava nel suo tempo tanto divinamente, che egli era spesso per quello adoperato a diverse musiche e ragunate di persone nobili.'

52 Another almost contemporary example of an artist identifying himself with the figure of Christ is Dürer; see E. Panofsky *The Life and Art of A. Dürer* (Princeton 1943) 59.

53 Quoted by Ridolfi; see Pignatti *Giorgione* 136.

54 As for Giorgione it has to be remembered that a meaning somehow related to

Orphism has been detected by Hartlaub (1953) in the controversial 'Three Philosophers in Vienna'; see for a discussion of his thesis R. Wischnitzer-Bernstein, 'The Three Philosophers by Giorgione' *Gazette des Beaux Arts* 87 (1945) 193ff; and Pignatti *Giorgione* 105. Giorgione dealt with the myth of Orpheus in another lost panel; O. Kurz, 'Holbein and others in a seventeenth century Collection' *Burlington Magazine* 82–3 (1943) 281. This panel represented Orpheus in the Underworld, a theme that was not very novel in itself; but we have no idea of how the subject was treated. W. Sheard 'The Widener Orpheus' 212 has therefore the right to say, with O. Kurz, that the theme of Orpheus was rather popular in Giorgione's circle.

55 H.E. Wethey *The Paintings of Titian* III (London 1975) 16f catalogue no 28, with complete bibliography. It is worth reporting Wethey's description: 'Despite its ruinous state the originality of the artist's macabre interpretation remains. The sense of terror here evoked is unique, especially the Bosch-like gate of hell with its smoke and red flames at the upper right. The anguish of the grief-striken Orpheus, who glances back ... adds to the dramatic intensity, which is exceptional in Venetian mythological paintings of this period.' The author adds that Titian might have read Ovid and Vergil, but he ignores completely Giorgione's role as a precursor of Titian. Ziegler 'Orpheus in Renaissance und Neuzeit' 244 believed that this painting (which he attributed to Giorgione) could have been influenced by a woodcut in the Bruges Ovid of 1484; the similarity between the two works, however, is hard to detect.

56 For Apollo and Daphne, see W. Stechow *Apollo und Daphne* (Darmstadt 1965).

57 G. Bräkling-Gersuny *Orpheus der Logos-Träger* (Munich 1975)

58 The anonymous *Orphei Tragoedia*; the play by Tebaldeo; the anonymous *Favola di Orfeo e Aristeo*: see Marrone 'Il mito di Orfeo' and Pirrotta *Li due Orfei* 18 and 50ff.

59 One formerly in the Spiridon Collection, the other in the Musée des Arts Decoratifs. See Schubring *Cassoni* no 547, 948, pl cxxiv. Two more examples of Aristaeus following Eurydice are provided by E. Langmuir 'Nicolò dell' Abate's "Aristeus and Eurydice"' *Burlington Magazine* 112 (1970) 107f.

60 *Nicolò dell' Abate* Exhibition, Bologna 1969, catalogue by S.M. Béguin 85ff.

61 I tend to reject the interpretation given by Martin of this medallion; J.R. Martin *The Farnese Gallery* (Princeton 1965) 98ff. A better interpretation is provided by D. Posner *Annibale Carracci* (New York 1971) I 93, who sees in the medallions of the vault 'the theme of the violence, frustrations, and even the catastrophes brought about by the capricious nature of Love.'

62 As Ripa reminds us, poetry is for Plato 'expression of divine things'; therefore there is no basic contradiction, in the Platonic tradition, between Orpheus the theologian and Orpheus the poet. Theologians of the Church during the

sixteenth century quoted Orpheus with the greatest respect. A. Pio *Tres et viginti libri in locos Lucubrationum D. Erasmi* (Paris 1531) f 32ʳ states that Orpheus did not eat meat and set an example of the highest spirituality; Cochlaeus *De Sanctorum invocatione et intercessione* (Ingolstadt 1544) cap v, f Diiᵛ saw in Orpheus an example of Poetic Theology. But later on, the Counter-reformation tried to dispel the magic of this tradition. Vittorio Giselino, a famous theologian of the late sixteenth century, explained in detail the reasons why the reading of poets like Musaeus or Orpheus had to be avoided; A. Possevino *Tractatio de poesi et pictura* (Rome 1594) 46.

63 On this, see especially W. Sheard 'The Widener Orpheus' 208ff.

64 For the main guidelines of Renaissance views on Orpheus, see Walker 'Orpheus the Theologian' 100 and Sheard 'The Widener Orpheus' 212.

65 Quoted by Sheard 'The "Orpheus" in the Widener Collection: Giorgione's role,' a paper read at the Symposium on Venetian Art, Johns Hopkins University, March 1974.

APPENDIX

The Myth of Orpheus: A List of Works Done in Italy between 1400 and 1600

Bibliographical references are given for works not mentioned in the article. Abbreviated references are to studies cited in full in the notes. The works are listed in rough chronological order.

1 Anonymous Veronese (?). Orpheus. Illustration of Albericus, *De deorum imaginibus libellus*, c1420. Vatican, Library. Seznec *Survival of the Pagan Gods*.

2 Leonardo da Besozzo. Orpheus. Illustration of a *Picture chronicle*, 1435–42. Formerly in the Norbio collection.

3 Luca della Robbia. Music (Orpheus). Marble relief, 1437–39. Florence, Campanile le of the Cathedral. (figure 1)

4 Anonymous Florentine. Orpheus. Illustration in a *Picture chronicle*, 1440–50. Cockerell collection.

5 T. Finiguerra (?). Orpheus. Illustration of a *Florentine chronicle*, 1460–70. London, British Museum. (figure 2)

6 A. Mantegna. Orpheus and the animals; Orpheus in Hades; death of Orpheus. Frescos, c1470–74. Mantua, Palazzo Ducale.

7 A. Mantegna. Stories of Orpheus. Frescos in Marmirolo (lost).

8 A. Mantegna. Death of Orpheus. Drawing or engraving (lost).

9 Bertoldo. Orpheus (?). Bronze, 1470–90. Florence, Bargello. (figure 3)

10–12 Bertoldo. Orpheus and the animals; Orpheus in Hades; death of Orpheus. Bronze plaquettes, c1470–90.

13 Marco Zoppo. Death of Orpheus. Drawing, c1470. London, British Museum.

14 Anonymous Ferrarese. Death of Orpheus. Engraving, 1470–80. (figure 4)

15 Anonymous Florentine. Orpheus. Drawing, 1475–1500. London, British Museum.

16 A. del Pollaiolo (cirle of). Orpheus. Drawing, 1480–1500. Turin, Biblioteca Reale. Warburg *Der Tod des Orpheus* 56.

17 Anonymous. Death of Orpheus. Majolica dish, c1500. Venice, Museo Correr.

18–19 Pesellino (school). Two stories of the Argonauts with Orpheus. Panel paintings, c1460–70. New York, Pierpont Morgan collection.

20–22 J. del Sellaio. Aristaeus and Eurydice (figure 5); Orpheus and the animals (figure 6); Orpheus and Pluto. Panel paintings, c1480–90. Rotterdam, Museum; Vienna, Lanckoronski collection; Kiev, Museum.

23 P. Perugino (school). Orpheus and Eurydice. Painting, c1500. On the Parisian market in 1903.

24 Francesco di Giorgio. Orpheus (?) among the animals. Marble intarsio, c1488. Siena, S Domenico. (figure 7)

25 Francesco del Cossa (?). Orpheus. Drawing, c1470. Florence, Uffizi (figure 8).

26 L. Costa (died 1535). Cosmos and other gods with Orpheus. Panel painting. Paris, Louvre, no 1262.

27 L. Costa. The court of the Muses of Isabella d'Este with Orpheus (?). Painting, c1505. Paris, Louvre, no 1261. Winternitz *Musical Instruments* 224.

28 L. Costa. Triumph of Death with Orpheus (?). Fresco. Bologna, S. Petronio, Bentivoglio chapel. Winternitz *Musical Instruments* 181.

29 F. Francia (died 1517). Orpheus. Niello print.

30 Timoteo della Vite (attributed to). Orpheus and Eurydice. Majolica dish, early sixteenth century. Venice, Museo Correr. Pirrotta *Li due Orfei* plate 5.

31 Pellegrino (or Peregrino) da Cesena. Orpheus. Niello print, beginning of the sixteenth century.

32 Anonymous Venetian. Death of Orpheus. Woodcut in Ovid, *Metamorphoses*, printed by G. Rosso for L. Giunta, Venice 1497. Warburg *Der Tod des Orpheus* 56; Henkel 'Illustrierte Ausgaben von Ovids Metamorphosen in 15., 16., u. 17. Jahrhundert' *Vorträge der Bibl. Warburg* (1926–7) 70; Ziegler *Orpheus in Renaissance* 241.

33 Giovanni Bellini (circle of). Orpheus and Circe. Painting, c1500. Washington, National Gallery.

34–35 Nicoletto da Modena. Orpheus. Two etchings, beginning of the sixteenth century.

36 Giorgione (died 1510). Orpheus. Lost. Copy by David Teniers, formerly New York, Suida collection. (figure 9)

37 Giorgione. Orpheus in the underworld (lost).

38 Titian. Eurydice. Panel painting, c1510. Bergamo, Accademia Carrara. (figure 10)

39 Cima da Conegliano (died 1517–18). Orpheus. Drawing. Florence, Uffizi. L. Coletti *Cima da Conegliano*, Venice 1959, 82 no 59. (figure 11)

40 Cima da Conegliano. Mythical subject with Orpheus. Painting. Vienna, Lanckoronski collection. Reinach *Essai* 148.

41 Anonymous Venetian (V. Carpaccio or G. Mocetto). Orpheus. Paintings, c1500. Formerly in Vienna, Lanckoronski collection. Schubring *Cassoni* no 765; Heinemann *Bellini e i belliniani* 259 no 283.

42–44 Anonymous Venetian. Marriage of Orpheus and Eurydice; Orpheus playing in front of the animals; death of Orpheus. Woodcuts from Ovid *Metamorphoses*. Rusconi 1509. Ephrussi *Dürer et ses dessins* 19ff; same blocks used for the editions of 1510 and 1517. (figures 12–14)

45 Pseudo-Melioli. Orpheus and the animals. Bronze plaquette. Pope-Hennessy *Renaissance Bronzes* 60 n 201.

46–47 B. Montagna. Orpheus. Two etchings. M. Pittaluga *L'incisione italiana nel Cinquecento*, Milan 1934, figure 113; Hind, *Early Italian Engraving* II 178 plate 745.

48 B. Carrari. Aristaeus and Eurydice. Painting. Paris, formerly in the Spiridon collection. (figure 15)

49 B. Carrari (?). Death of Eurydice (?). Dublin, Murnaghan collection.

50–54 Moderno. Orpheus descending into Hades; redeeming Eurydice; losing Eurydice; playing to the animals; Death (figure 16). Bronze plaquettes. Pope-Hennessy *Renaissance Bronzes* 52f nos 171–5.

55 B. Peruzzi. Orpheus and the animals; Orpheus and Eurydice (figure 17); death of Orpheus. Frescos, c1509–10. Rome, Farnesina, Sala del fregio.

56 Marcantonio. Orpheus and the animals. Engraving. Bartsch *Le peintre graveur* 14, 314. (figure 18)

57 Marcantonio. Orpheus and Eurydice. Engraving, Prior to 1506. Bartsch *Le peintre graveur* 14, 282. (figure 19)

58 Marcantonio. Orpheus and Eurydice. Engraving, c1507–8. Bartsch *Le peintre graveur* 14, 295. (figure 20).

59 Giulio Romano. Orpheus in the underworld. Frescos. Mantua, Palazzo del Te, Sala delle Metamorfosi.

60 Giulio Romano. Orpheus. Drawing. Paris, Louvre. Warburg *Der Tod des Orpheus* 56.

61 B. Luini (?) (died 1532). Orpheus and Eurydice, two episodes. Painting, formerly in the Somzée collection (sale 1904 no 405). Reinach *Essai* 148.

62 Agostino Veneziano, Orpheus in Hades. Engraving, 1528. Bartsch *Le peintre graveur* 14, 259. (figure 21)

63 Marco da Ravenna (?) (died 1527). Eurydice leaves Hades. Engraving. Bartsch *Le peintre graveur* 14, 262.

64 Anonymous. Eurydice leaves Hades. Engraving. Bartsch *Le peintre graveur* 14, 262.

65 L. Cambiaso (died 1585). Orpheus (?). Drawing. Florence, Uffizi. *Mostra strumenti musicali* 35 no 23; Winternitz *Musical Instruments* 45 identifies it with Apollo. (figure 22)

66 F. Salviati (died 1563). Orpheus. Drawing. Florence, Uffizi no 1092. L. Parigi *I disegni musicali del Gabinetto degli Uffizi*, Florence 1951, no 1011. (figure 23)

67 G. Stradano (died 1605) (also recently attributed to S. Scorza). Orpheus. Drawing. Florence, Uffizi. Parigi *I disegni musicali* no 1099. (figure 24)

68–69 G. Vasari (died 1574). Orpheus. Two drawings. Florence. Uffizi no 2722; and Biblioteca Nazionale. Parigi *I disegni musicali* nos 1171 and 1370.

70 Anonymous Venetian. Orpheus and the animals. Engraving, 1558. Florence, Uffizi, volume 10169. (figure 25)

71 Francesco Bassano (died 1592). Orpheus. Painting. Rome, Galleria Doria no 125. (figure 26)

72 Francesco Bassano. Orpheus. Drawing. Florence, Uffizi. Parigi *I disegni musicali* no 99. (figure 27)

73 B. Bandinelli (died 1560). Orpheus (lost statue; known from a drawing by Cherubino Alberti in Florence, Uffizi no 93695 c 21). Parigi *I disegni musicali* 5f; Winternitz *Musical Instruments* 27.

74 Primaticcio. Orpheus. Fresco, c1570. Fontainebleau, Galerie d'Ulysse (lost). L. Dimier *Le Primatice*, Paris 1900, 299; Reinach *Essai* 148.

75 Nicolò dell' Abate. Aristaeus and Eurydice. Painting, c1560–70. London, National Gallery.

76 A. Boscoli (died 1606). Death of Orpheus. Drawing. Naples, Museo di S. Martino. G. Scavizzi 'Su alcuni disegni delle raccolte pubbliche napoletane' *Bollettino d'Arte* 47 (1962) 76 figure 6.

77 Annibale Carracci. Orpheus and Eurydice. Fresco, c1600. Rome, Farnese Palace. (figure 28)

78 C. Stati. Orpheus playing before Pluto. Sculpture executed for Palazzo Corsi in Florence, c1600. New York, Metropolitan Museum.

79 Agostino Carracci. Orpheus and Eurydice. Engraving, prior to 1602. V. Casale and M. Calvesi *Le incisioni dei Carracci* Catalogue of the exhibition, Rome 1965, 41, no 135.

80 Anonymous. Stories of Orpheus. Frescos, c1600. Mantua, Palazzo Ducale, Camerino d'Orfeo. N. Giannantoni *Il Palazzo Ducale di Mantova*, Rome 1929, 83f.

ACKNOWLEDGMENTS

The author wishes to thank the following for permission to reproduce the works of art in their collections: the Trustees of the British Museum (figure 2); the Boymans–van Beuningen Museum in Rotterdam (figure 5); the Biblioteca Nazionale, Florence (figures 12–14). The author also wishes to thank the following agencies for providing photographs: Alinari, Florence (figures 1, 3, 7, 16); Soprintendenza alle Gallerie, Florence (figures 8, 11, 22–5, 27); Gabinetto Fotografico Nazionale, Rome (figures 17, 26, 28).

Orfeo and *Euridice*, the First Two Operas

INTEREST IN THE REDISCOVERY of ancient Greek culture was a common European preoccupation during the Renaissance. Musicians as well as all other humanists participated in the pursuit of antiquity, and therefore it should be no surprise that the first opera, a product of that investigation, should have as its subject matter a Greek myth.[1] The Orpheus legend was the subject not only of the first opera, but of the first three operas: *Euridice* by Jacopo Peri, 1600, on a libretto by Ottavio Rinuccini, *Euridice* by Giulio Caccini, 1600, on the identical libretto, and *Orfeo* by Claudio Monteverdi, 1607, on a libretto by Alessandro Striggio. The similarity among these works is more than the same subject matter; both the second and third operas depend heavily upon the first.

The second opera, that by Caccini, can be dismissed quickly. It was the result of a rivalry between Peri and Caccini. Jealous of Peri's work, Caccini rushed his own setting of Rinuccini's libretto into print, actually beating the publication of Peri's work by several months,[2] although Caccini's was not performed until a year after its printing.[3] Caccini's work is musically inferior to that of Peri, and substandard in comparison to his own works, such as the madrigals in his *Le nuove musiche* of 1602.[4] The libretto for both operas is the same in all but a few details, and both men followed the same compositional procedure. The only difference between the two works is one of quality; and therefore, since this essay will deal with similarity and difference in structure and compositional style, Caccini's opera will not be considered further.

The occasion for Peri's opera was the marriage of Maria de' Medici to King Henry IV of France in October 1600. *Euridice* was one of a number of festive presentations that took place on that occasion but was by no means the focal point of the festivities.[5] It was performed in the Pitti Palace on 6 October 1600, with limited scenery for a small audience in the private rooms of Don

Antonio de' Medici, brother of the bride,[6] and was overshadowed by the more elaborate production of *Il Rapimento di Cefalo* by Caccini on a text by Gabriello Chiabrera, which was presented in the much larger great hall of the Uffizi Palace three days later. There is, however, reason to believe that, in spite of its humble setting, *Euridice* was quite successful. It was repeated for several years and was selected, rather than *Cefalo*, to be printed immediately after its initial appearance and again in 1608 (a fact that must have added fuel to Caccini's jealous fire).

There is no record that Claudio Monteverdi or Alessandro Striggio saw the first production of *Euridice*. Dignitaries from many locations were present at the wedding and among them must have been Vincenzo Gonzaga, duke of Mantua and employer of both Monteverdi and Striggio. (Monteverdi was attached to the Mantuan court as court musician and had been one of the musicians accompanying the duke on other occasions such as the 1595 campaign against the Turks and the trip to Flanders in 1599. Striggio was the duke's chancellor). In any case, as the following comparison will attest, both Monteverdi and Striggio were familiar with the work of Peri and Rinuccini and must have had access to a copy of the printed score. In 1607 they produced *Orfeo* in Mantua for a celebration at the Accademia degli Invaghiti during carnival time. The production was an unqualified success and was repeated a number of times afterwards.[7]

Having chosen the Orpheus legend, librettists Rinuccini and Striggio were both faced with the same plot problem: the occasions for the operas were both joyful, but the traditional form of the legend has a tragic ending. The version of the Orpheus legend known in Florence and Mantua throughout the Renaissance was the 1480 play by Angelo Poliziano which ends with the Bacchants slaying Orpheus.[8] The librettists were obliged to alter the ending, therefore, in order to present a love story suitable for the happy occasions. Consistent with the symbolism, it is reasonable to conclude that reason for the selection of the title *Euridice* for the Medici occasion, rather than Poliziano's *Festa d'Orfeo*, or perhaps *Orfeo ed Euridice*, was the desire of the Florentine artists to honour the Medici member of the wedding: Euridice was Maria de' Medici. (The groom, Henry IV, did not attend the wedding ceremony in Florence but met his bride in Lyon on 17 December for the official church wedding.) The reason for the choice of the Orpheus legend for the Mantuan celebration of 1607 is not clear, for there is no known relationship, symbolic or otherwise, between the subject matter of the text and the occasion of its first performance. It may well be, as Schrade has suggested, that the story had been a favourite of Mantuans since Poliziano's presentation, and also that Striggio and Monteverdi wished to try their hand at the already existing opera topic.[9]

Striggio and Rinuccini each solved the problem of the ending differently. Rinuccini merely omitted the condition traditionally placed upon Orpheus: that he should not look back at Euridice while leaving the underworld. Thus, in the new version, once he is permitted to retrieve Euridice, nothing stands in the way of their happiness. Striggio rejected this simple solution, retained the traditional condition, and created a somewhat more complicated ending: Orpheus loses Euridice a second time and the happy ending is provided by the intervention of Apollo who takes Orpheus to join Euridice in heaven.[10]

Rinuccini probably used Poliziano's play as his source, for the bare outlines of the literary work may be found in his libretto. Rinuccini kept the idea of a prologue but changed Poliziano's Mercury into a personification of Tragedy, thus introducing more of a dramatic element to the opening statement of the drama. He also saw fit to tidy up the incident leading towards Euridice's death. In Poliziano's play she is bitten by a snake while fleeing from the amorous advances of Aristaeus. Rinuccini has her killed by a snake while she is picking flowers. Otherwise, the general outline up to and including Orpheus' confrontation with Pluto is kept fairly close to Poliziano's model. With the ending changed, Rinuccini's libretto moves quickly from the confrontation to the happy ending. Once Pluto has been convinced to change his mind, the scene changes to a sustained praise of happiness and love by all characters – not surprising considering the purpose and the occasion of the opera.

Aside from the difference in the endings, Striggio's libretto is structured very much like that of Rinuccini. There are no lines of text common to the two plays, but the assignment of lines to characters, the sequence of elements, and the emphasis on certain scenes all suggest that, from the beginning up to the confrontation scene (scene 3), Striggio used Rinuccini's play as his model. The elements taken from Poliziano are common to both libretti.

In Striggio's libretto, a prologue is kept but, again, the character delivering the message is changed. Where Rinuccini chooses the personification of Tragedy to open the opera, Striggio chooses Music. The change is a small one; both characters are able to enter into the story emotionally and remind the audience that they have the power to change events. Striggio follows Rinuccini's model further by writing the prologue in rhyme: four-line stanzas with end rhyme ABBA.

Additional correspondence between the two librettos may be seen in their use of chorus (totally absent in the Poliziano play). Both librettists choose approximately the same dramatic moments for the chorus, and in both works its function is to comment on the action.

In general, throughout the first two acts, Striggio assigns similar kinds of lines in similar quantities to the same characters as does Rinuccini. Perhaps the most noticeable similarity is in the scene in which Euridice's death is announced to Orpheus. In both operas the scene begins with a reflection on happiness by Orpheus' entourage; the joyful moment is interrupted by a messenger. In Rinuccini's play the messenger announces that she brings sad news. Rather than announce it directly, as in the Poliziano play, the messenger must be coaxed by Orpheus and Arcetrus. Finally, she relates the unhappy death of Euridice in an extended monologue. Arcetrus replies first, and then Orpheus sings a lament 'I neither weep nor sigh' (see example 2). Striggio organized his scene in a strikingly similar way. The scene of happy shepherds with Orpheus is identical, as is the entrance of the messenger who announces that she bears bad news. Again there is a long exchange with various shepherds attempting to elicit the information from the messenger. Orpheus coaxes, and finally she tells. At that point, Striggio departs from Rinuccini's model. Instead of having the messenger deliver her sad tidings at the end of her monologue, he has her first state 'your beloved bride is dead' to which Orpheus reacts immediately with one word, 'alas.' The messenger then relates the story in an extended monologue, to which the shepherds react and Orpheus sings his lament 'You are dead and I live' (see example 3).

The similarities are too great to be accidental. Striggio improves on the drama of the earlier libretto by having Orpheus informed of the death before the monologue of the messenger, allowing him to utter the poignant 'alas' and then to fall into shock for the duration of the messenger's monologue – a minor change but a major dramatic improvement.

The confrontation scene in *Orfeo* also shows the dependence of Striggio upon Rinuccini's model. In both operas the scene is begun by a spirit who escorts Orpheus to the gates of Hell (there is no escort in Poliziano). Rinuccini chooses Venus, goddess of love – a choice quite in keeping with the occasion of the opera. Striggio, however, decides on 'Speranza,' Hope personified, which fits the drama better (although in an amusing lapse of taste he compromises the serious dramatic impact of the scene by having Hope leave Orpheus at the sign 'Abandon Hope all you who enter here').

In the confrontation scene Orpheus must persuade Pluto to allow him to descend into the underworld and bring back Euridice. Rinuccini structures his scene similarly to that of Poliziano: after several exchanges between Orpheus and Pluto, Proserpina is moved by the plea and convinces Pluto to relax his law. Striggio changes the scene to a confrontation with Charon, guardian and boatman of the river Styx. Proserpina again intercedes in Orpheus' favour, but the confrontation for Orpheus is with Charon, and it is at that point that the prophecy of Music in the Prologue is actually realized:

> I am Music who, with sweet accents
> can calm all troubled hearts
> and with noble anger or with love
> can inflame the most frozen minds.[11]

Charon is charmed and convinced by Orpheus' song, and thus the drama is much tighter in terms of action, reaction, and motivation.

After the confrontation the two operas differ in their plot resolutions and therefore the resemblance ends. For the final scene both operas conform to the general custom of the time in which festivities and presentations ended with chorus and dancing. From the third to the fifth and final act there is no scene-for-scene correspondence between the two librettos because of the change in story, but Striggio maintains the basic scene construction used by Rinuccini in *Euridice* (and in his previous work with Peri, the *Dafne* of 1594): the scenes are composed of some strophic verse, some freely alternating seven- and eleven-syllable lines, and choral endings.

There is little doubt that Striggio used Rinuccini's libretto as a model for his own, just as Rinuccini had used Poliziano as his basic source. Each man in turn depended on the writer before him for the basic scene divisions and flow of the drama. Rinuccini adapted a century-old drama for a setting in the new monodic musical style.[12] Striggio was imitating a recent success, undoubtedly showing his ability with the same material. An investigation of the music for the two operas discloses a similar dependence of Monteverdi on the music by Peri.

The association of music and drama was not new to the late sixteenth century; the tradition dates from the liturgical dramas of the ninth century. Music had always been associated with festive occasions, and in Florence, from the early decades of the sixteenth century, accounts exist of entertainments known as *intermedii* which combined music and dance during intermissions of spoken drama.[13] The musical style of the Renaissance, however, impeded the development of a real union of music and drama until later in the century. The polyphonic style – the interweaving of several voices to achieve a total melodic-harmonic fabric – did not lend itself to furthering the development of music dramas. Changes in musical style were necessary before opera could come about.

Example 1   Excerpt from *Zefiro torna* by Luca Marenzio

Renaissance music was for performance by several voices, as may be seen in example 1. The most popular vocal form of the sixteenth century was the madrigal, a form written phrase by phrase to express the text. Two basic styles of writing can be found in the madrigal (and in most of the other forms of the time), the imitative style, as seen in measures 1 to 7 of the example, and the homophonic style, in measures 8 to 12. In the imitative passages the voices enter one at a time with the same melodic phrase, and the listener hears the texture grow thicker and more complex, both melodically and rhythmically, with each succeeding voice. In the homophonic sections all voices declaim the text simultaneously with similar rhythmic patterns, and the result is a single, united impression furnished by the entire ensemble. The two techniques were used side by side in an attempt to represent the text.

Madrigals were sung as parts of various entertainments such as the *intermedii* described above. Although most madrigals were individual works, occasionally several were written on a common subject or were linked together to tell a story (as in Orazio Vecchi's *L'Amfiparnaso* of 1597). There were, however, at least two features of the madrigal that made it unacceptable for musical drama (or opera as we know it): the imitative technique and the multi-voiced presentation. Thus, in measures 1 and 2 of example 1, as each voice enters it sings the text from the beginning, resulting in the simultaneous declamation of different words and an obscuring of the text. This would not be a problem in the homophonic sections, but even then a madrigal is not an ideal form for dramatic presentation. When four singers sing 'I love you' as part of a dialogue, the audience receives the correct message, but the delivery by several people is quite impersonal, and a group cannot act out its emotions effectively. To sing only one voice part of a madrigal yields only a partial solution, and a rather unacceptable one at that. Although the solo singer could act the part, and the sentiments would be personal, the madrigal style was still a multi-voiced composition and the singer's part includes only one portion of the musical interest. The remainder of the musical line would be included in the parts played by the accompanying instruments, which would direct much of the attention away from the soloist. The madrigal obviously would not serve. Another style was needed which would give particular emphasis to a single vocal line and reduce the role of the instruments to accompaniment only.

To the modern reader the solution seems simple: accompanied solo song. This is also the conclusion reached by the composers in the late sixteenth century, but, without pre-existing models to guide them, they had to experiment with various ideas before settling on the new style.

The new style of accompanied solo song was developed in several centres of Europe during the last two decades of the sixteenth century. In Florence it was an outcome of investigations into early Greek music by a group of writers, philosophers, poets, and musicians who met at the home of Count Giovanni Bardi from 1576 to 1581.[14] Their efforts were aimed at discovering the Greek tradition, and their researches resulted in the new style of solo song, which consisted of focusing all melodic interest in a single vocal line which is shaped according to the dictates of the text, and which is accompanied by a part which serves only to support that melodic line. It was the solo song, written for performance by a single voice to the accompaniment of a continuo (harpsichord, organ, lute, etc), that allowed the full union of music and drama, and it is upon the solo song that opera depends as its major vehicle.

The new solo song differed from the earlier madrigals in several important ways – or at least attempted to. For one, it aimed at expressing the basic sentiment of the text. This was in contrast to the current madrigal practice of musically describing only the individual word or phrase. (An example of the word-painting technique can be seen in example 1, measures 1 to 5, where the word *fiorir*, or 'flowering,' is portrayed musically as a flowery melodic figure.) Another excess frowned upon by the Camerata was the practice of ornamentation by division, that is, the addition of rapid vocal ornaments to fill in much of the melodic line. Caccini criticized these and other practices in his foreword to *Le nuove musiche*,[15] in which he also claimed credit for invention and development of the new song style. Borrowing a phrase from a treatise written by another Camerata member, he referred to the older practices as merely 'tickling the ears.'[16] He instead calls for greater concern with the 'conceit and the humour of the words.'[17]

If we set aside the bragging, the academic justifications, and the claims for historical precedent on the part of those who claimed its invention, it is clear that the new style of solo song was characterized by a new concern for the text. The composer showed this concern by writing solo rather than ensemble music, and by shaping the musical phrase to the textual phrase – another correction called for by Caccini: '... the old way of composition, whose music, not suffering the words to be understood by the hearers, ruins the conceit and the verse, now lengthening and now shortening the syllables to match the descant, a laceration of the poetry ...'[18] Caccini was also concerned about the placement of vocal ornaments so that they would express but not obscure the text. In actual practice, the last-named reform, that of not obscuring or interrupting textual meaning with ornaments, was only partly achieved, as may be seen in Caccini's own madrigals in *Le nuove musiche*, and in those of other composers of the era.

The new style of composition developed by members of the Camerata is quite different not only from that which preceded it, but also from the solo style that evolved later. Whereas in later opera and solo song the emphasis is upon a melody which is repeated several times, thereby giving a sense of unity to the song, in the early Florentine monodic passages that aspect is largely missing. The vocal lines are formed to the text and, since there is no repetition in the text, there is little repetition in the melody. Melody, too, has a different meaning in the Florentine style. The music is so completely wedded to the text that all aspects of the music are determined by the text: rhythm, rise and fall of the line, and even the placement of the harmonies. Rhythms are selected to portray closely the rhythm of speech, and both the melodic shape and harmonic consonance/dissonance are intended to emphasize the words.

From the operas of the eighteenth and nineteenth centuries we have become accustomed to separation of material into aria and recitative, the aria for the melodic emotional reflections on the plot, and the rapid-fire, non-melodic recitative for plot development. There was no such separation of solo material in early opera. Plot and reflection were set in much the same manner. That is not to say that there is no variety of writing in the early operas; besides the sections where text lines of irregular length are set in continuous melodic flow, *Euridice* has several instances of strophic lines which are set musically in strophes. For real contrast, the chorus sections are set not in the monodic style, but in the older Renaissance dance-related rhythms and phrase lengths. There are also more subtle differences in the approach of both Peri and Monteverdi to the setting of different kinds of texts, some of which will be mentioned below.

Peri expressed his intentions clearly in his foreword to *Euridice*:

Seeing that dramatic poetry was concerned and that it was therefore necessary to imitate speech in song ... I judged that the ancient Greeks and Romans ... had used a harmony surpassing that of ordinary speech but falling so far below the melody of song as to take an intermediate form ... For this reason, discarding every other manner of singing hitherto heard, I devoted myself wholly to seeking out the kind of imitation necessary for these poems ... I knew likewise that in our speech some words are so intoned that harmony can be based upon them and that in the course of speaking it passes through many others that are not so intoned until it returns to another that will bear a progression to a fresh consonance. And having in mind those inflections and accents that serve us in our grief, in our joy, and in similar states, I caused the bass to move in time to these, either more or less, following the passions, and I held it firm throughout the false and true proportions until, running through various notes, the voice of the speaker came to a word that, being intoned in familiar speech, opened the way to a fresh harmony.[19]

We may see in example 2 how Peri put his theory into practice in his setting of Orpheus' lament. In his foreword, Peri spoke of basing harmony on some notes and allowing certain others to pass. That is, he intended to fit only certain words into the harmony and leave others outside of the chord. In measure 2 he has set the first two and the last melody notes to fit the harmony, while the notes for *e non* are foreign to the chord. In measure 5 he even begins the melodic phrase on a repeated non-harmonic pitch, and thereby allows the

Example 2   Orpheus' lament from *Euridice* (numbers and signs over the bass line refer to the chords the accompanist is to fill in)

dissonance to persist for the full measure. This melodic style he believed to be used by the Greeks and Romans, an intermediate form which surpassed mere speech but was not yet song.

The rhythm, duration, and pitch selected for each syllable were guided by the dramatic intensity and importance of the word and by the natural inflection of speech. Both *piango* (measure 2) and *spiro* (measure 3) are placed in positions to allow their natural accent to coincide with the metric accent of the music. The first syllable of *sospiro* is set as a short note just prior to the accented beat of the measure and placed on a high note – all in imitation of natural speech patterns. There is, of course, more to this than merely a setting of speech inflection. As Peri intended, it surpasses ordinary speech. For exclamations such as *ohime* (measure 10), a short melodic phrase serves as a musical interpretation of the drama contained within the word itself.

One aspect of this kind of writing which Peri does not mention in his foreword but which is none the less important, concerns the nature of the accompanying line. Peri has chosen to accompany the melodic line with a spare use of accompanying chords which leads to an expressive delivery of the text-oriented melody. The bass notes have no set rhythm pattern of their own, unlike the regular rhythmic accompaniment used by other composers of the same era. A single chord often lasts for as long as a full measure or more without change – a feature which allows the performer a flexibility in delivery which would not be available if the bass line had its own rhythmic structure. This type of bass line may well have been Peri's invention.[20] In this first opera Peri applied his theory and set the example.

If we look now at Monteverdi's setting of Orpheus' lament (example 3), the similarities are obvious. The use of non-harmonic notes can be found in measure 7 where the phrase begins on a dissonance and does not move to a harmonically compatible note until half-way through the measure. As Palisca has pointed out, Monteverdi has derived his style from Peri.[21] The differences in the settings are due mainly to the differences in the poetry. Striggio used blank verse which allowed Monteverdi to ignore the line endings with ease, whereas Rinuccini rhymed his verse. The similarity between the two laments goes even so far as the dramatic juxtaposition of the same two contrasting chords to underline unhappiness: in Peri's lament the chords, E major and G minor, are found in measures 9 and 10. Monteverdi uses the same chords in measures 3 and 4 for a similar purpose – the contrast of happy thoughts of Euridice with the realization of her death.[22]

The relationship between the two laments is the most extreme example of Monteverdi's dependence on Peri's setting. It is one example where Monteverdi changed very little from the Peri model. In other instances of borrowing Monteverdi did change what he borrowed, and in the next example, the Prologue, he improved on Peri's writing.

The Prologue to *Euridice* is sung by Tragedy, who, in seven stanzas, sets the stage for the drama. Peri set the text of the first stanza to music but left the underlay of the other six stanzas to the performer (see figure 1). (The notes at the end of the prologue, marked *ritornello*, indicate a short instrumental interlude played between stanzas). The text is not as emotional as that of the lament and therefore it is set in a straightforward manner, without the

Example 3   Orpheus' lament from *Orfeo*

extremes of the rhythm and melody patterns seen in example 2. Even then, the performer would have some difficulty fitting each of the text lines to the music in such a way that the natural flow and accent of the word is maintained from stanza to stanza. For example, line 2 in stanza 3 requires a pattern of accents quite opposed to that in the first stanza. Instead of

♩ ♩♩♩♩ᖴ ♪ ♪ ♩.♪ ♩♩

Spars' or di doglia hor di minaccie il volto

in stanza 1, the line in stanza 3 requires

♩.♪♩♩ ♩♩♩ ᖴ♩♩. ♪♩♩

Simulacri   funesti,   ombre   d'affanni

The performer, if conscientious, would probably have rearranged the rhythm pattern, but he would also need some guidance from the composer if the melodic line were to closely follow the text.

In the strophic form a close relationship between music and text can be achieved for only one stanza, and this causes weaknesses in a style where that relationship is important. To avoid the problem, Monteverdi wrote out the setting of each stanza in his opera. The Prologue to *Orfeo* is sung by Music, and is written in five stanzas. Example 4 provides the settings of stanzas 2 and 3 in a format illustrating Monteverdi's improvement, a technique known as strophic variation. He retains the bass line and the harmonic sequence from stanza to stanza with very little change, while the rhythmic flow and pitch contour of the melody is adjusted from one stanza to the next to accommodate the needs of each individual line. The advantage of the strophic variation technique can be seen in measure 6. Monteverdi has decided to run together the third and fourth lines of verse 2 without stopping between 'Amore' and 'Posso,' whereas in verse 3 the lines are separated by a pause on the word 'sonora' and a break in the melodic line. By using strophic variation Monteverdi was able to retain the strophic nature of the setting, while also adhering to the principle of following the dictates of the individual lines of text.

He also used the technique of strophic variation for the musical highlight of *Orfeo*, the scene in Act Three in which Orpheus confronts Charon and proceeds to charm him with song. The text is set in the monodic style and the singer is accompanied by the usual instruments and also by pairs of melody instruments which insert elaborate instrumental passages during pauses in the melody (figure 2). Monteverdi included an ornamented version of the vocal

Example 4   Prologue to *Orfeo* (verses 2 and 3)

line in the printed score, and the vocal elaborations are even more lavish than those of the instruments. Together they make a rather spectacular impression.

The alternation of voice and instruments is known as *stile concertato*, which became a frequently used technique during the Baroque period. But the innovations do not end there. Monteverdi also added the element of change within what is otherwise a strophic aria. For the first four verses, while Orpheus states his case to Charon, the voice and instruments alternate with ornamented phrases in strophic variation. In the fifth verse Orpheus changes from demanding to pleading and the music changes with him. The fifth verse

PROLOGO
LA TRAGEDIA.

O che d'alti sospir vaga, e di pianti Spars'or di doglia
11. 10. 9.

hor di minaccie il volto Fei negl'ampi to atri al popol folto Scolorir di pietà volti, e sembian-

ti. Ritornello.
6
10. 11.

2
Non fangue fparfo d innocenti vette
Non ciglia fpente di Tiranno infano
Spettacolo infelice al guardo humano
Canto fu mefte, e lacrimofe fcene.

3
Lungi via lungi pur da regij tetti
Simulacri funefti, ombre d'affanni
Ecco i mefti coturni, e i fofchi panni
Cangio, e defto ne i cor piu dolci affetti

4
Hor s'auuerrà, che le cangiate forme
Non fenza alto ftupor la terra ammiri
Tal ch'ogni alma gentil ch'Apollo infpiri
Del mio nouo cammin calpefti l'orme

5
Voftro Regina fia cotanto alloro
Qual forfe anco nó colfe Atene, ò Roma
Fregio non vil fu Ionorata chioma
Fronda Febea fra due corone d oro

6
Tal per voi torno, e con fereno afpetto
Ne Reali Imenei m'adorno anch'io
E fù corde più liete il canto mio
Tempro al nobile cor dolce diletto

7
Mentre Senna Real prepara intanto
Alto diadema, onde il bel crin fi fregi
E i manti, e feggi de gl'antichi Regi
Del Tracio Orfeo date l'orecchie al câto.

Figure 1 Prologue from Peri's *Euridice* (1600)

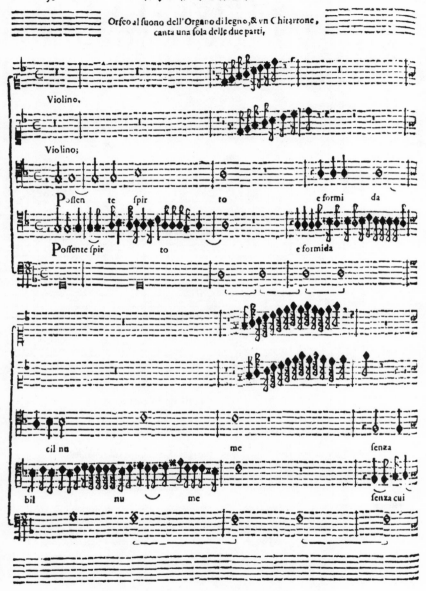

Figure 2   Monteverdi's *Orfeo* Act 3 (1615)

is set to a new bass line and chord pattern, and without the *concertato* instruments. In the sixth and final verse the strophic variation technique returns but with the melodic line accompanied by sustained chords in the strings. It is in this final verse that Orpheus refers to the sweet sound of his lyre and it is with this unornamented verse that Charon is charmed, in fulfilment of Music's prophecy in the Prologue. In this setting Monteverdi has added two new dimensions to the Florentine monodic style. He has introduced the idea of a rounded strophic form which includes a non-strophic verse within it, and he has included a consideration of instrumentation as a way of heightening the musical support of the text. Both ideas were used and expanded upon by the opera composers in the following centuries.

There is little doubt that Monteverdi used Peri's opera as a model for his own. The use of Florentine monody, especially the technique of sustained bass, and the similarity of the two laments give strong evidence that Monteverdi joined with his librettist in borrowing element from the earlier opera.

If Monteverdi and Striggio had been content merely to copy the earlier work, *Orfeo* would deserve little more than a footnote in history as an imitation of the first opera. In fact, neither man limited himself in that way, but used the basic format of the Peri-Rinuccini opera as a starting-point for his own creative ideas.

Both operas are still deserving of attention from an artistic point of view as well as a historic one. In terms of theatre, *Orfeo* is a more successful opera than *Euridice*. Striggio's libretto is more dramatic and Monteverdi's music contains imaginative changes to the basic monodic style as well as a more varied set of ingredients – more chorus sections and a number of instrumental interludes. *Orfeo* is an improvement over the earlier opera because Monteverdi and Striggio were able to see the flaws in their model and had the talent to improve on it.

Euridice and *Orfeo* began as attempts to re-create early Greek drama, and succeeded in beginning a new tradition of music drama that has lasted for nearly four hundred years. The style of opera writing has changed many times in those four centuries, but the basic ideal of the Florentines has remained: to represent the meaning of the text – what Peri describes as 'following the passions.'

NOTES

1 The involvement of musicians in Greek music and theory is related in D.P. Walker 'Musical humanism in the 16th and early 17th centuries' *The Music*

Review 2 (1941) 1, 111, 220, 288, and 3 (1942) 55; Claude Palisca 'Girolamo Mei, mentor to the Florentine Camerata' *Musical Quarterly* 40 (1954) 1–20; and Howard Mayer Brown 'Music – how opera began: an introduction to Jacopo Peri's *Euridice* (1600)' in *The Late Italian Renaissance* ed Eric Cochrane (New York 1970) 401–43.

2 Caccini's opera was printed in 1600, and Peri's in 1601, both by Georgio Marescotti in Florence. Some of the same initial blocks are used in both publications.

3 In December 1602, according to Nino Pirrotta 'Caccini' *Enciclopedia dello spettacolo* II (Rome 1954) 1447.

4 *Le nuove musiche de Guilio Caccini detto Romano* (Florence: Marescotti 1601 [1602])

5 This point is elaborated upon in Nino Pirrotta 'Early Opera and Aria' *New Looks at Italian Opera* ed William Austin (Ithaca, New York 1968) 39–107.

6 Ibid 39 and 40

7 Libretto published in Mantua by Francesco Osanna, 1607; score published in Venice by Ricciardo Amadino, 1609 and 1615.

8 Poliziano was one of the several artists shared by Florence and Mantua. For details concerning the date and the production see Nino Pirrotta *Li due Orfei da Poliziano a Monteverdi* (Turin 1969) 13–56.

9 Leo Schrade *Monteverdi, Creator of Modern Music* (New York 1950) 225

10 In the 1607 publication of the libretto the tragic ending is retained, but in the 1609 score the ending is changed to the scene with Apollo.

11   Io la Musica son, ch'ai dolci accenti
    So far tranquillo ogni turbato core,
    Ed or di nobil ira ed or d'amore
    Posso infiammar le più gelate menti.

12 Pirotta *Li due Orfei* 18–47; the Poliziano play is reported to have been sung as well, but no music has survived.

13 Discussed in detail in Howard Mayer Brown *Sixteenth-Century Instrumentation: The Music for the Florentine Intermedii* (American Institute of Musicology 1973), chapter VI

14 For additional information concerning the Camerata see Nino Pirrotta 'Temperaments and tendencies in the Florentine Camerata' *Musical Quarterly* 40 (1954) 169–89; Claude Palisca 'Girolamo Mei' and 'Musical asides in the diplomatic correspondence of Emilio de' Cavalieri' *Musical Quarterly* 49 (1963) 339–55.

15 English translation in Oliver Strunk *Source Readings in Music History* (New York 1950) III 17–32

16 A similar criticism was printed by Vincenzo Galilei *Dialogo della musica antica et*

moderna (Florence 1581). Portions in English translation in Strunk *Source Readings* II 112–32.

17 Caccini in Strunk *Source Readings* III 20
18 Ibid 18
19 English translation in Strunk *Source Readings* III 14
20 Brown 'Music – how opera began' 424
21 Claude Palisca *Baroque Music* (Englewood Cliffs NJ 1968) 39–45
22 Ibid 39

PEDRO LEÓN

Orpheus and the Devil in Calderón's
El divino Orfeo c 1634

C ALDERÓN DE LA BARCA wrote two short plays on the Orpheus theme. They represent a fascinating combination of a backward-looking medievalizing interpretation of the myth with an advanced and sophisticated reformulation of the traditional story. Here the allegory of Orpheus as the word of God, Eurydice as the bride of Christ, Aristaeus as the Devil, is given its final and fullest statement. In this essay I want to examine in particular Calderón's treatment of the Devil in these two *autos sacramentales*, especially in the earlier of the two. Here Aristaeus, who represents the Devil, is the dominant figure in the drama. His dominance might at first seem paradoxical. However, I believe that it can be explained in terms of the Pauline doctrine that God and the things of God appear to be weak but are really strong; and in terms of Calderón's understanding of Thomistic ideas about the nature and relative power of the Devil. The creation of a dramatically and poetically magnificent Devil shows the extent of the Devil's devices and the futility of such devices in the face of the final victory of God. This theological argument has allowed Calderón to 'go all out' in the play in his poetic depiction of the Devil.

But first I should try to explain what an *auto sacramental* is. It could be described as a short devotional play, 'sermon puesto en verso' (a poetic sermon) to use Calderón's own words.[1] It is dramatic poetry used to convey a theological dogma. Calderón wrote more than seventy *autos*, each taking a story and producing an allegorical representation of the Eucharist. The plots were drawn from philosophical and theological sources, mythological and Old Testament stories, historical and legendary subjects, and from parables and other biblical material. Among the mythological stories used by Calderón are those of Andromeda and Perseus, Jason and the Argonauts, Theseus in Crete, Cupid and Psyche, and Orpheus and Eurydice. Calderón saw the myths through Catholic dogma and adapted their content to suit his theological purpose, for Calderón was a conscientious theologian as well as a great poet.[2] Moreover, he was also a brilliant dramatist whose work is best understood in production. In his terms a ' "concepto imaginado" becomes a "práctico concepto" through a "medio visible" – an idea is "seen" as well as "heard." '[3] The ideas are better retained when seen dramatized on the stage and converted into images or 'phantasms,' for by continual association they permit reflection to take place. This 'theory of imagination' is, according to A.A. Parker, the basis for Calderón's dramatic technique.[4] The dramatic picture which Calderón has created on the stage is the 'visual illustration of the [objects] as they exist in the imagination,'[5] and these 'phantasms' are the driving force behind the dramatic experience. Since imagination is not bound by time and space, Calderón can thus overstep the limits of verisimilitude. Imagination can 'clothe its fancies in any way it pleases,'[6] and it can also accept 'the personification of abstractions.'[7] The boundaries of this imaginative drama based on theological ideas are only those of its ideology. The *autos* are therefore conceived within the imaginative limits of accepted metaphysical truth and consistency.[8] At the narrative level, the action of the *autos* is conveyed through the allegory. The allegory is the link between abstraction and objectivization. It is also the link between two different planes of reality: 'the visible reality of the stage' and the 'invisible reality' of which 'the stage action is only the representation or reflection.'[9]

There are, as has been mentioned, two versions of *El divino Orfeo*. The version dated 1663 was printed for the first time in 1677 in Madrid, and is included by Valbuena Prat in his chronological table.[10] The other version, officially undated, but which I have dated c1634, is also included by Valbuena Prat among those *autos* attributed to Calderón, and is presumed by Pablo Cabañas to have been written later than the 1663 version.[11] The c1634 version appeared for the first time in 1948 in an appendix to Cabañas's doctoral dissertation. It was later published in Valbuena Prat's edition of the *Obras Completas*.[12] Only the 1663 version, therefore, has been known until recent times in the major commentaries of the *autos* including that of A.A. Parker, who felt that it was theologically unsound.[13] It should be noted, however, that before Parker some critics had considered it an *auto* worthy of praise.[14] About the c1634 version we have only some rather general comments by Pablo Cabañas and J.M. de Osma, and some brief references by J. Páramo Pomareda.[15]

Both *autos* contain the basic elements of the myth, that is, the wooing of Eurydice by Aristaeus, her death from a snake-bite, and her rescue by Orpheus from Hades. Although the plots of both *autos* are fundamentally similar, the thematic emphasis, the tone, and the dramatic intent make them quite different from one another. The stage directions of the 1663 version are carefully, almost fastidiously, detailed. The various characters appear in well-defined, if somewhat mechanical, order. The theological message is conveyed in a system of statements, reiterated or commented upon by a character or a chorus, in which the outstanding rhetorical figure is repetition.[16] The directions in this version are detailed and complex, underscoring the sumptuous, decorative, pageant-like character of this *auto*.[17] The c1634 version, by contrast is eminently narrative. Stage directions are brief and simple, and the characters are given a greater role in developing the narrative thread.[18] This early version is written in a more 'natural' style, to which most of its audience would immediately respond. The 1663 version would likewise appeal in the first instance to a wide public on account of the complexity of its theatrical technique and of the decorative magnificence of its staging, but its sophisticated poetic conception would be best understood by an intellectual audience. The main theme in this version is the creative and redemptive power of God's voice and not that of the fidelity of Orpheus and Eurydice. The c1634 version is a narrative allegory, poetic and natural in tone, simply staged, conveying the descriptive and symbolic meaning of the myth in a deeper and different way.[19] What follows, for the convenience of the reader, is a summary of each *auto*.

Version of c1634 The play opens with Aristaeus stumbling on to the stage dressed as a courtly devil. Creation is about to begin. Orpheus appears, singing, and begins the creation of the world. Aristaeus comments on the creation of each day. After Orpheus creates Human Nature, Eurydice enters dressed as a peasant and accompanied by Love and Grace dressed as shepherds, and followed by Albedrío (Freewill), dressed as a yokel. Aristaeus expresses his intention to seduce Eurydice. She, meanwhile, comments on the creation, all the while eulogizing Orpheus. Orpheus replies to Eurydice in loving terms and invites her to his hut. Amor comments on the invitation by saying that in this way she will be free from the snakes hidden amidst the flowers. Eurydice adds that the apples are poisoned. Orpheus offers to point out to her the safe ones. Amor, Albedrío, and Gracia discuss free will in a humorous vein. They exit, and Aristaeus enters disguised as a courtly shepherd. Albedrío enters and discusses with Aristaeus the fall of Lucifer. Albedrío further explains that they are in Paradise, where Orpheus and Eurydice live in grace, and he proceeds to tell of Orpheus' ancestry. Aristaeus explains that he is a foreign shepherd who had the misfortune to be exiled. Albedrío, on learning his name, recognizes his true identity. Eurydice and Gracia enter. Albedrío, intent on mischief, introduces Aristaeus to her as a 'crazy man' with a talent for telling diverting stories. Eurydice feels disposed to hear Aristaeus. She observes, however, that in the measure in which he advances, Gracia retreats. Aristaeus begins by praising Eurydice's beauty and by expressing his love for her. Encouraged by her, he then tells his story in a long and detailed narrative which occupies about a fourth of the play's total length. In his story, Aristaeus says that he was a great prince, who knew the king's secrets. The king took him into his confidence and showed him a sketch of his wife, which made him desire her at once. Jealous, he began to speak ill of her to the king, to say that she was of ignoble blood, and finally he led a rebellion against the king. However, the king defeated him and caused him to flee. Emboldened, he now speaks ill of Orpheus, saying that he can captivate Human Nature but cannot give Eurydice anything extraordinary. He contrasts the simple, rude offerings of Orpheus, 'wheat, honey and milk,' with those he can give her, 'gold, silver, pearls and power.' On hearing Aristaeus, Eurydice rejects him because he has attacked her deity. She withdraws with Gracia. Aristaeus hides in a tree where the serpent is. Meanwhile a struggle ensues between Gracia and Albedrío, the former trying to protect, the latter helping to tempt Eurydice. After being bitten by Aristaeus-serpent, Eurydice reasons that it is Albedrío's fault and laments her loss of grace. Orpheus enters and asks Gracia where his wife is. He laments his loss. Amor bids him rescue her using a harp fashioned like a cross. Orpheus then meets Charon. Charon, moved by Orpheus' song, passes him a cross. Aristaeus appears in the Underworld and describes in sombre tones his domain to Eurydice. An earthquake announces Orpheus' entry into the Underworld. Everything is upset by his visit. Orpheus then appears on the cross. He sings and asks Pluto (Aristaeus) to give him back Eurydice. Pluto refuses, and Orpheus frees her with his song. Pluto warns him that if he turns his head she will return to him. Orpheus explains to Eurydice that he will always be before her in the host and in the Chalice. The *auto* ends with Aristaeus entering the mouth of the serpent and sinking into Hell.

Version of 1663 The *auto* begins with the Prince of Darkness who is seen on a *carro* (scenic device) in the shape of a ship, painted black, with black sails and flags and a coat of arms emblazoned with snakes. He is accompanied by Envy. He expresses his intention to seduce Human Nature. An instrument or a voice is heard. Orpheus appears in an elaborate *carro*, a celestial globe with stars, planets, and signs of the Zodiac. As soon as Orpheus starts his song, a third allegorical *carro* opens, with the seven days seemingly asleep, and in their midst appears Human Nature.

Creation begins with Orpheus, the God Creator, addressing the void and commanding each day to be born. The Prince of Darkness and Envy occasionally comment or express admiration. Human Nature then awakens. Orpheus calls her and mentions their betrothal and soon after exits inside the celestial globe. Human

Nature follows him inside the third *carro*. The Prince of Darkness then speaks of his love for the queen, whose portrait Envy showed him. His desire for her led him to rebel against the king, but he was defeated and had to flee. He asks Envy and later Lethe to help him to seduce Human Nature. He will enter the world disguised. The Days and Pleasure then sing, eulogizing the work of the Lord. Orpheus appears between Orpheus and Human Nature, witnessed by the Days, Pleasure, and the musicians, who repeatedly praise the glory of the Lord. Orpheus and Human Nature exit. Pleasure is left alone on the stage. The Prince of Darkness and Envy enter and immediately attempt to gain Pleasure's help to achieve their designs. Pleasure narrates a *fábula* about Orpheus and Eurydice which is designed to mislead the Prince of Darkness. He, however, is not misled, and instead explains the differences between the pagan story and the theological truth. Human Nature then enters accompanied by the Days and the musicians. The Prince of Darkness, with Envy echoing his words, tempts Human Nature. She succumbs and then laments her disgrace. The Days comment on Human Nature's fall. Bitten by the snake, Human Nature falls into the Prince of Darkness's arms, and later is taken away by Lethe. Orpheus enters, and the Days make repeated references to Human Nature's fall. Her redemption is anticipated in similar fashion. Orpheus appears once more carrying a harp on his shoulder. The harp's handle is shaped like a cross. Orpheus says that he will have to go through Calvary to reach his wife. He then calls Lethe, who refuses to let him cross alive. Lethe appears to wound Orpheus and both presumably die. (This is not altogether clear in the play.) Orpheus then rises and, on entering Hades, causes an earthquake. The Days comment in amazement. Orpheus asks the Prince of Darkness to free his wife, and when he refuses, Orpheus sings and redeems Human Nature. The *auto* ends with the Days singing praises of the Sacraments and of the Catholic Church.

Let us now examine Calderón's treatment of the myth in the version of c1634. As can be seen in the résumé of this version, we find here not only the story of Aristaeus, Orpheus, and Eurydice, but also the biblical stories of the creation of the world, the fall of man, and his redemption. The characters personify, in varying degrees of complexity, the concept or entity they represent on the stage. This allegorizing is, however, more than a mere visualization of an abstraction, for instance, Albedrío as free will. Rather it is usually a characterization which takes its initial outline from a source or sources and transforms it to suit Calderón's purpose. Thus, Albedrío who is the personification of free will also plays the part of the clown or *gracioso* in Calderón's secular drama.[20] The main characters in the story, Aristaeus, Orpheus, and Eurydice, have been transformed, and of their mythological personae we have but a narrative reminiscence.

This is understandable, given Calderón's intention to use them allegorically. Poetically and dramatically, *El divino Orfeo* c1634 is not so much the story of Orpheus and Eurydice as the story of Aristaeus the prince, the *privado* and the lover.[21] For although the play starts with the creation of the world, our attention is soon diverted to the quest of Aristaeus: the seduction of Eurydice. Orpheus' descent into Hades, after a brief, mournful dialogue with Amor, and his rescuing of Eurydice are, poetically and dramatically, considerably less striking than the story of Aristaeus. Correspondingly, his characterization is more complex and powerful than that of Orpheus. In mythical antiquity, he was the shepherd keeper of bees, of whom Virgil tells in the fourth *Georgic*. He appears there as an earnest youth who does not understand that he has caused great sorrow and who is 'startled' by Proteus' revelations.[22] In the medieval allegorizing tradition, Aristaeus 'stand for virtue, for *ares* is excellence.'[23] He is also the passionate lover, whose intensity of feeling is eloquently captured by Angelo Poliziano:

> Ier vidi sotto quello ombroso speco
> una ninfa più bella che Diana
> ch'un giovane amadore avea seco.
>   Com'io vidi sua vista più che umana
> subito mi si scosse el cor nel petto
> e mia mente d'amor divenne insana;
>   tal ch'io non sento, Mopso, più diletto,
> ma sempre piango, e 'l cibo non mi piace,
> e sanza mai dormir son stato in letto.

(Yesterday I saw beneath yon shady cave a Nymph more fair than Diana. With her was a youth, her lover, and as I gazed on her – more fair than mortal – of a sudden the heart in my breast so leapt and my mind so with love was torn that, Mopsus, I no longer know delight but ever weep. I crave not food and ever sleepless on my bed I lie.)[24]

Little survives of the mythical keeper of bees, however. Calderón's characterization of Aristaeus in *El divino Orfeo* c1634 is quite different from any other characterization known of him. Unlike the timid shepherd who unwittingly upsets Orpheus, in Virgil's story, Aristaeus is here the dominant dramatic figure who actively seeks to undermine the power of Orpheus. The earnest young lover is transformed by Calderón into an accomplished seducer; the startled youth is changed into the clever, scheming, and tragic rebel.

The characterization of Aristaeus in the c1634 version is achieved by the description of physical details in the stage directions and by comments from other characters, and it is defined through action, and even by the images and the metres he uses.[25] Aristaeus is a prince disguised as a shepherd, whose presence is impressive enough to move Eurydice to say: '... your appearance and your sheepskin jacket suggest that you are the overseer of a wealthy property.' She says, further, that he is well-mannered and courteous. He speaks eloquently in a rich, allusive language. His first words on the stage are uttered in *silvas*, an Italianate verse form. He uses *silvas* in other passages, and also the *octava real* (the Italian *ottava rima*). Thus, the Italianate forms used almost exclusively by Aristaeus provide a linguistic portrait of him which complements the physical description. Orpheus, however, is described as a shepherd, and he usually speaks in Spanish ballad metre. The down-to-earth character of this verse form reveals Calderón's intention to conceive Orpheus as a 'popular' figure, whose true, simple, unvarnished style contrasts with the ornate, 'foreign,' courtly speech of Aristaeus. For example, on learning of Eurydice's death, Orpheus laments:

> Anegue el llanto
> de los tristes ojos míos
> todos los campos presentes
> siendo los ojos dos fuentes
> de fuentes haré los ríos
> los ríos profundos mares
> los mares, montes de yelo
> porque en dilubios del cielo
> aneguen tantos pesares. (1806b)[26]

(May the tears that flow from my grieving eyes flood the fields that lie before me. Twin fountains are my eyes, and from those fountains I shall make rivers, and from the rivers deep oceans, and from the oceans mountains of ice, so that this grief may be drowned beneath a deluge from Heaven.)

The simplicity of this lament, both in thought and in language, contrasts with the baroque complexity of Aristaeus' rhetorical invocation to the mountains included below, and with the long, eloquent narrative in which he tells of his rebellion. His thoughts and his language are those of a courtier. Compare the following examples:

ARISTEO
Altos montes, que al cielo

gigantes de esmeralda alzais con saña
essa ar[r]ugada frente.
ajando el azul velo
que en la nevada espalda
asegura su fabrica eminente
donde la transparente
selva, que en luzes bellas
al sol causa desmayos.
y equibocando rayos
de flores y de estrellas
tanta noticia pierde
que al fin es monte azul o cielo verde.

(ARISTAEUS Mighty mountains, giants of emerald, lifting your rugged brows in anger and crumpling the azure veil, that pins upon your snowy shoulder the forest like a towering edifice; and the forest transparent makes the sun faint away in pools of light so that it cannot tell the rays of the stars from the rays of the flowers, and in the end it is a mountain of azure and a sky of green.)

Yo, bellísima pastora
cuyo blanco pie produze
a su contacto de nieve
flores moradas y azules
soy (aunque rústico trage
mi noble persona encubre)
por alta Naturaleza
Prínzipe altivo y ilustre.

(O beautiful shepherdess, whose white foot as it falls like a snowflake brings forth flowers sky-blue and purple, I am a prince (though my noble personage lies concealed beneath this rustic garb), a prince by lofty nature proud and glorious.)

Eurydice is so taken by Aristaeus' first loving speech, in which he praises her in subtle superlatives, that she scolds Gracia for being so timorous, and ends by saying: '... que el Pastor que ves discreto y gallardo es' (this shepherd is well mannered and courteous). In contrast with Aristaeus, the prince dethroned, well mannered and polite, Orpheus appears in a relatively secondary role. Indeed, Aristaeus occupies the dramatic foreground through most of the play. Orpheus remains in the background except for brief appearances in the beginning and in the last quarter of the *auto*. The naturalness of his speech and the apparent simplicity of his behaviour mask, however, a forceful, almost authoritarian attitude. Since he represents God the creator, Orpheus commands the creation of the world, and his use of the imperative is in agreement with the tone of the biblical text of Genesis. But, in his attitude towards Eurydice, his authority rather than his tenderness and love is most evident. Orpheus is here very much the master. His invitation, 'Ven, esposa, a mi cabaña para que todos te sirvan' (Come my wife to my lodging so that all may serve you), is somewhat detached and later, after Eurydice's loving, humble eulogy, Orpheus still remains somewhat distant:

> Tanto esposa, me enamoras
> quando tu hermosura humillas
> que con mi amor, y mi grazia
> has de tener companía. (1822b)

(You have made me love you so much, my wife, with your beauty made humble, that I shall give you my Love and my Grace to be your companions.)

He adds, however, in more tender, intimate terms:

> Sube, a mi cavaña, en ella,
> con las sombras te combida
> la siesta; para el rigor,
> del sol, dulze esposa mía
> en mis brazos. (1822b)

(Come now to my dwelling, my sweet wife; it is the time for rest, and the cool shade invites you. Let my arms protect you from the sun's fierce heat.)

His tone is however once more authoritarian when he tells Eurydice how to distinguish the poisoned from the good apples:

> Por esso Euridize mía
> Ilega sólo a la que yo
> te señalare, y permita;
> sígueme esposa. (1822b)

(I will show you which you may pick, Eurydice my wife; now follow me.)

There is in the characterization of Orpheus an intentional lack of stress on individualizing physical details. The 'courtly shepherd,' called later 'el más gallardo Pastor' (the most gallant of shepherds), is better known for the power and beauty of his voice. He is an orator, a 'divine musician,' and an 'instrumento templado' a tuned instrument).[27] His voice, identifying him metonymically, and all the other epithets used to eulogize him, succeed only in making an abstraction of him, a virtue or a mystery to be suitably conjoined with the mystery of the Eucharist. Fittingly, Eurydice says:

> Luego, Pastor, y Poeta,
> Músico, orador y lira
> heres, en grande misterio
> de todos ellos la enigma. (1822a)

(So you are shepherd and poet, musician, orator, and lyre – a blend of all, mysterious, unfathomable.)

Amor, at the end of the play, further emphasizes the enigmatic role of Orpheus and of his instrument when he explains:

> El instrumento que ves
> que al Abismo a de dar luz
> por aquesta parte es cruz
> y ataúd por esta es. (1831a)

(This is the instrument that will bring light to the abyss. Look on it. At one end there is a cross, and on the other a coffin.

Orpheus the singer is now Orpheus the Redeemer, who, with his *arpa-cruz*, will save Eurydice-Humanity from damnation. Orpheus represents, in fact, all the manifestations of God: creator, *logos*, and redeemer in 'grande misterio.' However, as a dramatic creation, Aristaeus reigns supreme in his earthiness in dealing with Albedrío, his cunning and in his Don Juanesque charm. Even at the end of the *auto*, although disconcerted by the power of Orpheus, he sets the conditions of Eurydice's freedom, in accord with the mythical story, and then exits in the grand style that fits his characterization: after calling the serpent a 'ferocious dragon' in appropriate hyperbole, he enters her mouth and disappears engulfed by flames!

Is Calderón unconsciously giving us a Lucifer larger than life?[28] Or is he trying to show us the extent of the Devil's power, of his inventiveness and deviousness, because he wants to instil in us a healthy respect for his capabilities? This is surely one of Calderón's aims. Perhaps he is also fascinated, like so many other great writers, by the energy and 'attractiveness' of the Devil. He is making the fall of Eurydice more plausible for us both theologically and dramatically. But Calderón tempers this fascination apparent or real with the Devil by means of an ironic undercurrent. Let us observe the manner in which Aristaeus first comes on stage. He enters 'falling from a rock,' in contrast with Orpheus who will later appear on high to sing his 'lowly' octosyllables. Aristaeus is accompanied by 'cajas destempladas y sordinas' (dissonant, distempered drums and muffled strings). Thus Aristaeus' entry colours his courtly utterances.

After this obvious device, Calderón uses a more subtle way to reinforce his point. He shows us that although the Devil appears heroic he is actually weak. Let us consider the text. Orpheus has begun the creation of the world. Aristaeus watches it with a mixture of admiration, envy, and perhaps scorn. He comments on the individual acts of creation, rephrasing Orpheus' words thus:

> ORFEO
> Háganse dos luminarias
> que eternamente enzendidas
> una presida a la Aurora
> y otra a la noche presida.
> ARISTEO
> ¡Qué dos lámparas tan bellas!   (1820b)

(ORPHEUS Let there be two great luminaries eternally aflame, one to watch over the dawn and the other to watch over the night.
ARISTAEUS Look at the two beautiful lamps hanging in the sky.)

> ORFEO
> y cruzen el viento, aves
> con música y armonía.
> ARISTEO
> Pájaros, y pezes ya
> las ondas y aire acuchillan.   (1821 a)

(ORPHEUS And let the winds be traversed by birds bringing music and harmony.
ARISTAEUS Look at the birds and fishes slicing through the waves and the air.)

Finally, Aristaeus comments on the completion of creation: 'et omne factum est ista.' Aristaeus appears to be genuinely admiring Orpheus' creation. Let us, however, isolate and compare certain words from the passages given above. Orpheus says *luminarias*, and Aristaeus echoes with *lámparas*; Orpheus commands 'cruzen ... aves,' and Aristaeus changes this to 'pájaros acuchillan.'[29] In every case we find a word which changes or attempts to refine or even redefine the word it replaces. A number of explanations could be found for this. It could be argued that Calderón is trying to show how Aristaeus attempts to diminish the value of creation, to 'upstage'

Orpheus, by substituting for Orpheus' words others which are on a lower stylistic level. For instance, both *luminarias* and *aves* are found in the Spanish text of Genesis, while *lámparas* and *pájaros* are not. This attempt would be in tune with Aristaeus' later effort to discredit Orpheus. It could also be maintained that Calderón was underscoring the futility of Aristaeus' attempt to tamper with the word of God.

This ironic undercurrent appears to run out, however, after the first one hundred lines of the play. From then on, Aristaeus appears to be drawn in heroic proportions. A.A. Parker discusses the portrayal of the Devil in Calderón in the *auto*, *El veneno y la triaca*, in these terms:

If we did not know what was behind the allegory, our sympathies would be entirely with the Devil. Purely on the level of poetic drama, that is to say, the Devil appears in a heroic light, as a faithful lover who has sacrificed everything for his beloved.[30]

We have shown, in note 11 and in the appendix, that *El veneno y la triaca* and *El divino Orfeo*, c1634 version, present virtually the same treatment of the Devil. Why should Calderón, a very orthodox Catholic, want to present us with a heroic Devil? Parker, echoing Valbuena Prat, argues that Calderón's portrayal of the Devil in both of these *autos* is an indication of his immaturity as a writer of allegorical drama and he adds:

The only thing that saves Calderón here from falling into Manichaeism is his failure to present his Evening Star as evil at all: the only sign of malice that he shows either in his account of his revolt or in his poisoning of the apple is, in terms of the allegory, nothing more than the jealousy of a lover fighting to win his beloved. The difficulty lies in the fact that if the Devil is to appear in person to woo Humanity, he must be made attractive to her and therefore to the audience.[31]

First, is it possible to say that Aristaeus is not evil at all? Second, is it admissible that the magnificent poetic creation which Calderón has achieved in the character of Aristaeus should be due solely to the fact that the Devil must be made attractive to woo Humanity? And, if so, how attractive? Is the extent of the poetic treatment not important in helping us to understand Calderón's attitude? For he was not only a good theologian, but also a great poet. And the poet in this double treatment of the heroic Devil (Aristaeus and Evening Star) not only repeats the characterization in two successive plays, but amplifies it and sharpens it in *El divino Orfeo*, c1634 version. Perhaps we will agree that Aristaeus is not evil at all. But whether we reach that conclusion or not, we shall still be justified in asking why he was drawn on such a heroic scale.[32]

Is Aristaeus evil? He is guilty of vanity, envy, jealousy, and deceit. He rebels against his king after being taken into his confidence and thus commits treason. He belittles Orpheus while trying to woo Eurydice and he finally poisons her. By the moral standards of the time, of which Calderón was keenly aware, and which are evident in his *comedias*, Aristaeus behaves in a very dishonourable way. He, like the original Don Juan, is guilty of excessive pride, a pride which makes him challenge the power of God. His attempt in his role of *privado* to subvert the authority of the king warrants a punishment similar to that of Don Juan: eternal damnation. Even if he appears to acknowledge generously the king's valour in defeating him, and even though he recognizes that his pride caused him to be exiled, Aristaeus behaves ignobly. His eloquence and gallantry, suitably exploited by Calderón the poet, are shown by Calderón the moralist to be the means by which he disguised his true self. The poetic paradox of a very attractive, powerful and eloquent courtier, who fails to conquer the innocent Eurydice and is defeated by the gentle, understated power of a humble shepherd, can be explained thus: the strength of Orpheus lies in the true quality of his being, reflected in his voice. His design can be explained in the words of St Paul: 'To the weak I became weak, that I might gain the weak. I became all things to all men that I might save all.'[33]

Indeed Calderón seems to have had St Paul's words in mind when conceiving of Aristaeus and Orpheus. He also understood, probably from St Thomas Aquinas' *Summa theologica*, the extent of Lucifer's qualities and of his power and the reason for his fall. Lucifer's splendour, and the sin which caused his fall, are described most lucidly by Father Walter Farrell in his article 'The Devil Himself.'[34] According to Farrell, Satan is pure spirit, independent of everything but God, perfect in his knowledge. These qualities are, however, magnified because of his position in the hierarchy of angels. He is the most perfect of all angels, the highest of an ascending order of perfection of which the Seraphim were 'the most perfect creatures God has made.' Lucifer, the 'morning star,' the 'bearer of light,' fell from the dazzling heights of his perfection to the equally dismal abyss of his wretchedness. However, he took with him his unequalled perfection, the gifts of which he now would use in the service of evil. Lucifer fell to his 'eternal doom by an act of his own free will.'[35] How could an angel of such perfection fall? Farrell puts it this way:

Caught by the undeniable beauty, perfection, goodness of his own angelic nature fully comprehended, Lucifer loved it; that was as it should be. But his love refused to budge a step beyond this, refused to look beyond the angelic perfection to its divine source; he insisted upon resting in that beauty to find there the fullness of happiness, to be sufficient unto himself, even from God. The sin, then, is to be found in his wilful ignoring of the further order of his own perfection to divinity; ignorance in the sense of lack of consideration was in the sin, surely, but in not preceding it, a part and parcel of the free choice that sent the angelic ghosts into hell. Lucifer's sin consisted in loving himself (as pride insists) to the exclusion of all else; and this with no excuse: without ignorance, without error, without passion, without previous disorder in his angelic will. His sin was a sin of pure malice.[36]

Soberbia or excessive pride is, then, the sin of Lucifer, a sin committed wilfully. Farrell, using St Thomas, has shown us Lucifer's pride developed. That Calderón, through his reading of St Thomas's work and other texts, understood the celestial hierarchy is evident throughout the play.[37] In the light of this theological doctrine of Lucifer's fall the 'heroic' Aristaeus, gallant and loving, can be seen as the evil Lucifer, in love with himself. If we reread the play with the above in mind, we find that Aristaeus' first utterance includes *soberbia*: 'Fiera soberbia mía ... caballo desbocado' (O my unruly pride ... unbridled horse). He seems soon after, in line 15, to brag about the chaotic darkness which he has created by saying: 'la densa sombra que enzendí yo mismo' (the thick shades that I myself set ablaze). The emphasis which reveals his pride lies in the 'yo mismo,' which Calderón places at the end of the line. We have already mentioned Aristaeus' attempt to redefine or change Orpheus' words in the creation of the world. His seemingly innocent linguistic substitutions could be said to hide a desire to upstage God. Later, in line 96, Aristaeus recognizes his own wickedness when he says: 'siendo yo la envidia misma' (seeing that I am envy itself). This awareness of his own capacity of evil shows that he knows the sins which have caused his downfall, and his attitude underscores the wilfulness of his behaviour.

In line 108, Aristaeus expresses his desire to conquer Eurydice. He says that she will be the object of his quest: 'venga a ser empresa mía.' 'Empresa' means 'enterprise' and also 'symbol.' It further contains the reason for the enterprise, the 'presa' or 'prize.' His conquest, like his later rebellion, will be the means of obtaining glory, of showing his power. Eurydice will be both the prize and the symbol of his enterprise. Later, in lines 503–16, Aristaeus says that he wants to have a gigantic symbol of his love carved on a tree, and, in lines 672–3, he describes in detail the emblems that he displayed on his tent before his battle against the king. In line 338, he appears to be proud of the wickedness of his flock when he refers to it as follows: 'a de ser el rebaño más perdido' (the most wicked of flocks). Immediately after, he seems to be maliciously accusing God for his fall instead of recognizing his own guilt. He says, in lines 364–5, '... la luz me faltó / y por eso me perdí' (the light failed me, and that is how I got lost). The implication is that he did not have the right kind of guidance. In lines 404–5, Aristaeus tells Albedrío that he is a foreign shepherd who 'en otro campo mejor / conduje el ganado mío' (used to lead my flock to pastures better than these). The emphasis on 'mejor' and 'mío' underscores his pride, particularly since it follows Albedrío's description of Orpheus' domain and ancestry.

Aristaeus' first 'loving' speech to Eurydice, in lines 487–516, indeed contains expressions of praise for her. He says that he intends the symbol of his love, the letter carved on a tree, to grow with it until it becomes immortal, an original, unrepeatable letter which the whole world would see. The lover's gesture, in view of the evil character of Aristaeus, should be seen to be related to his earlier attempt to gain prominence. His *empresa* will be gigantically and immortally advertised. His rhetorical 'vengo a servir y merezer' (I come to serve you and deserve my reward), in lines 493–4, with which he began his speech, shows nothing but false humility.

Aristaeus' long narrative, in lines 537–888, in which he appears to woo Eurydice while telling his own story, contains numerous expressions of self-praise. Indeed, while appearing to woo her, he is in fact, like Narcissus, looking at himself. He says that he is an illustrious and proud prince, 'prínzipe altivo y ilustre,' whose brightness and beauty was imitated by the sun. He stresses that his person is majestic. The empire of which he was a part is conceived in terms commensurate with his greatness, and it is described in a language reminiscent of that used in the description of Jerusalem in St John's Apocalypse.[38] He lists the inhabitants of this empire, explaining that of the angelic hierarchies, which include Cherubim and Seraphim, he was the most perfect example. He says that in this exalted state he was the closest adviser, the *privado* of the king, and was familiar with his secrets. Having gained the king's confidence, he tells how he was shown a portrait of the queen, and, compelled by jealousy, sought to demean her. When describing this demeaning of the queen, he includes a statement about his own nobility in contrast with her inferior quality. He acknowledges that it was his envy that caused him to belittle the king's wife, but there is always in everything he says a recognition of his superior quality: 'que siendo yo de mejor / esencia, adorarla escuse' (I, being of a higher essence, would excuse myself from worshipping her 648–50).

Narrating his war against the king, Aristaeus puts in doubt the loyalty of the king's followers and questions their right to punish the acts of rebellion of his own followers who were trying to free themselves from the royal yoke (657–64). The key word in this narrative is *presumir*. While Aristaeus accuses the king's followers of *presunción*, he is himself presuming by adopting a righteous attitude. The final comparison between the rustic gifts of Orpheus and his own extravagance emphasizes once more his *soberbia*. This comparison ends: 'Yo sí que puedo servirte como Rey ... 'Imperios tengo que la competencia sufren de los cielos' (But I can serve you as a king ... I am the lord of empires that stand in competition with the heavens 837–8, 865–7).

Eurydice rejects Aristaeus because of his *soberbia*: 'pero cuando sobervio / a mi deidad te atreves' (but as soon as you dare to raise your pride against my Deity 899–900). She recognizes that his speech was an attempt to disparage Orpheus' quality and to emphasize his own.

We should mention two more examples of Aristaeus' pride at the end of the play. The *soberbia* which, at the beginning of the play was termed 'caballo desbocado,' is now called 'hipogrifo alado' (winged hippogriff 1337). There seems to be an almost pathetic inability on his part to face the reality of the situation. By attempting to mythologize his pride he is actually trying to turn his back on the cause of his wretchedness. His flashy and fiery exit through the mouth of an equally hyperbolic serpent, called by him 'dragón feroz' (ferocious dragon), is the final statement of his attitude: he will have immortal, perfect unhappiness.[39]

The humble, apparently weak, and unobtrusive Orpheus can be similarly followed through the play. We have mentioned instances in which the authority of the God creator contrasts with the rusticity of the shepherd, as in Orpheus' exchanges with Eurydice at the beginning of the play. His humility and apparent weakness are best illustrated after he has discovered Eurydice's fall and he prepares to sacrifice himself in order to rescue her. He shows his vulnerability when he says: 'triste estoy, rendido y solo' (I am sad and alone, and all my strength is spent). He then asks his father for help.

His rescue of Eurydice, however, shows that his meekness and apparent weakness hide the strength to conquer the king of the dead. His power and authority are shown in his song, which opens all doors. Aristaeus recognizes Orpheus' powers when he says: 'quién / es este ... que tiene poder tan grande?' (Who is it, who can it be who has such power? 1387–8). He is asking, in fact, who is this being whose presence I have not noticed, of whom I know nothing and who is able to perform such feats? He thus emphasizes the 'obscurity' and 'weakness' of Orpheus and the unexpected extent of his power. Orpheus frees Eurydice with the strength of his voice, and there is no doubt or hesitation in his 'Restituirla a mi gracia / podrá mi canto suave' (The charm of my song will restore her to my Grace 1381–2). His triumph is climactically shown in the repetition of the imperative 'abrid las puertas, abrid ... a vuestro Señor' (open the gates, open ... to your Lord), and in his final speech: 'Vuelve el Divino Orfeo resplandeciente y triunfante' (the Divine Orpheus is returning in splendour and triumph 1425–6).

The poetic paradox of a 'heroic' Devil can thus be morally and theologically justified by the triumph of a seemingly unheroic God. The poetic allegory and the doctrinal message produce *en suma* the harmonious whole which is representative of Calderón's best works.[40]

NOTES

1 On Calderón's *autos sacramentales* see E. Frutos Cortés *La filosofía de Calderón en sus autos sacramentales* (Zaragoza 1952); A. Valbuena Prat 'Los autos de Calderón: clasificación y análisis' *Revue Hispanique* 40 (1924), and also his prologue to Volume 3 of The *Obras Completas de Calderón* (Madrid 1952); A.A. Parker *The Allegorical Drama of Calderón* (Oxford 1943). In this essay I shall be continually referring to Professor Parker's work, and attempting to respond to his analysis of Calderón's dramatic theory.

2 'Particularly when approaching the *autos* (because of their doctrinal character) it is essential to assert that the quality of their poetry is not independent of the quality of their 'content'. However fine the literary form of any one *auto* may be, however great the "passion of mind" pervading it, if the theme itself is nonsense, or if it is insignificant, with no bearing on any important aspect of life, it will not be great and vital poetry. If the dramatic treatment given to it is clumsy, and if its poetical form is crude, or diffuse, or merely decorative, however splendid the theme may be in itself the play as a whole will be unconvincing.' Parker *The Allegorical Drama* 40.

3 Ibid 75

4 Ibid 75

5 Ibid 76

6 Ibid 78

7 Ibid 78

8 Ibid 76

9 Ibid 80–1

10 Valbuena Prat, prologue to *Obras Completas* 36

11 Pablo Cabañas *El mito de Orfeo en la literatura española* (Madrid 1948). Cabañas presumes, without providing us with any evidence, that the undated version was composed later than 1663. Both Valbuena Prat, in a preliminary note to the edition of *El divino Orfeo* (Madrid 1952), and A.A. Parker, in a note to his article 'The Devil in the Drama of Calderón,' in *Critical Essays on the Theatre of Calderón* (New York 1965) 9, are of the opinion that the undated version was written in the 1630s and not later. Valbuena Prat further points out the youthful quality of *El divino Orfeo*, the undated version, in a series of rather uninfor-

mative footnotes to the text of this *auto*. It might be possible to date, if only approximately, *El divino Orfeo*, early version, by comparing it to another *auto, El veneno y la triaca*, published, according to Valbuena Prat, in 1634. (There is a reference by Valbuena to another *auto* by the same name published in 1651; see *Prólogo* to the edition of 1952, III 36.) There are numerous reasons for saying that *El divino Orfeo* and *El veneno y la triaca* (1634?) are of the same period, whether it be the 1630s or later. First, the plot in both *autos* is basically the same: the attempted seduction of human nature (Eurydice or Infanta) by the Devil (Aristaeus or Evening Star), with the assistance of Free Will and the impediment of Gracia or Inocencia. The death of Eurydice and her final redemption from Hades by Orpheus mirror the illness of the Infanta and her cure by a Pilgrim with the water of Baptism and the Holy Communion. Second, the language of these plays is remarkably similar. Whole crucial passages appear in both plays almost word for word. On the basis of a brief textual comparison, I believe it is possible to establish a relative chronological order between these two plays. (See Appendix.)

12 Valbuena Prat cites it as '*El divino Orfeo*, segunda parte. Citado en el Catálogo de La Barrera. Debe ser el del ms. 14.849 de la Biblioteca Nacional' (*Obras completas* II 29).

13 'Much later Calderón was to produce a still more beautiful allegory in *El divino Orfeo* (1663), an *auto* poetically so lovely that after the first reading one is tempted to rank it as the finest of all. But when analysed, its appeal is seen to reside only in the poignant delicacy with which Calderón is able to exploit the charm of the myth. Here too the allegory is acceptable as a pleasing analogy of the dogmas, but it is little more; dogma is presented in terms of a myth and no new or special significance is extracted'; Parker *The Allegorical Drama* 200.

14 Valbuena Prat, in his *Calderón* (Barcelona, 1941) 196, says: 'En el asunto mitológico realiza Calderón una síntesis de poesía, contenido teológico y fausto decorativo en una de sus obras más ricas y famosas *El divino Orfeo* (1663).' George Ticknor, in his *History of Spanish Literature* (Boston 1849, rpt New York 1965) vol II, p 323 comments favourably on the 'considerable poetical merit' of certain passages in this *auto*.

15 Cabañas *El mito* 165–76; Jose M. de Osma, 'Apostilla al tema de la creación en el auto *El divino Orfeo* de Calderón de la Barca' *Hispania* 34, 2 (1951) 165–71; Jorge Páramo Pomareda 'Consideraciones sobre los autos mitológicos de Calderón de la Barca' *Thesaurus* (Bogota) 12 (1957) 51–80

16 Dámaso Alonso 'alludes to the stylistic echo of the baroque defining it as "repetition, constant repetition, constant variation"'; translated from H. Hatzfeld *Estudios sobre el barroco* (Madrid 1966) 148.

17 For a full description of the *carros* devised for this *auto*, see N.D. Shergold

and J.E. Varey *Los autos sacramentales en Madrid en la época de Calderón, 1637–1681* (Madrid 1961) 169–70.

18 J.M. de Osma considers that there are two large speeches in this version which, given the brevity of the play, detract from its beauty; 'le afean,' he writes. Since he does not indicate precisely which passages these are, we should presume that in addition to Aristaeus' narrative, perhaps Eurydice's early speech is here censured; De Osma 'Apostilla' 165. These speeches, far from detracting from the beauty of the play, are crucial to the appreciation of Calderón poetico-philosophical conception.

19 Helmut Hatzfeld, in his *Estudios sobre el barroco* 151, says that the Christian desire to find the equilibrium between reason and faith and between grace and free will is reflected in a style which is characterized by a contrast between purpose and execution, high and low, external and internal elements. To this 'paradoxical' style is added a concept of the sublime, of the magnificent. Man, according to Gracián, is like the sun, 'criatura de ostentación.' Further, a style characterized by the use of oxymoron, antithesis, repetition, and metonymy is also distinguished by the use of the 'metáfora-enigma,' and by mastery in the use of visual elements, colour, tone, and arrangement. Although we do not here have space to illustrate the various facets of this style in *El divino Orfeo*, we should mention the magnificence and grandeur in the staging of the version of 1663, the use of 'metáforas-enigmas' in both versions, the elaborate rhetorical arrangement of passages such as Eurydice's speech in the beginning of the early version, and the importance of colour and tone in this version, particularly in the speeches of Aristaeus.

20 The *gracioso* is one of the stock characters of the Spanish *comedia*. He is a clownish figure usually introduced for comic relief. He is fond of eating and drinking and of keeping out of danger, like Brito in *El príncipe constante*.

21 The *privado* or favourite was the man closest to the king. The most famous *privado* in the history of Spain was the Duke of Olivares, a contemporary of Calderón.

22 An interesting retelling of Aristaeus' story appears in Michael Grant's *Myths of the Greeks and Romans* (New York 1962) 266–72.

23 According to William of Conches; see J.B. Friedman *Orpheus in the Middle Ages* (Cambridge, Mass 1970), 107ff. Probably the most important Golden Age Source used by Calderón is Juan Pérez de Moya's *Philosofía secreta* (Madrid 1585). Perez de Moya follows Virgil, Ovid, and Boethius in his narration of the historical Orpheus. According to Pérez de Moya, Orpheus means 'sabio' or wise and Aristaeus means virtue or thing that has virtue 'cosa que tiene virtud' (220).

24 *Fabula d'Orfeo*, lines 26–34; tr Louis E. Lord (London 1931) 76.

25 For example, popular verse forms such as the *redondilla* and the *letrilla* might be used to convey humour. The speaker using them would not normally be a nobleman. If a nobleman were to use them, he might place himself 'out of character,' and his attitude would have to be explained in the context of the play. In Lope de Vega's *Peribáñez*, the hendecasyllable is used to elevate the peasant, Peribáñez, whose qualities are described by Leonardo, the Comendador's servant. This verse form would not usually be used by a peasant. Peribáñez uses it, however, after he has been ennobled by the Comendador. Similarly, when the Comendador, who wants to seduce Casilda, Peribáñez's wife, speaks to her disguised as a labourer, he uses *redondillas*, a popular verse form. His intent has lowered him and therefore he cannot speak like a nobleman. See verses 824–6 for Peribáñez, and 1535–53 for the Comendador.

26 I have followed the spelling and punctuation of Valbuena Prat's edition.

27 In the play, Orpheus is called, among other things, 'músico divino,' 'gallardo pastor,' 'verbo divino,' 'músico excelente,' 'maestro de capilla,' 'instrumento templado,' 'grande músico,' 'Rey,' 'señor soberano,' 'deidad,' 'cisne,' and 'santo.'

28 William Blake, in his *Marriage of Heaven and Hell* in *Complete Writings* ed. G. Keynes (London 1966) 150, says: 'The reason Milton wrote in fetters when he wrote of Angels & God, and at liberty when of Devils & Hell, is because he was a true Poet and of the Devil's party without knowing it.' See also Shelley's comment on Milton's interpretation in A.A. Parker's 'The Devil in the Drama of Calderón' 6.

29 He also appears to misuse the Latin, putting *ista* instead of *ita*. This, however, could be due to a copyist's mistake. The manuscript, in the Biblioteca Nacional in Madrid, is thought to be an eighteenth-century copy of an undiscovered original.

30 A.A. Parker 'The Devil in the Drama of Calderón' 8

31 Ibid 9

32 Valbuena Prat *Calderón* 12

33 1 Corinthians 9:22. There are numerous instances in St Paul's epistles to the Corinthians, where God appears to be weak but really is strong, for example, 1 Cor 1:25 and 27, 2 Cor 10:1, 10:10, 12:10, and 13:3; *The New English Bible* (Cambridge 1970).

34 Walter Farrell, O.P. 'The Devil Himself' in *Satan* ed J.M. de Bruno (London 1951) 3–18

35 Ibid 11

36 Ibid 14

37 Parker *The Allegorical Drama* 70 gives evidence of Calderón's Thomistic education.

38 Although the description of Jerusalem in the Apocalypse is more complex than Aristaeus' description of his king's realm, the richness of detail and the tone of magnificence in Calderón's play recall St John's description.

39 Donald F. Bouchard, in *Milton: A Structural Reading* (Montreal 1974) 124, explains Lucifer's actions in *Paradise Lost* as characteristic of those of an unrequited lover. Lucifer's love for God is rejected because it is considered unworthy, and this rejection causes his rebellion. 'This stance is not intended as a final position, but should be understood in terms of the characteristic sulking of the lover. The rebellion, then, simply indicates the extent of Satan's love and attachment of God and the continuation of his desire to be noticed.'

40 I would like to acknowledge gratefully the illuminating suggestions made by Father A.E. Synan and by my colleagues David Mosher, Peter Richardson, and John Warden concerning various interpretative questions in this paper.

APPENDIX

Comparison of *El veneno y la triaca* 1634? and *El divino Orfeo* c1634

The first passage occurs early in the plays. Evening Star in *El veneno y la triaca* and Aristaeus in *El divino Orfeo* invoke the help of the mountains.

EVENING STAR	ARISTAEUS
Altos montes que al cielo	Altos montes, que al cielo
gigantes de esmeralda	gigantes de esmeralds alzáis con saña
alzáis con ceño la arrugada	essa ar(r)ugada frente,
frente, ajando el claro velo que en la	ajando el azul velo
nevada espalda asegura su fábrica	que en la nevada espalda
	asegura su fábrica eminente
eminente, donde la transparente	donde la transparente
selva, que en luces bellas	selva, que en luzes bellas
al sol causa desmayos, equivocando rayos	al sol causa desmayos,
tanta noticia pierde,	tanta noticia pierde
que trueca en nube azul el monte verde	que al fin es monte azul o cielo verde
Así privilegiados	Así privilegiados
siempre, alegres y hermosos	siempre alegres, y hermosos
duréis, siendo del sol bellos faetones	duréis, siendo del sol, verdes faetones
tanto que, aunque anegados	tanto, que aunque anegados

con montes de agua y piélagos de montes,	en montes de agua, o piélagos de montes
atentos horizontes,	hasta en los horizontes
vecinos os respeten	vecinos os respeten
las injurias del hado	las injurias del hado,
y al cielo, coronado	y al sitio coronado
de espumas, se sujeten,	de espumas te sugeten
levantando los hielos	levantando con yelos
murallas de cristal hasta los cielos	murallas de christal, hasta los cielos
Así, después del agua	Así libres del agua,
no pueda en tanto abismo	no pueda en triste abismo
profanaros tampoco tanto fuego	profanaros tampoco, tanto fuego
como mi pecho fragua	como mi pecho fragua
mi aliento expira cuando a veros llego	los ojos llegan, quando a veros llego
triste, confuso y ciego;	triste confuso y ciego;
y el diluvio segundo	y el dilubio segundo
que ha de borrar la esfera	que abortará la esfera
no os abrase ni hiera	no os abrase ni yera
sino, pompa del mundo	y sin ruina del mundo
os dejen sin desmayos	os dejen sus desmayos
incendio de agua y tempestad de rayos	
que en vuestros campos bellos	
un pastor disfrazado	
admitáis (que pastor también he sido);	admitáis; que también pastor herido
a vivir vengo en ellos	a vivir vengo en ellos
donde mi ganado	a donde mi ganado
a de ser el rebaño más perdido,	a de ser el rebaño más perdido;
cobarde y atrevido;	cobarde, aunque atrevido
amo a la Infanta bella	amo a Euridize bella
que hereda el ancho imperio	que es la esposa de Orfeo,

(Aristaeus' speech may be translated as follows: Mighty mountains, giants of emerald, lifting your rugged brows in anger and crumpling the azure veil that pins upon your snowy shoulder the forest, like a towering edifice; and the forest transparent makes the sun faint away in pools of light so that it cannot tell the rays of the stars from the rays of the flowers, and in the end it is a mountain of azure and a sky of green. Such is your privilege; and so may you remain, joyous and beautiful, green Phaethons of the sun, and even though mountains of water immerse you, or oceans of mountains, a watery abyss stretching to the horizon, your neighbours may respect you for the injury that fate has dealt you holding you within a coronal of foam, walls of crystal hewn from the ice stretching to the skies. Once you are free from the water let nothing profane you in that gloomy abyss. No, not even the fire I gorge within my breast, a volcano in itself, but one look from you and it smoulders dismal and without light. And that second deluge which this globe will bring to nothing let it not burn you or do you harm; let it fade away without the world's collapse, leaving you with its rainstorms blazing and its lightning falling in showers. Will you allow a shepherd in disguise to enter your fair meadows? (For I have been a shepherd too.) Here I shall live and pasture my flock – no sheep more lost than they. I am a coward, yet not without audacity. I am in love with the beautiful Eurydice, she who is the wife of Orpheus. My love and my desire have dragged me here to see her. It is the wife I yearn for – the wife of the musician who is in love with grace.)

We can isolate the following verses:

EVENING STAR	ARISTAEUS
Alzáis con ceño	Alzáis con saña
ajando el claro velo	ajando el azul velo
que trueca en nube azul el	que al fin es monte azul o cielo
(monte verde)	(verde)
Así después del agua	así libres del agua
y el diluvio segundo	y el diluvio segundo
que ha de borrar la esfera	que abortará la esfera
sino pompa del mundo	y sin ruina del mundo
cobarde y atrevido	cobarde, aunque atrevido

The passage in *El divino Orfeo* is more precise and better balanced. 'Saña' is stronger than 'ceño,' and fits better in the poetic context. 'Azul' is more definite than 'claro.' The contrast of the mountain piercing the background is more dramatically conveyed with the use of 'azul.' The baroque arrangement, 'monte azul o cielo verde,' expresses a range of possibilities in the image, a movement of colour and of texture. One could say what Dámaso Alonso says, referring to Góngora's *Polifemo*: 'El pensamiento poético ... sigue avanzando bifurcado y dudoso entre las dos posibilidades ...' The same range of possibilities exists in 'cobarde, aunque atrevido,' compared to 'cobarde y atrevido' where the artistic ambiguity is not present.

In a second passage, the Devil approaches and Gracia-Inocencia retreat. Infanta/ Euridice remark:

INFANTA	EURIDICE
Mirando en los dos está	Mirando en los dos está
mi atención varios efectos	mi pecho varios efectos

Esta huyendo, aquél llegando	Esta huyendo, aquél llegando
los pasos se estan midiendo	et tiempo se estan midiendo
y lo que él tarda viniendo	y lo que él tarda viniendo
se apresura ella apartando	ella se tarda apartando

There is more poetic intensity in the use of 'mi pecho' than in 'mi atención.' The syntactical arrangement which mirrors the parallel reactions of the characters is maintained in *El divino Orfeo* in the last two verses: 'tarda viniendo ... tarda apartando.' The combination 'tarda ... apresura' in *El veneno y la triaca* is awkward and destroys the balance.

Finally a third example. Evening Star/Aristaeus tell their stories:

EVENING STAR	ARISTAEUS
Pues enseñándome un día	Quiso enseñarme a su esposa
entre uno y otro perfil,	entre rasgos, y vislumbres
un retrato de su esposa,	de un bosquejo, de un retrato
desde el punto que la vi	en cuyas sombras, y luzes
empecé, celoso y triste,	puso menos fuerza, el Arte,
a padecer y sentir,	que yo admiraziones puse
porque en la pintura estaba	
con vida y alma el matiz	

The intensity of Aristaeus' desire is reflected in the repetition 'puse ... puse.' The whole sequence of poetic tonalities is better conveyed and climatically developed in 'rasgos,' 'vislumbres,' 'bosquejo,' 'retrato,' 'sombras.' It is a synthesis of his quest.

On the basis of the above comparisons, and with further evidence from the text, I believe that it is possible to argue that *El divino Orfeo* is a later *auto* than *El veneno y la triaca*. The plot in *El divino Orfeo* is more complex; Aristaeus' speeches are more polished; there is more variety of narrative and dramatic material; and there is more care in the development of the characters and of the imagery. Whether *El divino Orfeo*'s development indicates a period even later than 1634 is something that I believe is still open to question.

PATRICIA VICARI

The Triumph of Art, the Triumph of Death: Orpheus in Spenser and Milton

I N REVIVING THE IDEA of *prisca theologia* and the supremacy of Plato among ancient philosophers, the Florentine Academy sought to recapture not a lost classical age but the syncretism of the third to sixth centuries. Their enthusiasm for 'Platonism' led them back to the old veneration for the 'ancient theologians' as a means of reconciling their philosophy with their Christianity. At the same time, the craze among the learned for 'hieroglyphs,' enigmatic symbols supposedly based on Egyptian hieroglyphs, reinforced the contemporary taste for riddles and secret languages involving pictorial symbols or myths. On the one hand, Orpheus and his fate could be just such a 'hieroglyph,' and on the other, Orphic rites and Orphic 'wisdom,' as found in the Orphic fragments and hymns, could be used by the judicious few, not to the danger but rather to the enriching and exciting of their Christian faith.

As we have seen, it is difficult to be precise about what these men – or, for that matter, even the ancients who wrote about it – thought was specifically Orphic in 'the ancient theology.' I surmise that what they thought they owed to Orpheus was a specific mythology clothed in the language of the Orphic hymns and exemplifying the doctrines of theocrasy and the triads, and the ideas, shared by Neoplatonism, that opposites coincide and that the part is in the whole and the whole in the part.[1] The centrality of Venus (or Amor, or Eros) in the economy of the world is perhaps the most important point. To this we must return briefly. Finally, the idea of the importance of keeping wisdom secret seems to have been thought of as especially enjoined by Orpheus, who was, after all, the supposed founder of the Mysteries. Thus Orpheus was ranked with Moses and Dionysius the Areopagite, and his authority reinforced by theirs. Esoteric truth was to be both partially revealed and partially concealed through enigmatic language or imagery which both 'speaks' and is 'silent.' As a rhetorical strategy this lends more authority to what is being taught; it was also part of an elaborate learned game which these men both took seriously and did not take seriously, in the Renaissance spirit of *serio ludere*.

Because of the importance of Love in Neoplatonic cosmology and in Empedoclean physics, the Florentines placed Venus and Amor at the centre of the pantheon. In so doing, they invoked the authority of Orpheus, in whose theogony and cosmology Eros is a major figure. To be sure, he usually goes under other names (Phanes, Dionysos, Pan) and in ancient Orphic writings has no ethical character, but the Eros that Ficino and Pico saluted as Orphic was made to embody, among other things, the Christian notion of the God of Love. Naturally, Eros, or Amor, still retains his sexual function and also his Platonic character as the motive for the philosopher's quest for wisdom. Love is always the same force, but it operates on three planes, sexual, intellectual, and religious. In the sexual realm, love is both a painful servitude and an ecstatic release from the self; so, on the highest plane, it leads to painful death of the self and a joyous merging of the soul in God. Amor is thus of a double nature; Sappho and Hermias had called love 'bitter-sweet,' and Ficino revived the epithet.[2] Love is also a god of death because a true lover dies to everything but his love, and through love and death is united with the One towards which all love is ultimately directed.

Spenser's philosophical debt to Italian Neoplatonism is well known,[3] as is his emulation of Chaucer, whom in the *Shepheardes Calender* he calls 'the God of shepheards, *Tityrus* ... Who taught me homely, as I can, to make' ('June' 81–2). Through Chaucer's treatment of Dame Nature in the *Parlement of Fowls,* Spenser was acquainted with Alanus de Insulis' *De planctu Naturae,* which, in turn, derived from Boethius and the Neoplatonists.[4] In the cosmology which he learned from both ancient and Renaissance Neoplatonists and adapted for use as a central myth in his own poetry, elements deriving from the Orphic hymns play a prominent part, in particular, bits from the 'Hymn to nature [*Physis*]' (Hymn 10), 'To Aphrodite' (55), and 'To Eros' (58). Eros, who is also Phanes in Orphic mythology, is the Firstborn of the gods (Protogonos) and first creator. In the *Symposium* Plato calls him the eldest of the gods. Spenser addresses him as born of Venus yet 'elder then thine owne nativitie;/ And yet a chyld, renewing still thy yeares;/ And yet the eldest of the heauenly Peares' ('Hymne in Honour of Love,' 11.52, 54–6). In his *Commentary on Plato's Symposium,* Ficino remarks that Orpheus, taught by Hermes Trismegistus, had sung that Chaos had been before the world and that 'Love was the heart of Chaos.' 'The oldest and wisest of the gods, accomplished in himself, is Love – that is the doctrine which Orpheus teaches in *Argonautica.*'[5] Venus, in Spenser's

'Hymne in Honour of Beautie,' is the necessary companion of Love: she bore him, but he was older than she; she lent him the light whereby he formed the cosmos ('Hymne in Honour of Love' 71–3); she is that Beauty which is the pattern by which he, the 'worlds great workmaister,' created the world. This same Venus, we read in the *Faerie Queene*, Book 3, Canto 6, has devised a 'ioyous Paradize' for herself, in which she may forever enjoy Adonis. She and Adonis, 'the Father of all formes,' forever joined in copulation, are at the heart of the Garden. Together they perpetually generate 'infinite shapes of creatures,' Venus' 'deare brood.' This is Nature's seminary, presided over by 'Old *Genius,* the which a double nature has.' 'He letteth in, he letteth out to wend' the souls which clamour to be incarnate in flesh and which return to the Garden after each incarnation; he, as servant of Venus, keeps the keys of life and death. All things are born, die, and return to the Garden, where they live 'some thousand yeares' and then go forth again to inhabit a different body. The 'nucleus of nature,' here, as in Alanus de Insulis' poem and Orphic theology, 'is sex,' as Gustav Fredén succinctly puts it.[6] This doctrine of Nature, which we also find in the *Faerie Queene*, Book 4, Canto 10 (stanzas 20–9) and in the *Cantos of Mutabilitie* is certainly not Christian, nor is it Platonic. The Garden of Adonis differs from Plato's and Pythagoras' world of disembodied souls in that in the latter there is an important prospect, for some souls, of escaping from the Wheel of Generation, whereas Spenser's souls never can. Like 'Nature' in the Orphic Hymns, then still thought to be by Orpheus, this is a world of monistic materialism.[7] The whole of Nature consists of a unity of bodies and souls and it is never changed, never augmented or diminished by so much as one soul. It is certainly quite probable that this peculiarity is owing to Spenser's dependence (through Ficino and Pico) on specifically Orphic ideas, although it is also likely that Lucretius was also an influence. In any case, his language recalls that of Orpheus. The Garden of Adonis is 'the first seminarie of all things': in the Orphic hymns this idea is rendered by *pammateira* ('the mother of everything') and *spermeia* ('he who rules over the seeds of life').[8] Spenser's Venus and Adonis also resemble the first two hypostases of the second Orphic triad (of which Phanes is the third hypostasis), the 'hermaphroditic Duad' (the Egg) and the Seeds. Furthermore, the Venus represented in the third and fourth books of the *Faerie Queene* is very like the *Physis* of the tenth Orphic hymn. Orpheus calls this divinity 'all-parent, ancient and divine,' 'immortal, first-born, without a father,' 'thyself the father whence thy essence came,' 'Father of all, great nurse, and mother kind / Abundant, blessed, all-spermatic mind,' 'from whose fertile seeds / And plastic hand this changing scene proceeds.' Her creation 'whirls' forth in a never-changing circle (9–10); she is the destroyer and creator (28). The Eros of the Orphic

Venus is described as 'twofold' and 'keeper of the keys' (Hymn 58). Spenser's Venus is veiled, like Chaucer's Dame Nature; the reason for the veil given in Book 4 is to hide from the vulgar (though not from her priests, of whom Spenser, as a poet, is one) the fact that she is hermaphroditic:

> she hath both kinds in one,
> Both male and female, both vnder one name:
> She syre and mother is her selfe alone,
> Begets and eke conceiues, ne needeth other none.   (st 41)

Like Orpheus' Aphrodite, she is pacifier of storms, 'the ioy of Gods and men,' 'the root of all that ioyous is,' 'mother of laughter, and welspring of blisse' (st 44 and 47; cf Orphic Hymns 55.1 and 5). Orpheus' Aphrodite joins the world in harmony (Hymn 55.5); she is 'Goddess of marriage,' 'source of persuasion,' who joins mortals in 'necessary bands'; Spenser's Venus has the same functions. On the porch of her temple stands Concord, joining Hatred and Love hand to hand, a more 'mystical' and inclusive expression of the same ideas as are to be found in Orpheus' 'Hymn to Aphrodite.'

Spenser's philosophy, as I hope will now be apparent, was deeply imbued with the mythology and theology of the Orphic hymns, and his imagination was also touched by the figure of Orpheus himself, the musician, the lover of Eurydice, and, above all, the poet. As a poet, Orpheus possessed some of the qualities which he ascribed to divinities in his hymns. In Canto 2 of Book 4 of the *Faerie Queene* (st 1–2) Orpheus the Argonaut is mentioned in connection with the theme of discord and harmony. Spenser evokes the power of his music to soothe the rage of the Argonauts against each other and reconcile them as friends again. Here Spenser makes the old comparison between Orpheus and David, who cured Saul of his mad fit with music.[9]

In the 'Hymne in Honour of Love,' Spenser says that Orpheus was provoked by love to descend to Hades. He was therefore an example of the special working of the life force (or love) in man, a rational creature. It does not merely urge him to propagate his kind, but inspires him with desire for a higher kind of immortality (103–5). In the October eclogue of the *Shepheardes Calender* he alludes to Orpheus in connection with the idea that love teaches the soul to ascend and has a specially potent effect upon poets. In *Colin Clouts Come Home Againe* he describes love in the same way as Protogonos or Phanes is described in the Orphic hymns. Love rules all creatures, each according to his kind. It impels and enables Colin Clout, Spenser's representative poet, to pour 'forth these oracles so sage,/ Of that high power, wherewith [he is] possest' (825–6). Orpheus was able to tame the 'hellish hound' with 'his musicks might' ('October' 26–30), but the music's power was also the power of love; love is poetic inspiration and the 'divine madness' of the priest, poet, and sibyl. That is its mode of operation in their special case.

In *The Ruines of Time* Spenser is haunted by what Sir Thomas Browne was to call 'the iniquity of oblivion' that 'blindly scattereth her poppy, and deals with the memory of men without distinction to merit of perpetuity.'[10] 'Many ingenious lovely things' are not only lost but forgotten. Where is now the glory of Verulam? Here Orpheus appears first as one who has escaped the ordeal of time through death, and in '*Elisian* fields so free' 'with *Linus* and the choice / Of all that ever did in rimes reioyce' enjoys the only fame that is lasting and true, the praises of his fellow poets, the best that might be from every age (330–6). In death Orpheus escapes from the conditions that hedged him about while he was alive. Spenser is picking up an idea of Ovid's who, at the end of his account of Orpheus, suggested that in dying Orpheus achieved what he really wanted, free and untrammelled union with Eurydice. Now he need not fear looking back as he sports with her.

But we, the living, must be concerned with what is right in this world. It is only just and fitting that we should remember those to whom we are indebted. This is the business of the Muses: they hold in check the ravenous appetite of time. They only can preserve fame and thus confer immortality, as they did on Hercules (379–92). 'Daughters of Dame memorie, / And *Ioue* the father of eternitie' (368–9), it is they who set men on fame's golden throne; they raised the Dioscuri to heaven and set them shining there as stars.

> The seuen fold yron gates of grislie Hell,
> And horrid house of sad *Proserpina*,
> They able are with power of mightie spell
> To breake, and thence the soules to bring awaie
> Out of dread darkenesse, to eternall day,
> And them immortall make, which els would die
> In foule forgetfulnesse, and nameles lie.   (372–8)

It was they who

> for pittie of the sad wayment,
> Which *Orpheus* for *Eurydice* did make,
> Her back againe to life sent for his sake.   (390–3)

Although he seems to be saying that Orpheus succeeded literally in bringing

Eurydice back to life, the 'life' here is a metaphoric one in heaven or the starry sphere. Spenser is evoking a paradise of art and poetry, something like the eternal world of Yeats' Byzantium, where all the glorious productions of the Muses,

> freed from bands of implacable fate,
> And power of death, liue for aye aboue,
> Where mortall wreakes their blis may not remoue. (395–7)

This recalls Boccaccio's interpretation of the story that Orpheus' head and lyre continued to sing and play after death: that symbolised the posthumous fame of poets. But Spenser's is not such a simple idea. It is closer to Milton's definition of true poetic fame in heaven in *Lycidas*:

> *Fame* is no plant that grows on mortal soil,
> Nor in the glistering foil
> Set off to th' world, nor in broad rumour lies,
> But lives and spreds aloft by those pure eyes,
> And perfet witnes of all judging *Jove*;
> As he pronounces lastly on each deed,
> Of so much fame in Heav'n expect thy meed. (*Lycidas* 78–84)

Spenser then goes on to oppose to the arts of poetry and music, which are spiritual, the crass attempts at self-perpetuation that produced vain monuments, 'Pyramides,' 'Colosses,' 'brasen Pillours,' 'Shrines' (408–11). Made of mere matter, they cannot endure. Art is something different. Like love, it seems to depend on a physical medium and sensation, but it communicates with a higher level of reality. It is a greater force than magic. It little availed Achilles to have been dipped in Lethe: he is remembered now only because Homer sang of him. It is Memory and her daughters that have the keeping of the gate to Elysium. We are reminded that the Orphic initiates were taught that the only way to escape from the Wheel and enter Elysium was to resist the temptation to drink of Lethe.[11] Therefore Mnemosyne is invoked in the seventy-seventh Orphic hymn as

> Free from th'oblivion of the fallen mind,
> By whom the soul with intellect is join'd (3–4)

where Intellect is a higher order of being than the Mundane. In the visions that follow, the poet sees the dead Philisides' (Sir Philip Sidney's) 'Harpe stroong all with siluer twyne' (603–9) swimming down the river Lee. It

> seemed to haue been
> The harpe, on which *Dan Orpheus* was seene
> Wylde beasts and forrests after him to lead (606–9)

and, like Orpheus' lyre, it was caught up to heaven and stellified, all the while its strings, 'stirred with the warbling wind' (an obvious symbol for poetic inspiration), gave out 'most heauenly noyse' 'that wrought both ioy and sorrow in my mind' (612–14). Through the symbol of the harp, Sidney, now The Poet, is assimilated to Orpheus, and translated into the celestial realm that Orpheus inhabits.

Thus Orpheus symbolizes the power of poetry to redeem from death, oblivion, and time. In the October eclogue of the *Shepheardes Calender* Piers praises the songs of poets as civilizing influences, restraining 'the lust of lawlesse youth.' Poetry lifts the mind beyond the realm of sensation and the body, which is the empire of death and time, just as Orpheus' music brought Eurydice back from hell. Here, in Renaissance dress, is something like the medieval 'moral' interpretation of the Orpheus and Eurydice story, but with Art now taking the place of Reason as the liberator of the soul. Hades is the state of death, which is part of the kingdom of time: Time-Death-Oblivion are, as it were, the infernal triad for the Renaissance artist or poet. In his *Epithalamion*, written to be presented to Elizabeth Boyle, Spenser says that he is going to sing *for* her on the occasion of their wedding (not 'to' her), 'So Orpheus did for his owne bride' (16). Aside from the parallel drawn between himself and Orpheus, Spenser is again making the point that such song is an antidote to oblivion, death, and other disasters of the fallen state of man. It is a 'song made in lieu of many ornaments, / With which my loue should duly haue been dect,' but it is a better ornament because it does not partake of the materiality of the pyramids and pillars of *The Ruines of Time*. Therefore it can be

> vnto her a goodly ornament,
> And for short time an endlesse moniment. (432–3)

To sing for one's bride and to sing in order to escape from time and death are not at odds but, as it were, two different ways of saying the same thing. Obviously, Spenser had a highly idealized conception of love and marriage, and he took seriously his own version of the Platonic metaphor of climbing the scale of love to arrive at the summit of knowledge of and union with the truth. Despite the palinodes in the hymns to Heavenly Love and Heavenly Beauty, Spenser believed that the proper way to heaven for a mortal lay in pursuing and refining human goals, one of the most important being the union of true lovers, for that was the way God had appointed man to function. Eurydice, then, and the stellified lyre do not represent opposed ideals, but demonstrate the unity of life and the nisus towards transcendence in all human striving. Thus Orpheus the Musician-Poet-Theologian and Orpheus the Lover are not separate, but the one is a metaphor for the other.

The seventeenth century witnessed the decline and fall of classical mythology as a branch of knowledge, as a subject for poetry, and even as a rhetorical ornament. As the medieval world-view faded into a curiosity, so did the doctrine of hieroglyphs, that 'sacramental view of nature' which upheld the mystical significance of the creatures made by God and the myths made by God's image, man. Men began to feel that 'our flowers are merely – flowers' and that, if they require an explanation of their existence, a valid one will have to be framed in a new vocabulary, the sterilized one of 'science.' Even the words 'science' and 'philosophy' shrank their borders and narrowed their meanings, and the hunt was up after 'objectivity' and what John Donne called 'unconcerning things, matters of fact.' No matter how true the morals or natural laws that tradition and ingenuity have wrested from the tales of the 'fabulous Greeks,' such ideas (so ran the new current of thought) could as easily – and more wittily – be expressed with less hackneyed materials. After the scientific battle with myth had been won, the aesthetic attack began. The stories were old and *fade*, mere commonplaces on every poetaster's tongue. They were 'but the Frigidities of Wit' which 'become not the genius of manly ingenuities.'[12] The poet Carew praised Donne in his 'Elegy for Dr. Donne' for his new, more masculine style, in which 'the goodly exiled train of gods and goddesses' did not spoil the effect.

There had never been lacking moralists, prudes, and heavy-witted literalists to attack poetry as profane, lascivious, immoral, and so on. Thomas Aquinas' repudiation of the idea that such poets as Orpheus were ancient theologians had revived the hostility between poetry and philosophy in the thirteenth century, and the Reformation and subsequent religious quarrels did the same for the sixteenth and seventeenth centuries in all Protestant countries. In England the attack was renewed with special vigour in the late sixteenth and seventeenth centuries by the Puritans. Poetry was again accused of lying, vanity, idolatry, and sheer immorality: according to Prynne (*Histriomastix*, 1633), its subject-matter was 'Rapes, Adulteries, Murthers, Thefts, Deceites, Lasciviousnesse, and other execrable Villanies of Dung-Hill, Idole, Pagan-gods and Goddesses.' Nor did the likes of Prynne and

Gosson hesitate to carry the attack *ad hominem*: to be a poet was a reproach, poets were 'the very caterpillars of the Commonwealth.'

In the midst of this, the youthful Milton proudly proclaimed his calling to the high honour of being a poet in his sixth Latin elegy written to Charles Diodati in December 1629, when the twenty-one-year-old poet was busy writing his 'Hymn on the Morning of Christ's Nativity':

But the poet who sings of wars and of heaven ... and of pious heroes and leaders half divine, ... of the sacred conference of the high gods, now of the abysmal realms where barks a savage dog, that poet should live sparingly as did the Samian teacher [Pythagoras]. Let him have, in addition, a youth chaste and free from evil, uncompromising standards, and stainless hands. Such is your character, augur, when, bright with sacred vestments and lustral waters, you rise to approach the angry gods. In this fashion we learn that wise Tiresias lived after he lost his eyesight and Ogygian Linus and Calchas, ... and aged Orpheus, taming wild creatures amid those lonely caves. So Homer, eating but little and drinking but water, carried the Dulichian hero over the long stretches of sea and ... through thy realms, O King of the Lower World ... For the poet is sacred to the gods and is their priest. His inmost soul and lips breathe Jove.'[13]

The old tradition of 'that divine Orpheus' was obviously not dead yet. We have seen that the Spanish poet Calderón, writing at the same time as Milton, was still confidently preaching the 'ancient theology,' and in his *auto El divino Orfeo* (1634 and 1663) treating Orpheus as a Christ-figure as Byzantine artists had done long before.[14] In Milton's poetry, chronologically, we have three Orpheuses. The first, in Elegy 6, is Orpheus the priest-magician-philosopher, aged and austere, in the lonely mountains of Strymon taming the animals. The second is Orpheus the lover and musician, seeking his beloved even in hell and liberating her with his charming song. The third is the torn poet, victim of the maddened crowd. In the period from the end of the Roman Empire to the end of the Renaissance, these portraits of Orpheus succeeded each other in more or less the same order.

Milton devoted no entire work to Orpheus, but no attentive reader can fail to notice his remarks on Orpheus, their evolution, and their relevance to Milton's own poetic career. Orpheus has a highly personal, as well as emblematic, significance for Milton. Elizabeth Sewell finds the beginning of Orpheus' progress through Milton in the youthful companion pieces 'L'Allegro' and 'Il Penseroso,' and she says that they 'are primarily secular and have no deep bearing on the nature of the poet or of poetry. Orpheus can come and go freely, in connection with music, as if he were freed from content and could appear as pure form.'[15] In each of these poems Milton addresses a goddess or presiding spirit who is also a mood and a muse. If Mirth will adopt him into her crew, he says in 'L'Allegro,' he will see poetic visions. Mirth it is who can

> Lap me in soft *Lydian* Aires,
> Married to immortal verse
> Such as the meeting soul may pierce
> In notes, with many a winding bout
> Of lincked sweetnes long drawn out,
> With wanton heed, and giddy cunning,
> The melting voice through mazes running;
> Untwisting all the chains that ty
> The hidden soul of harmony.
> That *Orpheus* self may heave his head
> From golden slumber on a bed
> Of heapt *Elysian* flowres, and hear
> Such streins as would have won the ear
> Of *Pluto*, to have quite set free
> His half regain'd *Eurydice*.   ('L'Allegro' 136–50)

These are haunting lines. Bush calls them 'cool, plastic, economical, achieving a sensuous effect with hardly a sensuous word,' like Ovid in their 'decorative objectivity,' but unlike him in evoking, with a not-too-glamorous magic, 'the ideal beauty.'[16] The ideal music, of course, can never be heard: even Orpheus, who appears here as the consummate poet, could make music only half as good. The important thing to note, however, is that the function of music is to set Eurydice free. Orpheus did not succeed in doing it. Might Milton? He does not, of course, directly compare himself with Orpheus as a competitor: he will not make the music but merely 'hear' it. But there is no difference, in fact, since the ideal is not made, it is conceived.

Since Mirth rules only half of human experience, her companion Melancholy is then evoked. In the midst of pleasing fancies of the occupations ruled over by this 'goddess, sage and holy,' thoughts of Orpheus recur. Milton wishes that Melancholy might have the power to

> raise Musaeus from his bower,
> Or bid the soul of Orpheus sing
> Such notes as warbled to the string,
> Drew iron tears down Pluto's cheek,
> And made Hell grant what Love did seek. ('Il Penseroso' 104–108)

This is all in the optative subjunctive, suggesting that in fact the ideal is out of the reach even of the imagination. However, the function of Orpheus' song (now imagined as successful) remains the same. To make hell grant what Love seeks has Christian connotations; it also reminds us (quite intentionally) of Spenser's Orpheus who saves his bride from time, death, and oblivion.

Milton wrote one poem that makes systematic use of an Orphic type of fable and of Orphic themes. *Comus*, a masque written to be performed by the Earl of Bridgewater's children at his seat of Ludlow Castle in 1634, continually recalls the Renaissance and Spenserian Orpheus, although there is not one allusion to Orpheus in the entire work.[17] The story is of a nubile virgin (Amoret, Spenser's version of this character, as a virgin bride is closer to the original Eurydice) who is held captive by an evil magician in a dark wood that later metamorphoses into a sinister palace like Dis's gloomy hall or Busirane's palace in *Faerie Queene*, until another figure magically liberates her and restores her to home and safety. The story might sound too general to be specifically Orphic, were it not for the fact that the chief magic in the poem is music. Indeed, according to Angus Fletcher, who has written a book about it, 'The triumph of song is the main thing that happens in *Comus*.'[18] Professor Fletcher sets forth an interesting argument that the poem is less like a masque than like one of the early Italian operas, a genre that was founded on the myth of Orpheus.[19] The resemblance between, or even identity of, poetic metred language and music was a commonplace. Ficino wrote, 'There is ... a twofold imitation of that divine music among men, a lower one through voices and instruments, and a higher one through verse and metre. The former kind is called vulgar music, whereas the latter is called by Plato serious music and poetry.'[20] In 'Ad patrem' Milton contrasts mere melody of an instrument or voice with the true Orphic music: 'the empty modulations of the voice, when devoid of words and their meaning and of rhythmical language' 'befits the choruses of the woods, not Orpheus, who checked the course of streams and added ears to the oaks, by his poetry, not by his lyre, and by his singing reduced to tears the ghosts of the dead.'[21] The dramatic *agon* in the masque, the conflict between the Lady's divinely reinforced virtue and Comus' power, is projected in terms of music. There is a musical contest between Comus' rout's 'noise' of 'jocund Flute' and 'gamesome Pipe' (170–3) and the Lady's 'Echo' song, and later the songs of the Attendant Spirit and the nymph Sabrina. Not only that, but the verse-rhythms of Comus' speeches, as opposed to those of the Spirit and the Lady at her Orphic best, reflect and represent the two embattled types of magic.[22]

The general theme of the story – the power of chastity to overcome the allurements of wanton lust – recalls the medieval allegorizing of the myth as a confrontation of carnality and the rational powers of the higher soul.[23] Not only is the concern for purity Orphic, but chastity connects the Lady both to Orpheus and Sabrina. The latter's story was told in the *Faerie Queene* (2.10.17–19), but Spenser did not make her, as Milton did, a special patroness of virgins (*Comus* 855–6), nor did he tell of her 'quick immortal change' in Nereus' hall. Sabrina died because of the unchastity of her mother and father, and according to one version, Orpheus met his fate because the Thracian women could not tolerate his celibacy. Both were immortalized when they were thrown into their respective rivers. Under the topos of chastity Sabrina is a type of Orpheus.

It might be well here to recall that Milton's notion of chastity (or virginity) was neither the Stoic nor, exactly, the Christian one. In *Comus*, chastity is equated with charity, the highest of the theological virtues, and presented as an emblem of divine grace.[24] It is the saving virtue. But Milton also identified it with poetic inspiration, or the necessary conditions for it.[25] Thus he did not think of it as a mere negation, or capacity for remaining unmoved, but, as Spenser did, as a vital, energizing force. Perhaps the source of this now apparently odd idea was the old courtly-love idealization of the willing refraining from sexual enjoyment of the beloved as productive of all the virtues and the accomplishments (chiefly artistic) of the lover. But there is a difference. Both Spenser and Milton see it as an appropriate preparatory stage for a later fruition in mature married love. Spenser's symbol of chastity, Britomart, the heroine of the third book of the *Faerie Queene*, is already in love, and is spurred on by her 'chastity,' or love – the two terms are almost synonymous – to seek her true mate through hard adventures and long wandering. She is destined to be the mother of illustrious progeny and she is full of a vital energy that takes the form of chastity, or 'truth' in love, and will in future be transmuted into fertility.

It is impossible not to notice that *Comus* is the 'prime descendant' of the *Faerie Queene*, where, as we have seen, a Neoplatonic-Lucretian-Orphic myth was created to show the controlling place of love and fertility in the cosmos. The 'chastity' celebrated in Book Three was shown as having its authentication in natural fertility, and the ending of *Comus* makes the same point. Despite her championing of the 'sublime notion and high mystery' of virginity, the Lady is no more destined to a life of perpetual celibacy than is Britomart. The poem does not end in a vision of the 144,000 virgins but in a country dance in a domestic setting, an emblem of fertility and a foreshadowing of the Lady's eventual happy marriage. She says she possesses 'the unblemish'd Form of Chastity,' and the use of the striking word 'form' here indicates that we are to think of chastity as a generating pattern, a divine creative principle. It is in this respect that the philosophical argument of

Comus comes close to Spenser's Orphic ideas. The controlling principle that presides over his Garden of Adonis takes most obviously the shape of Venus and Adonis joined as the divine Orphic hermaphroditic Eros, forever generating all the forms of nature. Cupid appears here only as a naughty boy, one of Venus' ambivalent attributes. Love does have the power to torment, but in the happy garden he lays aside his 'sad darts' that do not belong to unfallen nature and plays happily with Psyche, long since reconciled to Venus and already the mother of Pleasure. In *Comus*, the corresponding final vision of cosmic fertility resembles Spenser's but varies from it, no doubt in order to 'correct' it. The garden now is not the rather earthy one of Adonis but the less-easily-located Garden of Hesperus. Adonis is still unrecovered, and Venus does not have much to do:

> ... young *Adonis* oft reposes,
> Waxing well of his deep wound
> In slumber soft, and on the ground
> Sadly sits th' *Assyrian* Queen;
> But farr above in spangled sheen
> Celestial *Cupid* her fam'd Son advanc't
> Holds his dear *Psyche* sweet intranc't,
> After her wandring labours long,
> Till free consent the gods among
> Make her his eternal Bride.   (999–1008)

As in the Orphic hymns and in Spenser's 'Hymne in Honour of Love'[26] Cupid transcends his mother, for this is the 'celestial Cupid,' who can be identified even with Christ himself in the Renaissance Platonic tradition. He is not yet married to Psyche. He holds her, but she is still 'entranc't,' and the reason is the same as that for which the Red Cross Knight, at the end of Book 1 of the *Faerie Queene*, could not yet be married to his Una. Time and history must first come to an end.

Despite its resemblances to various Spenserian stories – of Guyon's crusade against Acrasia, of the rescue of Amoret and of Florimell – *Comus* is not about the triumph of philosophic virtue or of love but of art or magic. It is also true, however, that virtue, love, and art were so closely connected in the Platonic tradition that they almost, if not quite, reached the condition of metaphoric identity. As the enchanting singer, Orpheus is the saviour, who in various ancient versions brought not only Eurydice but many others as well back from death by the power of song. As priest, philosopher, and initiator into the mysteries he is also a saviour, for the cult of Bacchus, like that of

Christ, is a soteriological one.[27] Here Sabrina initiates the Lady by baptizing her. The Lady's heavenly virtue of virginity enables her to keep a free mind, but it is not enough to save her from having her 'corporal rinde' 'immanacl'd' (664–5): she is riveted to a 'marble venom'd seat / Smear'd with gumms of gluteous heat' (916–17). Neither her brother nor Jove's Spirit can break the spell, although they frighten away Comus himself. Only a more powerful magic can undo it; only the nymph Sabrina, 'if right invok'd in warbled Song,' can release the Lady with her song, her ritual touches 'with chaste palms moist and cold' and ceremonial lustrations. The latter clearly represents the rite of baptism, a symbolic death by and rebirth from water, through which the earthy Adamic nature, the body of death, is washed away. Just as Sabrina herself was purged of her mortal part by entering the water, so the Lady, entering Sabrina's waters symbolically, emerges a changed creature, one who can bring home 'a crown of deathless Praise' (970–3).[28] The centre of the story hinges on magical enactment as against mere philosophizing, grace versus reason and moral argument. Though there certainly is a great deal of preaching and moralizing, the solution of the Lady's difficulty is brought about mimetically. On the one hand, the story is a sort of moral allegory, in which we are taught that sensuality is a delusive good, an artificially maintained evasion of life. 'To roll with pleasure in the sensual stye' is not to get on with the business of life. Not only are Comus and all his revellers barren (in his illustrations of the masque Blake draws them as virtually sexless): they are incapable of human society and have withdrawn from the world. All this and its converse, the power and potency of virtue, the Elder Brother knows quite well, and rather tiresomely imparts to the other. For all that, he is unable to do one single thing of use until the Spirit arrives and takes charge. Indeed, he is infatuated with his own wise speeches, and lulled into a false sense of security. 'How charming is divine philosophy,' exclaims the Younger Brother at first, but then, hearing of the actual plight of his sister, asks 'Is this the confidence you gave me, Brother?' There seems to be a justice that surpasses compliment in the Lady's likening of her brothers to Narcissus (237). 'Divine philosophy' has its inadequacies. The Lady herself can philosophize better than Comus (756–79), but it is when she threatens to leave this vein and soar into the Orphic raptures of ecstatic utterance (780–99) that we and Comus know that her words would truly acquire power to bring all Comus' 'magic structures' tumbling down.

That magic power and not just knowledge alone can save us from such potent charms as Comus' obviously expresses the Protestant distinction of grace from 'works' or knowledge. The magic herb haemony that the Spirit gives the brothers, symbolizes the lesser sort of power possessed by reason and right thinking.[29] It enables them to enter Comus' presence unharmed, but not to undo his spells.

Magical power is, above all, the power to effect metamorphoses. The high point of the myth of Orpheus could be seen as the transformation of Orpheus' mutilated body into the eternally singing head and lyre, the transcending of tragic earthly experience by art. Several transformations are alluded to or narrated in the poem, Ulysses' sailors' and Comus' followers', Sabrina's, Narcissus', Echo's and Psyche's. The transformation of the Attendant Spirit into Thyrsis, a local shepherd of Orphic powers, and of Comus into a villager take place on stage. Initiation is itself a metamorphosis. The cult worshippers of Bacchus were supposedly transformed into the god himself through their rites, which involved among other things acting out the events of his life. Therefore drama was part of the worship of Dionysos. Poetry in *Comus* clearly has magic power: the Spirit's incantations and songs conjure up Sabrina, and their power is at least partly due to their quality as poetry. But I cannot agree with Fletcher that Sabrina is merely 'Ariel to Thyrsis' Prospero;'[30] she is a more powerful magician than Thyrsis. He can only pray to her to come; he is in no sense her master.

All the main characters in the masque, except Comus himself, reflect aspects of the Orphic *persona*. Most obvious is the Attendant Spirit as Thyrsis, a role taken when the masque was first performed by Henry Lawes, the composer of the score. Even the country swain whose outward shape the Spirit takes is an Orphic musician. The Lady, too, the first singer in the masque, is a kind of Orpheus. Her song is so enchanting it surpasses those of Circe and the Sirens, according to Comus (245–65). It smoothes 'the Raven down / Of darkness till it smil[es]' (251–2), a compact reference to Orpheus' charming the beasts and Hades. The Attendant Spirit says her song could 'create a soul / Under the ribs of Death' (561–2). But the art of this fledgling Orpheus calls up not even Echo, only Comus. At this point the Lady becomes a Eurydice, even, indeed, a Ulysses. The darkness and the monsters in Comus' wood suggest not only the Underworld but also Circe's island.

Since every story of pagan myth was supposed to be another attempt to express the obscured truth, in each of them Milton would have thought it natural that the Orpheus story in some ways resembled the story of the *Odyssey*, particularly the Circe and Calypso episodes, both of which are evoked in *Comus* through congruence of poetic image and verbal echoes. The Lady is certainly a detained traveller like Ulysses, and Comus is the son of Circe. 'The navel of this hideous Wood' (520) not only echoes Homer's epithet for Calypso's isle, *omphalos thalasses* (the navel of the sea), it also suggests the body of the huge beast Leviathan. Both were taken in the

tradition we have been following to mean carnality, death, and the body of
Satan, into which the entire race has been brought. When the medieval and
Renaissance interpretations of Eurydice and Circe as carnality are brought
side by side, a parallel is being drawn. It is no mere simple equation:
differences are more obvious than similarities. And yet, however virtuous the
Lady may be, she is still a daughter of Eve, possibly a temptation to others and
certainly a frail human being in need of the help from above so graciously sent
to her.

The Lady tries to call forth Echo, and with Echo we are reminded of
Narcissus; he is somehow connected with the other mythical personages of
the poem. The brothers are narcissistic, Comus extremely so. There seems,
moreover, to be some sort of traditional connection between Narcissus and
Orpheus. Narcissus could give away nothing of himself; according to Plato,
Orpheus failed because he would not give himself up for love totally, as
Alcestis did. He gave only his art. Perhaps the severed head and lyre resemble
Echo's disembodied voice. In a sense, too, Echo is the opposite of Narcissus;
whereas he is totally self-absorbed, she is completely 'out of herself'; he
belongs only to himself; she belongs to everyone. Above all, she communicates, she redoubles communication. Thus, she undoubtedly represents a
benign force, though by herself she has no power. (In a sense we could call
Echo a failing saviour; if Narcissus had loved her he would not have died, but
he didn't.) The principle of an echo is embodied in the Spirit's successful
invocation to Sabrina, and we conclude that Echo has something to do with
magic. Probably Milton is drawing on everyone's early impressions of the
uncanniness of an echo, but there is more to it than that. The reader should
refer to Fletcher's treatment of the various ways in which the idea of an echo
works in the art of the poem, both in the text and in the music.[31]

The mythological texture of *Comus* is dense. At this point in his career
Milton is still rejoicing in classical stories. Orpheus, Eurydice, Ulysses,
Circe, Calypso, Cupid, Psyche, Narcissus, Echo, Bacchus, Venus, and
Adonis do not exhaust the list. The use of various myths by converting them
into one another is a poetic method of the Humanist tradition. All mythological allusions, even small details of a story, come fraught with their burden of
meaning that has evolved – accumulated, one might say – through centuries
of interpretation. And, in accordance with that Orphic doctrine of the whole
in the part, even the details radiate facets of the central myth and its meaning.
Angus Fletcher cites as an example of Milton's fusing and focusing power his
treatment of the herb haemony. We recognize it as Ulysses' 'moly,' a charm
against Circe's arts, which represents reason, according to Cleanthes the
Sophist. But the use of 'haemony,' not 'moly,' invites a contrast between the

powers of reason and of Apollo's son. It is an allusion to Ovid's *Remedia
amoris* where Ovid discusses the remedies for sensual frenzy or lovemadness.
He says that the 'herbs of Haemonia' and magic arts were of old thought able
to cure love, but as for him, he will put his faith in the aid of Apollo, invoked
in sacred song.[32]

Milton's next important reference to Orpheus is in *Lycidas*, where he is
dealing with the duties, difficulties, and privileges of poets. The first part of
the poem, tortured with the seeming inexorableness of time and fate, comes to
a harsh climax with the question

> What could the Muse her self that *Orpheus* bore,
> The Muse her self, for her inchanting son
> Whom Universal nature did lament,
> When by the rout that made the hideous roar,
> His goary visage down the stream was sent,
> Down the swift *Hebrus* to the *Lesbian* shore?   (*Lycidas*, 58–63)

Orpheus is a symbol for the failure of even miraculous poetry to control the
'rout.' Phoebus replies that true poetic fame 'is no plant that grows on mortal
soil,' 'but lives and spreads aloft' in the eyes of 'all judging Jove.' Wherever
that might be it is not quite Spenser's eternal world of art, but something
perched rather uneasily between that and a Christian heaven. This is not the
first time that God has appeared as Milton's 'great Taskmaster' and ultimate
critic; but if the certainty of his just appraisal is a consolation it fails to assign
any special sort of praise to specifically poetic achievement. Milton does not
appear to have exorcised the spectre that Orpheus' fate evoked for him.

In *Paradise Lost* (1667), he attempts to do so again, this time by
contrasting the kind of poetry he is writing with that of Orpheus. The theme
is that of Calderón's *auto El divino Orfeo* (see previous chapter). But whereas
Calderón could make the myth of Orpheus support the Christian message by
identifying Orpheus completely with Christ (his poetry and music are not
merely metaphors but sacramental symbols for Christ's works and achievement), Milton at this stage in his career must deliberately reject the myth for
this purpose. He tells us that he intends to 'soar above the Aonian mount' and
sing 'with other notes than to the *Orphean* Lyre' (3.17), although he also
obviously recognizes his kinship with Orpheus. His subject matter is the
same as Orpheus' (Chaos and ancient Night), and like Orpheus, he is a
voyager,[33] a quester, who has visited 'the *Stygian* Pool,' a nightingale singing
in the dark.[34] Like Orpheus he is engaged in a dangerous enterprise. The
danger lies in

> the barbarous dissonance
> Of *Bacchus* and his Revellers, the Race
> Of that wilde rout that tore the *Thracian* Bard
> In *Rhodope*, where Woods and Rocks had Eares
> To rapture, till the savage clamor dround
> Both Harp and Voice; nor could the Muse defend
> Her Son.   (7.32–9)

Thus, Milton identifies himself with Orpheus even while rejecting him on the ground that he represents false pagan knowledge and art. Now, instead of being connected with ideal beauty and the art that redeems from death, Orpheus represents to Milton the precarious situation of the poet, the fact that he is always exposed to the danger of being torn in pieces. The only safety is in driving far off the wild rout (who, unfortunately, are the most in need of his song) and finding 'fit audience', 'though few.' Although at this despairing point Milton seems to be yielding to the temptation to isolate himself from the unregenerate mob, such a retreat would not be good enough for the man who wanted his poetry to be 'doctrinal to a nation' and to enlighten, not spurn, those who dwelt in darkness. Poetry must be relevant to the fundamental concerns of humanity, otherwise it would be a selfish indulgence. If the 'truth' now can no longer include Orphic doctrine and Orphic poetry, Milton must repudiate Orpheus and find a new model for a poet. The reason why Calliope could not save Orpheus was that she did not have the right kind of knowledge: she was, after all, only a pagan muse. So he begs *his* muse, Urania,

> fail not thou, who thee implores:
> For thou art Heav'nlie, shee an empty dreame. (*Paradise Lost* 7.39–40)

In his early poetry Orpheus' significance for Milton lay in the fact that as a poet he had a high role to play, one which Milton adopted for himself. He visited the Underworld and charmed the forces of death with his song. He sang of the Creation, of chaos and ancient night, and of the divine gods. It is the poet's task to do so, a task that is as much religious as aesthetic. But it turned out that Hades or the forces of death were not so dangerous to Orpheus as were human beings, with their unregeneracy, their general tendency to reel back into the beast. So in Milton the part of the Orpheus myth that finally receives the most emphasis is the *sparagmos*. But at first he does not accept it as a necessary part of a poet's career. He detaches himself from Orpheus. The *sparagmos* leads him to question the power of Orpheus' muse and of poetry in general. Poetry is knowledge and true knowledge is power. But false knowledge sets its deluded purveyor up for destruction, and so Milton proceeds to pit the Christian muse against the pagan and blame the latter for the failure of power or magic in pagan poetry.

The reader will remember that, according to one medieval tradition of long duration, Orpheus was a culture-hero, and his failure and death symbolized the impotence of pagan civilization. The negative aspect of Milton's treatment of Orpheus is similar, and it may be worth while to pause here to consider the difference in this respect between Milton's Orpheus and that of another famous compatriot, Sir Francis Bacon. *Of the Wisdom of the Ancients* (first published in Latin in 1609) is about the relationship of poetry to universal knowledge, and as such is a very Orphic book.[35] Bacon, who was thoroughly grounded in classical learning and professed to despise it, adopted the old allegorical method (ostensibly) to salvage what fragments of truth there were in ancient learning while advancing his own ideas. 'The story of Orpheus,' says Bacon, 'which though so well known has not yet been in all points perfectly well interpreted, seems meant for a representation of universal Philosophy. For Orpheus himself, – a man admirable and truly divine, who being master of all harmony subdued and drew all things after him by sweet and gentle measures, – may pass by an easy metaphor for philosophy personified.'[36]

Orpheus' music is of two sorts, Bacon continues, neatly separating the two layers of the myth. The one kind appeals to the infernal powers and pries out the secrets of nature: that is natural philosophy. The story of Eurydice has to do with this. Bacon takes the resuscitation of a dead person quite literally as a scientific possibility (as did many other 'philosophers' even later): 'the most noble worke of naturall philosophy' is the restitution of things corruptible and the preservation of bodies in their first estate. This can only be done (if at all by mortals), by 'harmony,' or 'exquisite temper of nature.'[37] But Orpheus fails, as science has so far failed, because of 'curious diligence and untimely impatience.' Foiled in the grand attempt, philosophy turns to more modest 'humane obiects,' such as the establishment of a just and ordered society. Thus we have the second kind of Orphic music, that addressed to the listeners in the 'theatre' on Pangaeus, which is civil or moral philosophy. It makes people obedient to the moral law, as long as they listen to its precepts. Just so long, also, are they happy, peaceful, and productive. The death of Orpheus was not caused by any desire on the part of the Maenads for vengeance (Bacon does not even glance at such an idea), but by the apparently accidental silencing, or drowning out, of Orpheus' music by their loud playing of cornets, the 'hideous roar' referred to by Milton, who also thinks of it as being somehow the cause of the fatal accident. The spell is broken, because no one can hear the music any longer; the animals return to the hunt and Orpheus is torn apart.

Spenser saw Orpheus as a symbol of the eternal life of art. Bacon sees him as the symbol of the eternal failure of human culture. It is not merely pagan culture that fails. It is simply not in the nature of earthly things for any stability or harmony to last long. Orpheus dies, not because his music is not good enough (as Philosophy he is 'admirable and divine,'[38] and his miracles as far outdo the labours of Hercules as the works of wisdom surpass the works of fortitude), but because civilization itself can never last. All things have their periods. Tumults, seditions, and wars inevitably arise and laws are then silenced. Men return to the depravity of their nature; fields are laid waste, and finally philosophy and learning are torn apart. In Bacon's hands the myth becomes an allegory of the historical process quite secularly understood. It is a pessimistic view; Bacon saw no hope for the human race except through science, if men could ever discipline themselves to pursue it long enough. Perhaps even then, Bacon said, the ultimate truth would not be capable of human comprehension. Although no culture can last, there is at least some consolation in the fact that the scattered remnants of knowledge (Orpheus' head and lyre) will be found after cataclysmic upheavals, and though a barbarous age must succeed a civil one (the river Helicon hides its head and later raises it in Asia Minor), in another country the ruins of philosophy will be put together again and a new civilization will arise – and, of course, inevitably decline in its turn.

Bacon's interpretation is a newer, more modern one. His relativism and secularism are quite at odds with Milton's comparatively medieval view of history. History, for Milton, was a procession towards the New Jerusalem, a winning warfare with the forces of error and evil. Milton thought his duty as a poet was to use his special gifts in the 'wars of truth,' and his humanism was a casualty in the fray. It is ironical that this great modern humanist and poet should in the end revert to a position very like that of the Christian apologists of the fifth century who denounced all heathen culture. Orpheus' muse is an 'empty dream.' Does Milton for a moment wish the dream were true? Many readers have felt so. But there can be no mistaking the stern tone of the Son of God in *Paradise Regained* as he condemns the songs of Greece, half-learned and perverted from the true Hebrew wisdom.

> Ill imitated, while they loudest sing
> The vices of thir Deities, and thir own
> In Fable, Hymn, or Song, so personating
> Thir Gods ridiculous, and themselves past shame.

> Remove their swelling Epithetes thick laid
> As varnish on a Harlots cheek, the rest,
> Thin sown with aught of profit or delight,
> Will far be found unworthy to compare
> With *Sion*'s songs, to all true tasts excelling,
> Where God is prais'd aright, and Godlike men. (4.339–48)

But the myth of Orpheus had sunk deeply into Milton's mind and although he consciously repudiated the Humanist tradition the ideas that had given power and eloquence to the old poetry remained. The unique feature of the Orpheus myth is that in it art enters life as a means of dealing with death. In so doing it steps upon the tragic stage. The artist must sacrifice not only his own personal 'happiness' but even his very self. 'The Orphic voice is committed equally to salvation and self-destruction,' as Angus Fletcher says.[39] Milton's increasing emphasis upon the sacrificial triumph of the poet led him to his 'ultimate Orphic hero,' no fiction of the fabling Greeks, but the Hebrew Hercules, Adam and Christ in one, 'that invincible Samson.'

With the Renaissance an era in the life of pagan fable ended. Orpheus was to reappear on the European stage in the Romantic period with the new upsurge of faith in mythology, nature, and art, and since then he has had an active career.[40] To follow the course of any major classical myth through its permutations would be to trace the history of European culture, but that is perhaps especially true of the Orpheus myth, as it has had such a long career and seems especially durable. If men of different times have been able to interpret it in strangely differing ways, that fact is an indication of the range of its significance.

NOTES

1 The Neoplatonic triads are well known. Theocrasy is the doctrine that all the gods are aspects of the one divine reality. The entire pantheon is in each god, according to the principle of 'the whole in the part,' as stated by Proclus (Proposition 67 of the *Elements of Theology*) and repeated by Pico (*Conclusiones secundum Proclus* no 17). Thus, the gods blend into one another and have no real independent character. When this idea is added to the Neoplatonic ones of reality's emanating in stages or 'orders' from the godhead and of the triads, the result for 'Orphic theology' is the doctrine that each god is one of a rank or 'order' of gods, in each of which he shares in the attributes of the ruling god of the rank (eg in the sphere of Saturn are the 'Saturnine Jupiter,' 'Saturnine Venus,' and so on); and

each god is one of a triad (eg Phanes-Zagreus-Dionysos, or Mercury-Apollo-Venus). The three gods of any triad also represent or 'unfold' the meaning of another god. Says Pico, 'He that understands profoundly and clearly how the unity of Venus is unfolded in the trinity of the Graces, and the unity of Necessity in the trinity of the Fates, and the unity of Saturn in the trinity of Jupiter, Neptune and Pluto, knows the proper way of proceeding in Orphic theology' (*Conclusiones de modo intelligendi hymnos Orphei* No 8; quoted by Edgar Wind in *Pagan Mysteries in the Renaissance* rev ed [New York 1968] 248–9). Furthermore, in each god opposites coincide and are reconciled, because each shares in all the others. Dionysos is mad and raging, yet he purifies; Hermes, the god of eloquence, advises silence; Venus loves Mars, and so on. To demonstrate this the Orphic teacher would depict Dionysos with the attributes of Apollo, or Venus with Diana's bow and quiver. This is the origin of the strange hybrids of Renaissance emblem art, double-sexed or triple-headed beings, a Venus-Diana, a Hermathena, a Hermercules, etc; see Wind, 200.

2 The reference is to Hermias Alexandrinus' *Commentary on the Phaedrus*; see Wind *Pagan Mysteries* 162.

3 See Robert Ellrodt *Neoplatonism in the Poetry of Spenser* (Geneva 1960).

4 Spenser refers to Alanus as an authority on Nature in *Faerie Queene* 7.7.9. For a summary of his indebtedness to Alanus, see *The Works of Edmund Spenser: A Variorum Edition* ed Edwin Greenlaw *et al* (Baltimore 1938) VI 396–9.

5 Gustaf Fredén *Orpheus and the Goddess of Nature* (Göteborg 1958) 51

6 Ibid 93

7 The inconsistency between the Orphics' monistic doctrine of Nature, on the one hand, and their ethical dualism, on the other, has often been noted. See A.W. Mair 'Suicide' *Dictionary of Philosophy, Religion and Ethics* ed James Hastings (Edinburgh 1926) XII.

8 Hymns to Nature (10.1), Demeter (40.5), and Apollo (4.3). All quotations in English from these hymns are from the translation of Thomas Taylor (Orpheus *Mystical Hymns* [Chiswick 1824]). See Fredén *Orpheus* 88 n 1.

9 Spenser treats Orpheus and David as equals. David's power was not truer or greater. Their gifts had been given to each by the same Giver and had an equally celestial origin.

10 *Urne-Buriall* Chapter v; *The Works of Sir Thomas Browne* ed Charles Sayle (Edinburgh 1927) I 139

11 Mair 'Suicide' in *Dictionary* ed Hastings XII 30b

12 Sir Thomas Browne *Pseudodoxia Epidemica* 1.9; *Works* ed Sayle I 181

13 Trans F.A. Patterson *The Student's Milton* (New York 1930) 92

14 Nor are Milton and Calderón unique in their century. In *Christ's Victory and Triumph* (1610), Giles Fletcher says that the 'obscure fables of the Gentiles' embody Christian truths. The myth of Orpheus meant more than its pagan

perpetrators knew: it foreshadowed the redemptive victory of Christ:

> But he that conquer'd hell, to fetch againe
> His virgin widowe, by a serpent slaine,
> Another Orpheus was then dreaming poets feigne.

(Stanza 7)

It is strange that Douglas Bush should remark, 'Only in the all-reconciling imagination of the Renaissance could "the second Adam" become a second Orpheus' (*Mythology and the Renaissance Tradition* [New York 1957] 166). This by no means happened for the first time in the Renaissance imagination. As Bush himself notes, an earlier poet writing in English, Gavin Douglas, speaks of Christ as 'that hevinlie Orpheus' (ibid 168).

15 *The Orphic Voice: Poetry and Natural History* 69
16 Bush *Mythology and the Renaissance Tradition* 265
17 At several places in the next few pages I am indebted to Miss Katherine Hines's unpublished paper entitled 'The Orphic Comus,' written while she was an undergraduate at the University of Toronto.
18 *The Transcendental Masque: An Essay on Milton's 'Comus'* (Ithaca, New York 1971) 166
19 Ibid 188. See also Joseph Kerman *Opera as Drama* 27–8, quoted by Fletcher.
20 P.O. Kristeller *Renaissance Thought* II (New York 1965) 157–8
21 'Ad partem' 50–5 trans Patterson *The Student's Milton* 102.
22 The musical effects of the poetry are rather hard to assess without knowledge of 'the metrical style Milton and Lawes together created' (Fletcher *The Transcendental Masque* 189), but Fletcher guesses that the power of the Spirit's speeches does not lie mainly in the words' poetical imagery but in their rhythmns or musical qualities.
23 Friedman *Orpheus in the Middle Ages* Chapter IV
24 Fletcher *The Transcendental Masque* 158, 168–9
25 See *The Apology for Smectymnuus* in *The Student's Milton* 694–5.
26 See above p 208.
27 A difficulty in associating Orpheus with Bacchus lies in the fact that for Milton, as for most Renaissance writers after the early phase, Orpheus was chiefly an Apollonian figure. That does not mean, however, that no one of them could have thought of him as also a priest of Bacchus, for the Renaissance science of mythology loves nothing so much as to contain contradictions or paradoxes. *Comus* could be seen as a treatment of the Apollonian-Dionysian polarity, although many modern readers perceive Comus as a parody of Bacchus, and therefore not a genuine 'balancing value' for the Apollonian side.
28 Although the brothers have not been initiated yet, courtesy and pragmatism required that the Spirit present them to their parents along with their sister.
29 Douglas Bush has shown that haemony cannot represent divine grace, because, in

that case, 'its efficacy would surely be less limited than it proves to be.' Other
critics as well have convincingly argued that it represents knowledge. See Fletcher
The Transcendental Masque 158–9 n 14.

30 Ibid 167
31 See especially ibid 169 and n 25, 187, 203.
32 Ibid 194
33 It was the travelling Orpheus of the *Argonautica* who sang of 'Chaos and ancient Night.'
34 *Georgics* 4.511–15. Cf *Paradise Lost* 3.38–40.
35 See Sewell *The Orphic Voice*.
36 *Of the Wisdom of the Ancients* Chapter 11; *The Works of Francis Bacon*, ed James Spedding XIII (Boston 1860) 110
37 Ibid 58
38 Ibid 54
39 *The Transcendental Masque* 191
40 For various discussions of later treatments of the myth see Pablo Cabañas *El mito de Orfeo en la literatura española* (Madrid 1948); Eva Kushner *Le Mythe d'Orfée dans la littérature française contemporaine* (Paris 1961); Arthur Hubens *La Legende d'Orfée et le drame musical* (Brussels 1910); Walter A. Strauss *Descent and Return: The Orphic Theme in Modern Literature*; (Cambridge, Mass 1971); and the anthology, ed Joachim Schondorff *Orpheus und Eurydike: Poliziano, Calderón, Gluck, Offenbach, Kokoschka, Cocteau, Anouilh* (Munich 1963).

Suggested Reading

Böhme, R. *Orpheus: Der Sänger und seine Zeit* Berne and Munich 1970
Buck, A. *Der Orpheus-Mythos in der italienischen Renaissance* Krefeld 1961
Cabañas, P. *El mito de Orfeo en la literatura española* Madrid 1948
Fredén, G. *Orpheus and the Goddess of Nature* Göteborg 1958
Friedman, J.B. *Orpheus in the Middle Ages* Cambridge, Mass 1970
Guthrie, W.K.C. *Orpheus and Greek Religion* 1934; rpt New York 1966
Joukovsky, F. *Orphée et ses disciples dans la poésie française et néo-latine du XVIe siècle* Geneva 1970
Kerman, J. *Opera as Drama* New York 1956
Kern, O. ed *Orphicorum fragmenta* Berlin 1922; rpt 1963
Linforth, I.M. *The Arts of Orpheus* Berkeley and Los Angeles 1941
Marrone, L. 'Il mito di Orfeo nella drammatica italiana' *Studi di letteratura italiana* 12 (1922)
Pirotta, N. *Li due Orfei de Poliziano a Monteverdi* Torino 1969
Parker, A.A. 'The devil in the drama of Calderón' in *Critical Essays on the Theatre of Calderón* New York 1965
Segal, C.E. 'Orpheus and the fourth Georgic: Vergil on nature and civilization' *American Journal of Philology* 87 (1966) 307–25
– 'Ovid's Orpheus and augustan ideology' *Transactions of the American Philological Association* 103 (1972) 473–94
Seznec, J. *The Survival of the Pagan Gods* (tr Barbara Sessions) New York 1961
Sewell, E. *The Orphic Voice: Poetry and Natural History* New Haven 1960
Strauss, W.A. *Descent and Return: The Orphic Theme in Modern Literature* Cambridge, Mass 1971
Walker, D.P. *The Ancient Theology* London 1972
– 'Orpheus the theologian and Renaissance platonism' *Journal of the Warburg and Courtauld Institutes* 16 (1953) 100–20

Index

This book
was designed by
WILLIAM RUETER
and was printed by
University of
Toronto
Press